Growing Up Mostly Normal in the Middle of Nowhere

A Memoir

John Sheirer

Published By
Foremost Press
Cedarburg, Wisconsin

John Sheirer
JohnSheirer@aol.com

Copyright © 2005 John Sheirer. All rights reserved. Reproduction of any part of this publication in any way requires written permission from the author.

Published by Foremost Press

ISBN 0-9748921-1-4

For Mom and Dad and Grandma

Thelma Mae Crites Mason Sheirer, 1923-1995

William Junior Sheirer, 1923-1982

Annie Katherine Stuby Sheirer, 1890-1987

All this, of course, cannot be verified.

Mark DeFoe, Bringing Home Breakfast

Prologue

I wasn't kidnapped as a child, never abused, abandoned, beaten, or sold to the highest bidder. My parents didn't lock me in the basement. The cults never got hold of me–not counting a pretty wacky Bible camp. I wasn't transgendered, interracial, or multinational. No president denied that I was his love child. No aliens abducted me (although sometimes I wished they would). I wasn't blind, deaf, mute, epileptic, dyspeptic, or unable to digest milk. I wasn't an altruistic autistic. No one in my family was a psychopath or a sociopath, but a few of my cousins definitely went down the wrong path. My worst disease was mumps, and the closest I came to physical tragedy was a bee sting on the lip.

I'm not a celebrity or related to one or sleeping with one.

I breathe air, drink water, eat food.

But on a Tuesday afternoon in fourth grade, I realized for the first time that I was only "mostly normal."

***

I was singing with my classmates in music class. My voice was years away from changing, high, sweet, and boyish. I would never make the Vienna Boys' Choir, but I wasn't awful.

Halfway through the class, the school secretary came into the room and whispered mysteriously to Mrs. Claudio, my music teacher.

Mrs. Claudio then pointed toward several spots around the classroom. "I need you and you and you and you and you to please go to the speech therapy room near the main office." She pointed quickly as if conducting a more talented class of singers, and her slightly crooked index finger left in doubt exactly which students she had singled out among my mumbling classmates.

After a moment, a few kids ventured forward with their heads down. All of them spent most of their school day in what at the time was called "special education"–"special-ed" for short or "sped" if you wanted to be cruel. They were mildly retarded or had pretty serious versions of what we now call "learning disabilities" and only joined the rest of us for lunch, recess, gym, and music. And they each spoke with a speech impediment–convenient ammunition for the jerky kids who liked to tease them–so the school had recently hired a part-time speech therapist.

After these kids dutifully gathered at the front of the classroom, Mrs. Claudio said, "John, please join them. Do you know where the room is?"

I nodded.

"Good," she continued. "Then you can take them there."

This was a very proud moment. Mrs. Claudio had appointed me to show the less advanced students where they needed to go for speech therapy. Clearly, she recognized my leadership potential and responsible nature and entrusted me to escort these kids to their speech therapy session. So I led the way, feeling very pleased with my new role as "teacher's assistant"–not "teacher's pet," a label that would have doomed me for a decade to come.

I walked the other kids to their assigned room, made grown-up sounding small talk along the way, and then pointed them to the door. Helping these kids was a pleasure. I liked them and was glad I could contribute in my own small way to their education. Speech therapy might help them fit in better and feel less isolated.

Beaming with accomplishment, I walked back to music class and returned to my place among my friends.

Mrs. Claudio, inexplicably, stared at me. "John," she said, not hiding her impatience, "why are you here?"

"I took them to the room like you said," I replied, confused. This was no way for her to speak to her new assistant.

"No, John," she said, striding over to take me by the elbow and hustle me toward the door. "You were supposed to stay there with them. You need speech therapy too!"

"Too, too, too . . ."

Her words echoed around me as I staggered into the empty hallway.

"Thpeech therapy?" I said to myself, stunned. "Thee thays I need thpeech therapy too."

From that day on, I missed an hour of fourth grade music class each Tuesday afternoon to attend speech therapy. The drills with the therapist eventually helped me learn to stop substituting "th" sounds for my "s" sounds–a problem I didn't know I had until then. And I learned an even more important lesson that first day of speech therapy: it hurts to be singled out because someone thought I didn't belong with everyone else in school.

I never again used the word "sped" … or "thped."

***

Missing so much music class that year might have adversely affected my singing ability. If there had been treatment centers for the singing-impaired, I would have been sent to one. Dad and I were by far the worst singers in church, back when I still went to church. My sisters rolled their eyes when we sang, then asked if I sang badly on purpose. In a way, I guess I did because I decided as soon as I hit puberty that I had a very deep voice. I dipped my chin into my collarbone and lowered my voice as much as I could, trying to sound like my naive perception of a very talented opera singer. Instead of praise for my rich tones, all I earned was a sore throat from the strain.

When my class chorus sang at our sixth grade graduation ceremonies, I was one of a handful of kids not allowed to sing with the group. Ironically, the only other people banned from singing were my fourth grade speech therapy friends. We sat in the audience while our classmates stood on stage and sang some dopey song about how we were all "blossoming" into young adults.

Mom asked me after the ceremony why I sat with, "those, um, kids, um, you know, the 'slow' bunch." I didn't really mind not singing with everyone else. Instead, I enjoyed the reunion with my speech therapy friends. We reminisced about our year of Tuesday afternoons and joked about how I thought I was just escorting them to therapy.

"The look on your face when you came back …" one of the kids said. I made that face for them again–an expression of overwhelming disappointment. We all laughed. Then we watched our miserable classmates up on stage as they muddled their way through dreadful practice sessions.

Maybe we couldn't always talk *and* sing as well as everyone else in our class, but we were certainly happy to be spared from taking part in that stupid blossoming song.

***

Chapter 1
Where I'm Going

I haven't called it home for a long time.

Not long before Christmas in 2002, one of my colleagues at Asnuntuck Community College saw me in the hallway and asked, "Are you going anywhere for the holidays?"

"Yes," I replied.

After a moment while we stared at each other, she asked the obvious follow-up question: "Uhhh . . . where?"

This is not an easy question. On the one hand, I plan to drive 450 miles to a specific location. My destination is Wills Mountain in the Laurel Highlands of the Allegheny Foothills of the Appalachian Mountain Range of southwest central Pennsylvania. On the other hand, there's more to consider than geological formations on a topographical map or lines on the dog-eared atlas under the driver's seat of my car.

This is the place where I grew up, but is it "home"?

***

I was born in the Bedford County Memorial Hospital in Everett, Pennsylvania, in the wee hours of May 17, 1961. Until I went away to college at age eighteen, I lived in a farmhouse in southern Bedford County in the village of Madley on Pennsylvania State Route 96. Going south on Route 96 at fifty-five miles per hour, you'll see the "Village of Madley" sign. If you count to five and look in the rearview mirror, you'll see the "Village of Madley" sign for northbound traffic. As the saying goes, you'll miss it if you blink.

To be fair, it's not really that small. If you turn west from Route 96 onto Madley Hollow Road, this paved but unlined road goes for several miles with dozens of houses, farms, trailers, barns, sheds, outhouses, cats, dogs, chickens on porches, kids playing in mud, and cars up on blocks in the front yard. That's all part of Madley.

If you turn east at Madley onto the dirt road that runs toward Wills Mountain rising a thousand feet from the valley floor, you'll pass a couple of two-story houses on your immediate right and left. About fifty yards beyond these houses is a third–my childhood home–a large white farmhouse with several small outbuildings and a barn. The only other building on the dirt road that loops about half a mile back around to Route 96 is a cabin a few hundred yards beyond the farmhouse.

I'm going to that cabin for the holidays.

Look up and to the east on Wills Mountain and you'll see a stone quarry, a reddish-tan rock scar marking the top of the ridge. Until the early 1950s, quarry workers mined Lancaster Limestone to be pulverized for making cement. The official topographical map of the area simply refers to this feature as a "sand pit." Historical documents reveal the actual name as Ganister Rock Quarry. In my youth, everyone simply called it "the quarry."

I plan to climb all the way up there too.

***

Janet and Fred now own the farm of my youth where they raise llamas, of all things. In 1985, Mom sold the farm to a woman named Miranda, one of my sisters' best friends. Miranda began to renovate the house but sold to Janet and Fred in 1988 when her marriage couldn't be renovated enough to avoid divorce.

The farm features the small cabin that we called simply "the log house." When I was young, I only knew that the log house was built in 1812 and that we rented it every fall to deer hunters from New Hampshire. I had no idea then why half a dozen men came all the way from that far north to rent an old, dank cabin in the middle of nowhere, but they always came and always hung their trophy deer on hooks outside the cabin for everyone to see.

During the Christmas season in 1999, I visited my sister Tam and her husband Dale at their home in Watsontown, Pennsylvania. Tam told me that Janet and Fred had started renting out the cabin to people other than hunters on a regular basis.

"You're kidding," I said. Long ago, our family "roughed it" overnight at the cabin once or twice each summer. To me, the place seemed tiny and old and dirty. I remembered that it had basic electricity and a wood-burning cook stove but no indoor plumbing. The water sources were an unreliable indoor pump and a pipe that Dad and I had suspended from a spring fifteen feet high on the steep bank of the little stream that flowed near the cabin.

"Who would want to stay there besides deer hunters?" I asked Tam.

"*We* stayed there," Tam replied. "You wouldn't recognize it. Fred and Janet tore out all that crappy old wallpaper downstairs. You can see the original log walls. They rebuilt the porch and added a modern kitchen and bathroom on the back. And remember, it's got three bedrooms upstairs. It's roomy and very comfortable. And they put in a hot tub and cable TV."

So I called Janet a few days later, and she remembered me. Janet grew up a few houses to the north but was closer in age to my older brothers, Ronnie and Norman. I didn't remember her well because of our age difference. She was intrigued that I worked as a college professor and described her experiences as a substitute teacher over the years. Within ten minutes, we were chatting like old friends.

Janet told me about the cabin. Not only had my sister Tam visited, but my brothers Ronnie and Norman had as well. She said she'd be delighted for me to come down and stay.

Then she told me the price: $80 per night. In my teens, I would have thought this was more money than God could spare for his favorite church. In my twenties, I would have grunted but paid, trying to figure how to afford gas for the trip. By 1999, I had a real job and was making more money than I ever dreamed. Of course, as a community college teacher, I had modest dreams.

Janet apologized for the fee and explained that they charged that much to make up for all they had spent on renovating the cabin.

"In New England," I told Janet, "A three-bedroom cabin would be a bit more than that. Put a one in front of that eighty." In fact, if the cabin happened to be in a tourist spot, people would happily pay $280.

I told Janet that I had some time off in January, and I'd call her soon to arrange a weekend stay at the cabin. That mythical time off, as often happens for teachers between terms, went by much too quickly, so I didn't call Janet back until July of 2002, *more than two years later*. By then, I had started seeing a wonderful woman named Jenny, and I wanted to go somewhere special with her.

I'd seen Jenny jogging the country road that meanders by my little house in Somers, Connecticut, and we'd sometimes waved and smiled at each other. I wanted her to stop and chat, but she never did. I didn't want to interrupt her run by offering her a glass of iced tea or something goofy like that. By coincidence, she enrolled in one of my classes that January. After the semester ended, we started e-mailing each other and discovered that she lived less than a mile from my house. We eventually went for ice cream on our first date.

Things have been good between us ever since. We both enjoy nature (Jenny's passion) and books (my passion). We're both athletic, artistic, progressive, and active. We both love to eat, at home and out. In fact, our favorite dates usually involve food. I'm glad she's not the type of woman who eats three bites of lettuce and then declares that she's gained five pounds.

Her two sons and I share an obsession for basketball that always gives us something to talk about when Jenny's in the other room. The only problem that might eventually come between us is that I've become a Red Sox fan during my years in New England, like Jenny's sons, her brother, and her father. Jenny, unfortunately, is a member of the "evil empire" of Yankee fans. But we'll survive.

We'd had a couple of weekends away together without a hint of an argument, so I thought we could risk being together for eight-hour drives to Pennsylvania and back, along with two nights of "roughing it" in the cabin.

We went to the cabin in August 2002 and had a terrific romantic getaway. One of the first things Jenny said when we arrived was, "The boys would love this." We went back again in December with her sons, Rob, fifteen, and Jim, eight. Instead of cramming ourselves into one of our little cars, we rented a Ford Expedition, a boat of an SUV. I could fit my car, a Geo Tracker, in the back of the thing and still have room for Jenny and the boys–maybe Jenny's Ford Escort too.

I felt somewhat guilty about the extravagance of the Expedition, but we needed a big reliable car to haul four people and all of our stuff to Pennsylvania and back, and none of us were interested in a minivan. We even brought along a little TV-VCR combination that I got for my office a few years ago. The kids watched videos the whole way down and back while Jenny and I drove and talked. We had a great time at the cabin–hiking, sightseeing, and hanging around the haunts of my youth.

During that wonderful December family visit, I rambled my way through a dozen "old home" stories to Jenny, Rob, and Jim. I was surprised when Jenny said, "You've got a lot to say about this place." I'd always felt odd about my isolated upbringing, even a little ashamed–and I didn't usually talk about it. But Jenny was right. I had a lot to say.

So I decided to come back alone and write about my experiences. This time, my time between semesters wouldn't fly away. Jenny and I had no special New Year's Eve plans, so she suggested I go the week after Christmas. I called Janet, reserved the cabin, and looked forward to three days of solitude, reflection, and writing.

***

Since leaving the farm nearly a quarter century ago, I've often had to play a strange little game to explain where I grew up. Imagine I'm at a party nursing a diet coke while standing near a potted plant with a curious new friend who wants to have a conversation. The game usually goes like this:

Curious New Friend: "So, John . . . where are you from?"
Me: "Pennsylvania."
Curious New Friend: "Really, what part?"
Me: "Sort of southwest central."
Curious New Friend: "Near Philadelphia?"
Me: "No."
Curious New Friend: "Near Pittsburgh?"
Me: "Not really."
Curious New Friend: "Near that place where the groundhog looks for his shadow?"
Me: "That's Punxatauny. I've driven through there, but it's not close to where I'm from."
Curious New Friend: "Well, what's the name of the town?"
Me: "There really wasn't a town."
Curious New Friend: "What do you mean, no town?"
Me: "It's kind of in the middle of nowhere."
Curious New Friend: "Well, what was your mailing address?"
Me: "Rural Route One, Buffalo Mills."
Curious New Friend: "So you lived in Buffalo Mills, Pennsylvania?"
Me: "No. That's where the post office was. We were a few miles south of there."
Curious New Friend: "Did you go to school in Buffalo Mills?"
Me: "No. I went to high school in Hyndman."
Curious New Friend: "Hymen? What was your nickname, 'the virgins'? Ha, ha, ha."
Me: "Hyndman. H-y-n-d-m-a-n. We were the Hyndman 'Hornets.'"
Curious New Friend: "So you lived in Hymen, Pennsylvania?"
Me: "It's Hyndman, and no, that's where the high school was. We lived a few miles north."
Curious New Friend: "Okay, I'm confused. Is this near any big cities?"
Me: "No."
Curious New Friend: "Big towns? Any place I might have heard of?"
Me: "Have you heard of Bedford?"

Curious New Friend: "No."
Me: "Have you heard of Altoona?"
Curious New Friend: "No."
Me: "Have you heard of Johnstown?"
Curious New Friend: "Hey, wait a second. Your name's 'John.' Did you live in 'John's' town?"
Me: "No. Have you heard of Cumberland, Maryland?"
Curious New Friend: "No. I thought you said you were from Pennsylvania."
Me: "Yes, very far in the south of southwest central Pennsylvania–close to Maryland."
Curious New Friend: "You know, I think I see someone I know over by the fondue. It's been nice talking to you John from the middle of nowhere in Pennsylvania."

***

This place is hard to call home, as in "I'm going home for the holidays."

Not long after I went to college, my twin sister June took over my bedroom. When I came "home" to visit, I slept in the guest room.

The experience was unsettling–sleeping in the guest room of my only home a short time after I'd left. I can't blame June for moving into my room. All her life, she shared a large bedroom with our sisters Pam and Tam (also twins) who are two years older than June and I. As the only boy at home (my brothers Norman and Ronnie were much older and already out of the house), I had a small bedroom to myself and felt immensely lucky every minute of my formative years because I could close that bedroom door and find solitude from everyone else in the house.

Since I've been gone, the house has been sold twice, re-sided, re-roofed, and extensively remodeled. Most of the furniture has been replaced–including the bed I slept in the whole time I lived there. Everything has changed: the people, the things, even my favorite apple tree is gone. How can I call it home now?

Home has been one of the dozens of apartments I've lived in over the years. Home is now a little two-bedroom house I rent on a country lane in Somers, Connecticut. When people ask me where I live, I like being able to say the name of a definite town and not have to play any versions of the "where-are-you-from" game.

***

So when my colleague at the college asked where I planned to go for the holidays, I replied, "Pennsylvania."

***

My trip begins in darkness at 7:30 a.m. on December 30, 2002, but the sun will be coming up soon. Even in the poor light, I can see blue sky and a few feathery clouds. Snow fell in Connecticut on Christmas and a couple of days afterward, recently enough that there are still patches of white in the fields. The roads are dry and safe, and the snow along the edges has that dirty brown and gray look from the interaction of mud and cars.

One minute into the trip, I realize that I forgot to leave the rent check at the usual place near my front door. I'll be gone until the evening of January second, and the landlord always comes by on the first to collect the rent. Because it's a holiday, perhaps he won't come until the second. Besides, I've paid early a few times, so I don't think an eviction notice will be nailed to the door when I return.

I'm leaving a great deal behind on this trip–Jenny most important. We've been seeing each other for eight months now, and this is the first time we're voluntarily going to be apart for more than two days. I'm also leaving my career behind. I still have some class planning to finish before the spring semester, only three weeks away. I'm also leaving behind a massive English department report–a dreadful project that I got stuck with. I promised to pull together a draft for my colleagues when we meet in two weeks. And I'm leaving behind my idea of the perfect vacation: sitting around the house and not going to work–reading, writing, watching TV, napping, hiking, going to the gym–all at my own pace. This is the most restful kind of vacation imaginable, partly because it doesn't involve a sixteen-hour round-trip drive in my rattling little car.

I've packed all kinds of healthy food (bananas, pears, clementines, apples) to eat on the trip, but my first stop is the McDonald's less than two miles from my house. My window hangs open for two full minutes at the drive-through speaker before anyone takes my order. The morning air is frigid, and my fingers begin to ache on the steering wheel.

A very odd bunch of folks work at this McDonald's (including a few of my former students), so I'm used to spotty service here. But they always smile and sometimes even give me the correct food and change. I order my usual: two sausage McMuffins (no egg), one hash brown, and one large orange juice. The orange juice is healthy. That's what

I tell myself as I try not to look at the banana pointing a judgmental stem at me from the bag of fruit on the passenger seat.

As I pull back into traffic, the warmth emanating from my fatty treasure begins to fog the windshield.

***

I've had a lifelong love/hate relationship with food. Mom called me a "snoopy eater" because I didn't eat everything she put in front of me. She was a great cook, especially considering she prepared nearly every meal for a husband and six kids over the course of almost forty years. But I simply didn't enjoy some foods. Here's a partial list of foods that I "hated" back then: liver, shrimp, eggs, seafood (especially anything with a shell or exoskeleton), cooked vegetables of most kinds, and mushrooms.

Sometimes when I hear Jim profess "hate" for a food, I tell him that "hate" is a very strong word and suggest that he only "dislikes" the taste of that food. When he replies, "No, I really *hate* this," I'm forced to remember that I didn't simply "dislike" some foods as a kid. No other word did justice to the "hate" I felt at being required to eat something that tasted repulsive.

Dad got very protective of Mom when it came to food. In the middle of a typical meal, he'd rub his belly and say, "Yum, yum, yum, this is delicious. Anyone who doesn't like this can go a house farther." If we were having liver, one of Mom and Dad's favorites, I looked at my plate and imagined what Margie and Ray, our sweet, retired neighbors in the mythical "house farther" were having for dinner. Our other neighbors, Dorothy and Earl, were a better possibility. Dorothy was a cook at our high school. Whatever she cooked for Earl, even if it might be the school's infamous "mystery meat," had to be better than liver.

Of course, my childhood happened before most parents simply took the plate and said, "Okay, you don't have to eat it," and let the child be hungry until the "hate" passed. Mom wouldn't let me leave the table until I had swallowed an appropriate amount of the food I hated. When I learned in school that different parts of the tongue specialized in different tastes, I chewed the offensive food with my front teeth so it touched only the tip of my tongue, hoping that might give it a sweeter flavor. I vaguely remember partial success with this method, but mostly I just bit my tongue.

Whether we liked or disliked or hated the food Mom cooked, Dad always made sure we gave her a kiss on the cheek and said, "That was good," after every meal. If we forgot and started toward the living room to turn on the TV, Dad called out, "Hold on there! What do you say to your mother?" and we rushed back with a kiss and a compliment.

Dad once announced that President Nixon himself probably didn't eat food as good as the dinners Mom served, so I secretly wrote a letter to the president and invited him to a meal at our home. I even enclosed a hand-drawn map to help him find our farm. A few weeks later, I got a package from the White House that contained a photo album of the president and his family along with a nice note from an assistant letting me know how much Mr. Nixon appreciated the invitation. Unfortunately, he couldn't accept because he was too busy planning his upcoming visit to China. The president was looking forward to sampling the native Chinese food, but the assistant assured me that the chief executive would have preferred my mother's cooking if he had the choice.

One of Mom's most aggravating habits popped up from time to time at the dinner table. She'd offer me a second helping of something–say, mashed potatoes–and I'd politely decline, having had my fill of mashed potatoes. Then Mom would look me in the eye and ask, "Are you sure?" I'd reply that, yes, I was sure, but she would continue, "Are you certain?" By this time, I couldn't keep the annoyance out of my voice when I'd tell her that I was, indeed, certain of my lack of desire for more mashed potatoes.

"Are you positive?" she would then ask, lifting the bowl of mashed potatoes from the table and holding it out toward me.

At this point, I almost yelled, "Of course, I'm positive! I'm not so stupid that I need to be asked a simple question four times!" Or I fantasized mumbling in my least intelligent voice, "Duh, gee Mommy, I'm too much of a dumb little baby to know if I want any more potatoes. Duh, golly, please tell me what to do." Instead, I usually just forced myself to take another blob of mashed potatoes.

When meat was on the table, I always accepted Mom's generous offer of second helpings. "Carnivorous" was a word I enjoyed learning in school because it described me well. I could eat anything back then and still stay rail thin. I weighed 155 pounds as a six-foot high school senior even though I'd eaten a lifetime supply of red meat by age eighteen. Our freezer was always full of beef, pork, poultry, and venison. A typical week of main courses included steak, ham, fried chicken, and "hash," three times, a meal mixing ground beef with whatever side dishes were left over from previous meals to form a new main course. Mom had this idea well before the invention of "Hamburger Helper."

Many meals consisted of actual burgers that Mom managed to make an inch and a half thick and nine inches in diameter. I've tried to make them like that as an adult, but they crumble to pieces. Mom fried her burgers in grease, but I can't in good conscience do that, so I broil mine–with mixed success. Mom spoiled me so much with her burgers that the first time I saw a fast-food burger, I lifted the bun and asked aloud, "Where's the rest of it?"

Sunday was the best food day of the week. After a big "dinner" (our term for lunch) around noon, Mom took the rest of the day off from cooking. I loved leaving the living room where Dad and I watched football all Sunday afternoon to ask Mom, "What's for supper?" Her reply always filled me with joy: "Tonight we're having 'Get What You Want When You Want It.' " My favorite meal!

So I'd open the refrigerator door and stare inside. A week's worth of leftovers usually stared back at me. Once again, my carnivorous instincts took hold. Nothing in the world tasted better than sinking my teeth into cold fried chicken or putting a slice of cheese atop a cold burger and eating it without a bun. This was before the invention of the microwave, and I had no interest in wasting time reheating anything in the oven, so I developed a real taste for cold meat. I sometimes even walked back into the living room (another Sunday treat–being allowed to eat in front of the TV) with a cold steak in my hand, eating it like a candy bar.

Between farm work, sports, not having my own car, and a teenager's metabolism, I could eat the way I did and not rise above my 155-pound limit. That all changed in college when I put on twenty pounds the first year, and food has been a source of struggle ever since. I have shoveled amazing amounts of food down my gullet over the years. Portion size has always been my problem because I once misheard someone say that a basic portion of food is about the size of your hand. I thought he said the size of your *head*. For years, my only goal was never to eat anything bigger than my head.

My weight rose to as much as 200 pounds in my twenties, fell to 150 when I had gall bladder surgery, then skyrocketed to 225 a few years after I got married. My late thirties gave way to the "divorce diet," when I hit 175 from depression and compulsive exercise. I'm back to about 190 now and trying to maintain a healthy balance of fruit and vegetables to go with fish, turkey, and veggie beef and pork substitutes.

Another problem is eating out. When I was a child, we went to restaurants so infrequently that, even now, I get a thrill from nice strangers bringing me food in a quiet, comfortable place. Even the McDonald's drive-through still strikes me as a miraculous thing from the happy land of dream-come-true.

***

Chapter 2
Wearing a Mask

I'm on the road for barely a minute after McDonald's when someone crosses over the center line on Route 190 and nearly sideswipes me. I can see him leaning over his steering wheel and squinting through a six-inch viewing portal scratched into the frost on his windshield. His side and back windows are completely iced over, and he has snow piled up on his bumper hiding his brake lights.

As a kid, I had four dream careers for what to be "when I grew up": basketball player, football player, baseball player, and police officer. Had I fulfilled the fourth dream, I would pull this jerk over and drag him directly to jail.

***

Today's drive should take about eight hours. I'll go through Hartford, Waterbury, and Danbury, Connecticut, on to southern New York State, then northeast Pennsylvania to Scranton, across the rural heart of Pennsylvania, and, finally, southwest to my destination in Bedford County. I've brought along a book on tape: *A Walk in the Woods*, Bill Bryson's account of hiking the Appalachian Trail (which my map tells me I'll cross on this trip somewhere in southern New York).

After my detour to McDonald's, I go a few miles along the "southern shortcut," a rural back route from my house leading to Route 91, a major interstate that leads south to Hartford, Connecticut, the state capital. Hartford is a nice but generic city, famous for being the hub of the insurance industry. Less well known is the fact that the poet Wallace Stevens worked for decades in that same Hartford insurance community. After puzzling over Stevens's poems for a graduate school semester, I have great empathy for my students who hate pondering the mysteries of poetry. Even more obscure is the fact that Mark Twain, a writer more closely associated with southern literature, lived in Hartford from 1871 to 1891. Twain did his most significant writing while a resident of Hartford, including such classics as *The Adventures of Tom Sawyer, The Prince and the Pauper, The Adventures of Huckleberry Finn, Life on the Mississippi,* and (appropriately) *A Connecticut Yankee in King Arthur's Court.* The Twain House still stands and is a first-rate museum and historic landmark.

I've gone to plays and concerts in Hartford, given presentations at the city's several colleges and universities, and watched my favorite sports team, the University of Connecticut's national-champion women's basketball team, play in the Civic Center. Hartford is home to the central office of the Connecticut community college system, my employer. Still, I feel no real connection to the city. I mostly drive around or through it to get somewhere else.

In Hartford, I switch from Route 91 South to Route 84 West. A few minutes later, I pass the town of Plainville, where my ex-girlfriend Amy grew up and where her parents still live. They're wonderful people who always treated me well during the few years of my on-and-off relationship with their daughter after our divorces. Sad as I was about the end of that relationship, losing her parents' friendship was almost as bad. Even an orphan as old as I am responds to good parenting. I have the urge to get off the exit in Plainville and visit them, but I resist. They'd probably look at me like I was nuts–but then they'd offer me some food. They're that kind of people.

Route 84 then takes me by Waterbury where I know some terrific people who teach at the community college there. To me, though, this is an ugly city with some ugly people, including a former mayor who is currently jailed and awaiting trial for having sexual relationships with minors. This horrible mess was plastered all over the news a year ago, and has popped up again now as the legal maneuvering continues. Maybe it's no coincidence that Waterbury's skyline is dominated by a hideous phallic clock tower.

From there, I'm on to Danbury, the last town in Connecticut on Route 84. A great highway rest area is hidden here, away in the woods with lots of trees and clean, well-maintained facilities. But only travelers entering Connecticut from New York have access, not those heading out. On the way back northeast, I'll be sure to stop here and jog around in the cold temperature to keep from falling asleep during the last leg of the trip.

***

After slightly more than ninety minutes of driving, I'm about an hour north of New York City, the lower part of "upstate" New York. Predictably, I taste my McDonald's breakfast again, and it's not as good the second time around. I should have had a couple of bananas instead.

I once made the mistake of stopping at a rest area off Route 84 in this part of New York at night and was propositioned by one man and offered drugs by another. Since then, I hold my bladder for the hour it takes to get through to Pennsylvania. Halfway across, huge prisons loom on both sides of the highway. One section looks like a college campus with a mix of modern and traditional buildings. The prison has a beautiful valley view from its hillside, and I'm sure I'd enjoy teaching there if it really were a college.

***

Considering I set foot on exactly one college campus before age twenty-two, I traveled a winding path to become a college teacher. I first had an inkling of the upcoming journey when I arrived at West Virginia Wesleyan College. I remember pulling my head out of a notebook long enough to look up at my teachers and think, *Maybe I could do that.*

I wasn't really intrigued by the thought of standing up in front of a room full of people and looking intelligent and respectable. In fact, that part intimidated me a little. Mostly, I liked seeing my professors on campus and having them come up to me and start a conversation. These educated, articulate, likable adults were interested in little old me–a kid barely removed from having dirt under my fingernails and hay in my hair. These people had an impact on my young life. I wanted a career that gave me the potential for that kind of impact on other people's lives.

My first actual teaching experience occurred a year before college during my senior year in high school. We had a student-teacher "switch day," and I got assigned one day's worth of history classes. Mom drove me to school an hour early so that I could hang out in the teacher's lounge wearing my powder-blue leisure suit and bantering with the day's other "teachers."

"Switch day" turned out to be one of the longest of my life. Although the "lectures" I had cribbed straight from the textbooks were nerve-wracking, they went well enough. The discussion parts of the classes, however, were like squeezing blood from a stone. I had very little success getting teenagers to say anything in class. (In fact, that's still the hardest part of my job–getting teenagers to use their minds and their mouths at the same time.)

A few years later, during my junior year at Wesleyan, I took a senior-level social theory seminar. Halfway through the semester, the professor asked me to organize a study group. I felt flattered and surprised and had no clue how to run a study group, but I couldn't say no. I walked home to my apartment that day in a fog, wondering what I had agreed to.

To prepare for the weekly study group, I re-read the assigned chapters five times and typed up what I called "big-idea outlines" to give to the group. The whole thing made me so nervous that I showed up an hour before our meetings just to arrange the chairs in our meeting room. I thought the seniors in the class would resent me, but they turned out to be grateful to have someone's help with the difficult material. We slogged through social theory together, memorizing dozens of German and French names and connecting seemingly unconnected ideas. Then I ran the study group the following year as well. The second time around, I felt like I knew what to do–at least a little.

Then I showed up at Ohio University in Athens, Ohio, to begin a master's degree in English. The first day of orientation, a Thursday, I was given a textbook and told that I would be teaching my own section of Freshman Composition beginning the following Monday. I didn't hear a word anyone said for the next half hour. The shock wore off by Friday night, and I spent the entire weekend making careful plans for the unsuspecting students unlucky enough to draw my name at registration–and picking out just the right necktie and sneaker combination to make me seem respectable but relaxed and approachable.

For the first class, I took roll, gave them my meticulous syllabus, showed them the textbook, and sent them home. They gleefully fled the classroom for far more important college pursuits: dorm naps, mating rituals, afternoon trips to the local bars, and pot smoking. When a few of them approached me after class to ask a couple of questions, my brain worked furiously to make up answers that, amazingly, seemed to satisfy them.

By the end of my career at Ohio U., I had taught every writing and literature course that graduate students were allowed to teach. I even took on a few classes at the medium-security prison extension program in Lancaster, Ohio. When I finished my degree, the administration invited me to stay another year as a barely paid adjunct faculty member. With each new class, whether in the prison or on campus, I planned obsessively to combat my anxiety. I couldn't imagine that they didn't know what a fraud they'd hired. I wasn't a college professor–just a farm kid from the middle of nowhere.

Fortunately, no one has figured out my masquerade. After Ohio U., I got a one-year teaching position at Parkersburg Community College in Parkersburg, West Virginia. I taught twelve classes for about $17,000 and drove an eight-hour round trip twice a week to work on a

Ph.D. that I could never seem to finish. After Parkersburg, I spent a year as assistant director of the college writing program at Bowling Green State University in Bowling Green, Ohio. My job included supervising graduate students who were teaching their first college class. Not only was I pretending to know what I was doing, but to know what they should be doing as well.

I left that job when I got married and moved to New England. The marriage never seemed to fit and ended after nearly a decade in my mid-thirties. Compounding the mistake, I had left a great job at Bowling Green to move to an area with lots of colleges but very few jobs available during a full-scale economic downturn. I spent several years working in a video store and a movie theater while living in a Mount Holyoke College dorm where my then-wife Stephanie and I served as "head residents," dorm parents for two hundred college women living in our building. At the same time, I taught part-time at American International College in Springfield, Massachusetts, did whatever odd jobs I could find, and combed the academic want ads looking for a full-time teaching job.

After a while, I got a bad job at a great college, Smith College in Northampton, Massachusetts. I edited and proofread every official publication sent out by the college, all the while envying the faculty members who taught five classes per year to honor students. The job was tolerable only because I had my own office and computer. I came in early each morning to print my resume and apply for teaching jobs in the area. In three years, I applied for seventy-five teaching jobs and interviewed twenty different places. Finally, Asnuntuck Community College (which I hadn't even heard of before I applied for a job teaching there) came to my rescue. I've been blissfully happy at this wacky little place with the goofy name ever since. For fun (and for the extra money), I sometimes even teach graduate writing classes at prestigious Wesleyan University, passing myself off not only as a teacher, but as a writer too.

Amazingly, no one has yet pulled the confident professor mask off my face to reveal the bashful farm kid underneath. With luck, I'll keep the charade going for another twenty years until I'm be eligible to retire into safe obscurity.

Until then, I'll probably still feel the anxiety that hits me as I walk down the hallway to each new class.

***

As I leave the western edge of southern New York State, Route 84 descends to the Delaware River, well north of George Washington's famous crossing, then passes into Pennsylvania. I've always liked the huge "Pennsylvania Welcomes You" sign here at the border. It looks so cheerful and friendly, bright blue and yellow shining in the sun. The license plates here even used to read, "You've got a friend in Pennsylvania"–which still feels true.

I'm barely three hours from my departure, but I'd be foolish to celebrate being in my home state. People driving from one end of Pennsylvania to the other have only one word for the state: *wide*. If I punch a time clock entering the New York side of Pennsylvania, drive the speed limit, then clock out when I reach Ohio on the other end, I'll have worked a full eight-hour day.

Many places in Pennsylvania sound familiar to the average American. Philadelphia–with the Liberty Bell and the "Founding Fathers" of this nation. Pittsburgh–with its professional football team and steel industry. Harrisburg–home of the Three Mile Island nuclear meltdown. (I was there that day, but it wasn't my fault. More on that later.) Gettysburg–pivotal battlefield of the Civil War. Lancaster–Amish country. Penn State University–home of the Nittany Lions football team. Titusville–home of the first oil well in the world.

But Pennsylvania is such a big state that my trip won't take me near any of these landmarks except Penn State, which I'll miss by a few miles.

I will pass within fifteen miles of the curiously named town of Centralia–not a landmark most people have heard of, but a place that shows how strange our world can get. Centralia is located in eastern Pennsylvania's anthracite coal region. Anthracite is the hard, long-burning kind of coal, as opposed to the more common, softer bauxite. In 1962, a year after my birth, an underground vein of anthracite ignited due to a fire in a trash dump in Centralia. And here's the amazing part: *It has been burning ever since.*

Anthracite coal is very difficult to extinguish once it starts burning. People tried to stop the fire, but nothing worked. So they let it burn, figuring that it couldn't cause any real problems so deep underground. Then in the late 1970s, people in Centralia noticed that the ground was hot. Then they began smelling vile fumes. Then huge holes started appearing in the town, swallowing chunks of roads and buildings–evacuation time.

Why Centralia is not in every school curriculum in the world, I have no idea. In a way, it's as stunning an example of how human beings can mess things up in our quest to dominate the environment as the Titanic, Chernobyl, acid rain, ozone, and Challenger. The really fascinating aspect of Centralia is that some people *haven't left.* Hard as it is to believe, they still live and walk and breathe (sort of, considering the fumes) atop a forty-year underground fire.

My sister Tam and her husband Dale live only a short drive from Centralia. They actually visited once, and Tam describes it as a place right out of *The Twilight Zone.* Many of the houses were tall, skinny, hillside row houses popular in working-class Pennsylvania communities. When the sane people left town, their houses were demolished. Some of the houses owned by the people who remain in town are row houses with the rest of their row torn down and missing from around them. Tam says they look like a gaping mouth with only one or two teeth left rising from the gums in a crazy smile. She says an enormous, beautiful Catholic church sits abandoned in the middle of town, streets collapsed around it, shimmering in the fumes.

Two other events in recent Pennsylvania history have made famous a couple of spots that are very close to my destination. Much of America saw the nine trapped Quecreek coal miners. Like me, most people thought they wouldn't survive, then breathed a soft "I'll be damned" when they were miraculously, joyfully rescued right there on TV. That happened in Somerset County, about an hour northwest of where I grew up.

And on September 11, 2001, if Flight 93 had stayed in the air on its flight path another five minutes, it might have crashed into the side of Wills Mountain overlooking our little farm.

I don't mind the inconvenience of explaining where Bedford County is, repeating again and again that my neighbors were not Amish, that I've never seen the Liberty Bell or even Punxatauny Phil. That's much better than hearing, "Oh my God, Flight 93. That's where you grew up?"

***

I enter Pennsylvania just in time for Bill Bryson to inform me that my home state contains what is widely considered the worst section of the Appalachian Trail. He writes in *A Walk in the Woods* that this part of the trail has no history, features the worst views, and misses the state's most scenic mountains–including, says Bryson, Tussey Mountain, the next range east of Wills Mountain. For hikers, like drivers, Pennsylvania seems to be one incredibly long and featureless state.

The most distinctive aspect of the Appalachian Trail in Pennsylvania is its felsenmeer, chunks of rock that poke up through the ground everywhere in roughly the size and shape of footballs. It seems Pennsylvania was on the edge of glacial advancement during the last ice age, so the ground here went through a long series of freezing and thawing, over and over again, until much of the rock was crushed and broken into little bits and strewn everywhere.

Dad and I shoveled through thousands of these rocks on our farm to dig fencepost holes. The blisters on my hands left scars that took years to fade. And I tripped over millions of these rocks during my own walks in the woods. Felsenmeer is not the huge erratic boulders or delicate and charming mica of the New England woods. It's just billions of clunky grayish brown rocks that always seem to be exactly where you want to put your foot for your next step–the place where healthy ankles go to die.

***

After an hour or so in Pennsylvania, I approach Scranton, the halfway point of my trip. Here I have to leave Route 84 and catch Route 81 south down the Scranton/Wilkes-Barre corridor for an hour.

Scranton is the setting for Harry Chapin's song, "Thirty Thousand Pounds of Bananas," detailing the adventures of a banana-hauling truck crashing into town–easy to imagine considering this is a terrible place to drive. A big electric sign reads, "Accident Ahead" in blinking neon. It has been on every time I've driven through here. Maybe it's always on.

The weather here is bad year round–even when beautiful everywhere else. Within ten miles of Scranton, things always turn ugly. The place is always shrouded in fog, and the roads seem icy even in summer. The signs are confusing, and the highway twists and turns up and down the mountains. More than once, I've experienced vertigo from the road hanging out on the edge of a cliff or claustrophobia where it cuts between two towering slabs of rock face.

Route 81 has about ten lanes in some places, with left and right exits and double exits stacked on top of one another. Thousands of trucks and millions of cars are all speeding or going thirty miles an hour under the limit. The huge trucks generate their own gravitational field, nearly sucking my little car under their wheels. And the trucks always do their mysterious light flicking when they pass each other. Does anyone know what this ritual means? I honestly think they're trying to confuse me.

Back in Connecticut, I live only a few miles from the New England Tractor Trailer Training School in Somers, Connecticut, so I know for a fact that some of the people driving these huge trucks are *beginners*. That scares me.

***

A few miles south of Scranton, a road sign reads, "Ashley Sugarnotch." One direction from the exit goes to the town of Ashley, the other to Sugarnotch. It's comforting to know that if I ever have a sex-change operation and then break into the adult entertainment industry, I won't have to worry about what stage-name I'll use.

***

Thankfully, this treacherous section of Route 81 quickly connects with Route 80–but that's no picnic to drive either. Many signs on Route 80 read, "Uneven Pavement." These signs bypass the merely obvious for the incredibly obvious.

Route 80 in Pennsylvania has probably driven more than a few people insane. It spans some three hundred miles from east to west and drones its own characteristic "tha-thunk, tha-thunk, tha-thunk, tha-thunk" that lodges in your brain and stays there. The whole road is one relentless rumblestrip in slow motion.

Tonight in my dreams, I will hear the endless Route 80 tha-thunk soundtrack. Judging by past trips, it won't go away for a week.

***

When Jenny, Rob, Jim, and I came through here a couple of weeks ago, we took a slightly different route. Rather than spending those long hours on Route 80, we kept going south on Route 81 to the Pennsylvania Turnpike. The detour added about half an hour to the drive, so today I've decided to save time by staying on Route 80, no matter how aggravating it can be.

Our turnpike drive took us near Harrisburg, the state capital and sight of the famous Three Mile Island nuclear reactor accident of 1979. As we drove by, I had the chance to tell Jenny and the boys that I had visited Harrisburg on the day of the reactor accident.

During my senior year in high school, two of my fellow school newspaper staffers and I got the day off to attend a high school journalism conference at the Harrisburg branch campus of Penn State University. The United States Army sponsored the conference, so the local army recruiter drove us there. He spent the entire trip trying (unsuccessfully) to talk us out of going to college and into joining the army instead.

I don't remember much about the conference itself, other than the fact that it took place in a gymnasium bigger than our whole high school. I do remember crossing a bridge over the Susquehanna River and seeing the nuclear plant set on a little island off in the distance. When I got home and went to bed that night, I could hear my parents watching television downstairs. Through my drowsiness, I thought I heard the words "Harrisburg" and "evacuate."

I got out of bed and went downstairs, something I rarely did, surprising my parents.

"What are you doing up?" Dad asked.

"Are they talking about Harrisburg?" I replied, pointing to the television.

"Some kind of problem with the power plant there," Dad said.

"They don't know much yet, but it looks like it might be serious," Mom added.

I stared at the TV as the screen kept cutting from shots of talking heads to the same power plant cooling towers I had seen earlier in the day.

"In Harrisburg?" I asked.

"Yes."

"Today?"

"Yes." They seemed irritated by my interruption, so I shut up for a few minutes. But I couldn't stay quiet.

"I was in Harrisburg today."

Mom and Dad both turned to look at me where I still stood at the bottom of the stairs.

"Are they saying anything about how dangerous it is?" I asked.

"They're not sure yet," Dad replied.

"How long were you there?" Mom asked.

"All afternoon," I said.

As we watched the news reports for an hour or so, I monitored my body closely. I had no idea what radiation sickness might be like. I felt no headache or upset stomach–just sleepy.

Finally, I went to bed. The next morning, I felt fine. The news reports were still vague, but no one in Harrisburg was falling over sick or dead or running around demanding brains to eat like the zombies in the original *Living Dead* movie filmed a few hours north near Pittsburgh– so I figured I would be okay.

I've long ago stopped worrying about whatever I might have been exposed to that afternoon in that college gymnasium listening to presentations about careers in journalism and in the army. I never grew armor plating or burst out of my clothes like the Incredible Hulk. But the experience makes a nice conversation piece on the long drive through Pennsylvania.

Half an hour after I finished telling my story, the boys were asleep in the backseat. So I leaned over toward Jenny and spoke softly.

"There's one thing I've never told anyone about Three Mile Island."

She leaned toward me, listening intently.

"You know that little tuft of hair on my lower back?" I asked her.

"Uh-huh," she replied.

"It's the strangest thing," I continued. "The morning after Three Mile Island, I noticed that tuft for the first time. I think the radiation made it grow overnight."

She stared at me for a few seconds before getting my joke. Later when she kissed me goodnight, she grabbed that tuft and gave it a little pull.

***

Chapter 3
Coming to See Me

About a third of the way through Pennsylvania, I drive near my sister Tam's house. She lives with her husband Dale and their two children in a wonderful old Federal-style house in Watsontown, just off Route 80. I feel slightly guilty that I haven't told them I'm passing through. I'd like to stop and see them, but I really want to get to the cabin as quickly as I can.

Tam is two years older than I am–twenty-six months, to be exact. Her twin sister is Pam, and my twin sister is June. Early in our lives, June and Pam were more like twins, as were Tam and I. June and Pam did okay in school but were more practical-minded than academic. Tam and I were honor students. I even looked more like Tam as a kid than I did like June.

When Tam was in high school, she spent part of a summer at West Virginia Wesleyan College in Buckhannon, West Virginia, attending a science program used to recruit new students. It must have worked because she enrolled there after graduation. On my first visit, I wanted to enroll too. I didn't even apply anywhere else. The campus was small and pretty, and all the people seemed attractive and smart and fun–especially compared with my high school classmates.

Sometimes today, people ask me why I went to college in such a backwater place as West Virginia. But Buckhannon had a movie theater, stores, restaurants, even bars. Considering the little farm I came from, it seemed like the big city to me.

At the start of my freshman year, Dad drove Tam and me to college in a huge purple Cadillac he had bought from his brother, my Uncle Glenn. This car was so big that I used it as a clubhouse in the summer, often reading in the comfortable front bucket seats or stretching out for a nap in the back when I had a free half hour away from farm work. And Dad had driven me to my senior prom in that car. The purple Cadillac, my *Saturday Night Fever* white disco suit, and my Venezuelan exchange student date made me a strange sight.

When I loaded all of my sister's luggage and belongings for college into the Cadillac, the trunk was full, and only about one foot remained in the backseat. Dad, Mom, and Tam sat in the front while I sat in the back, feet propped up on my one box of supplies as I hugged my single small suitcase.

Even in that cramped space, I spent the three-hour drive to campus quivering with joy. Throughout high school, I knew my life wouldn't really begin until college. I figured that college people would accept me for myself–a thoughtful but happy young man–not the nerdy farmer brain-boy that my high school classmates saw. From the first day at Wesleyan, as my parents drove away, I knew I was right.

Having an older sister at college was great. We even took a couple of classes together and had friendly competitions to see who could get the best grades. (She usually did, but I caught up by her senior year.) She introduced her shy brother to lots of really wonderful people. In fact, my first girlfriend was a friend of hers . . . also my second . . . and third. Two years passed before I started meeting girls on my own.

Tam liked having me there too. We got together a couple times each week, and she used to call me at my dorm room once in a while. Tam is quite a talker–and that's not meant as a criticism. I liked talking with her, but sometimes I had other things I needed to do.

About ten minutes into her call, I'd say, "uh-huh" and gently put the phone down on my desk while she continued to talk.

Then I'd clean my room, every now and then leaning down to the phone to say, "uh-huh."

Then I'd work on a paper, lean down to the phone, and say, "uh-huh."

Then I'd read a chapter in a textbook for the next day's class. "Uh-huh."

Then I'd go to someone else's room and call for a pizza. "Uh-huh."

Then take a shower. "Uh-huh."

Then go to the lobby to pick up the pizza. "Uh-huh."

Then grab the phone and say, "I'm sorry Tam, but I really have to go now."

She'd reply, "I'm so glad I can talk to you. No one listens to me the way you do."

When I get back to Connecticut, I'll give Tam a call. I promise I'll pay attention to every word.

**

I drove this same route from New England to Watsontown several times six years ago to see Mom when she lived with Tam and Dale during the last few months of her life.

When Mom sold our farm in 1985, she moved to a senior citizens' apartment complex in Corning, New York, close to Tam and Dale, who were living in that area then. Mom thrived in her apartment, making lots of new friends and feeling grateful not to have the big old farmhouse with too much upkeep and too many memories. In no time at all, she was one of the leaders in her building, keeping extra keys to help anyone who was locked out and organizing ceramics workshops in the recreation room. She even took a few bus trips with her building-mates to Atlantic City to try her hand at gambling.

Shortly after Tam and Dale moved to Watsontown, Mom moved to another senior citizens' building in Bedford where my Aunt Ethel (Dad's sister) lived. Mom renewed lots of old friendships and started many more, living a happy and independent life in her one-bedroom apartment. She even drove into her seventies–which wasn't as frightening as it might seem. She was such a terrible driver to begin with that she couldn't get much worse.

As a kid, I always thought Mom was fragile. From my limited perspective, she mostly seemed to sit at the kitchen table in the morning and evening or nap on the couch in the afternoon. Of course, I didn't know then the incredible toughness it took for her to cook and clean and care for a house full of kids while Dad worked away from home. And I can't even imagine the strength it took for her to put up with Grandma's complaints and bossiness all day as they waged their private war to see who was queen of the castle.

Although Dad and I did most of the farm work, Mom certainly did pitch in. She worked especially hard in the garden, weeding row after row of vegetables all summer long in preparation for the harvest. And she'd even drag a few haybales around to feed the cows when she had to.

When she was nearly fifty years old, she shocked me with her ruggedness. The whole family had gone to the state park for a picnic. When we were ready to leave, a summer thunderstorm suddenly blew in, so we packed and rushed toward the car to avoid the rain. My first surprise was seeing Mom run. I had never seen her run before and wasn't sure she could. But she outran my sisters and me even while carrying a heavy basket of picnic supplies on the way to the car. Her churning legs hypnotized me, so I didn't even have a chance to call out a a warning when she headed straight for a tree root jutting six inches out of the ground.

Her toe caught the root in mid-stride, and she fell. She had built up so much speed that she hit the ground face first and bounced a few times. The picnic basket ended up under her and smashed to pieces, fried chicken, paper plates, and plastic forks scattered across the ground.

I knew Mom was dead. I couldn't imagine someone her age and frailty surviving that fall. Already picturing the horrors of a motherless life, I ran to her side. The looks on my sisters' faces told me that they were just as frightened.

When we got to her, she was clearly alive and sitting up and–to our astonishment–*laughing.*

"Wow! That was fun!" she called out, laughing even more when she saw our terrified little faces. Then Dad helped her to her feet, and they started gathering the shrapnel from the picnic basket explosion, Mom chuckling the whole time.

Eventually, however, nearly sixty years of smoking caught up with her. She went to the doctor with shortness of breath and found a pretty advanced spot on her lung. At about the same time, she developed Parkinson's Disease and started to have trouble walking. Driving was out of the question. She needed help, so Tam and Dale took her in, converting their family room into Mom's bedroom.

They took wonderful care of Mom, and she benefited enormously from being around Tam and Dale's young children. I visited several times in the fall of 1994, sometimes by myself and sometimes with my then-wife Stephanie, who got along well with Mom.

During the Christmas holidays that year, Stephanie and I stopped at Tam and Dale's for a couple days before driving on to see Stephanie's family in Ohio. Near midnight the day after Christmas, Dale called Ohio to tell us that Mom had taken a very bad turn and that Tam had driven her to the hospital. We cut short our Ohio visit and headed back to Pennsylvania.

Mom was in good spirits when we got there, but annoyed that this visit to the hospital had interrupted her holidays. The immediate crisis seemed to have passed, but Mom was definitely on an overall downturn. Even though she held little hope that it would work, she decided to try an aggressive regimen of chemotherapy. Stephanie and I stayed a few days, then went back to New England, promising to come back soon.

Mom knew I had always detested her smoking, but she refused to believe that cigarettes were bad for her. When I complained about her smoking once many years ago, she said, "I work hard taking care of you kids and your dad. I like to smoke. Don't you think I deserve to do something I like?" How could I argue with someone who saw smoking as a reward rather than a health risk? But during our visit at the hospital, she told me, "The doctors say smoking did this to me . . . I don't know . . . maybe they're right." It was the worst thing she ever said about smoking.

Two more visits occurred during the next three weeks, first both Stephanie and me, then just me. Mom was in bad shape on the first of these visits. The chemotherapy had made her even sicker and more fatigued than she felt from the cancer and the Parkinson's. She slept often, even drifting off in the middle of a sentence, only to rouse five minutes later and laugh about her inability to stay awake. We brought her several silk scarves that she could wear over her head now that her hair had begun falling out. She liked them and told us she felt like a movie star in them. Her sense of humor had always been a comfort to her in hard times, and it hadn't abandoned her yet.

On the second visit, even her sense of humor didn't help much. I arrived on a Friday evening to find that nearly all of Mom's hair was gone. The slippery silk scarves wouldn't stay on her head, so she had stopped wearing them. She told me she felt like a bald old man, and then she tried to laugh. The laugh turned into a cough that didn't stop for an hour.

By Saturday, Mom was so weak that her dentures wouldn't stay in her mouth, so the nurses put them on her bedside table. Without them, she couldn't talk coherently. She slept for half an hour at a time, woke to see me, mumbled something, and then got frustrated that she wasn't making any sense. Then she drifted off to sleep again, exhausted by the combination of her diseases and medications, especially the antibiotics.

Mom slept almost all of Sunday, waking only occasionally to look at me while we held hands. Her breathing was so labored that each inhale was a surprise. Every exhale devastated me, torn between wishing she could rest and wanting her to stay. She kept going, little more than sheer stubbornness keeping her alive.

The nurses were having trouble finding veins in her arms to keep the antibiotics flowing. They didn't say anything, but their faces weren't hopeful. Before I left on Sunday, I called my brother Ronnie. We had drifted apart and hadn't spoken for several years. When his wife called out to him that "John" was on the phone, I could hear him in the background ask, "John who?" She replied, *"Your brother* John."

I told Ronnie that if he wanted to see Mom, he should come as soon as possible because she had very little time left. My brother Norman arrived at the hospital that day, so I visited with him for a while before I left. Norman wept openly in the hallway while we talked, but I felt numb. After a while, I walked to my car, sat down, locked the doors, cried for an hour, and drove home.

***

We've all seen the soap operas where a character discovers her "real father." It turns out that the man who raised her and whom she called "Daddy" all those years is not her real father at all–just some guy who made an "honest woman" out of her mother decades before. Her real father is actually the town drunk or the murderer recently paroled from prison or the town's richest oil baron or even–uh, oh–that nice older gentleman she started dating last month.

My story is not nearly as dramatic. For most of my life, I had a sneaking suspicion that Mom was not my "real mother." As a teenager, I had Dad's eyes and high forehead and muscles and usually calm temperament. Mom sometimes seemed to be an alien creature so much more like my sisters than me. Don't misunderstand me–she was a wonderful mother, dedicated and kind and generous and funny. But she wasn't *like me*. She was softer and rounder, had an unpredictable temper, a lack of patience, and an inability to drive a car effectively.

Dad was definitely Dad, but how could this woman be my *real mother*?

I understand that the biology behind this fantasy made no sense–not even soap opera sense. Finding out that your Mom is not your real mother is something that happens only in *Psycho* sequels. Because Mom told so many stories about what a difficult pregnancy and birth I had been, she clearly thought I was her biological son. And I have a twin sister, obviously Mom's child. The whole thing was beyond my powers of explanation, yet I held tightly to the not-my-real-mother fantasy for much of my life.

It took two unrelated moments in my late-thirties to put away my childish fantasy. One afternoon while I backed my car out of a parking space at the gym, my workout partner chuckled. I asked what was funny, and she told me that I backed the car "like an old lady." I immediately had a flash of Dad harshly criticizing Mom's driving. When I pondered that memory later in the day, I realized that I never criticize anybody's driving. People drive the way they drive–different styles for different drivers. Dad and I may have the same shaped hands, but when it came to criticizing drivers, we took very different roads.

Of course, the relative I resemble in the car is Mom. Her driving used to make me crazy even before I could drive myself. She was well into her forties when she finally got her license. Even at age twelve, I saw that she had very little idea what was going on behind her. She seemed content to travel down the interstate at forty miles per hour, confident that she would never run into anything or anyone. She was right. She never hit a thing with her car, but the drivers screaming past her and shaking their fists were running the risk of head-on collisions. This was a woman who stopped at green lights because she was afraid they would turn yellow. Mom was completely safe–just a terror for everyone else on the road.

I maintain and sometimes even exceed the speed limit when I'm on the highway, so that's not where the connection is. It's backing up. Mom inched backward a millimeter at a time, looking frantically over one shoulder, then the other, then back and forth again until she was dizzy. I'm not that bad, but I admit that I always make a tight U-turn in the driveway so my car points headfirst toward the street. And I'll walk an extra half a mile at the mall to find a "pull-through" parking space that requires no backing to enter or leave.

Not long after the driving revelation, I decided to shave the beard that covered my chin for nearly twenty years. I'd started growing it in my late teens and endured all the jokes about how scraggly it grew. Eventually, the bald spots filled in. People only occasionally ask me what I'm hiding behind my beard. I usually claim that I don't like shaving or that I'm tired of being a baby face.

The day I shaved it, however, I found what I had been hiding. As I wiped the steam from the bathroom mirror, I saw Mom's face staring back. I still had Dad's forehead and eyes and the top half of his nose, but from there down, I was my mother. In my amazement, I uttered a few soft curses and even saw Mom's words in the shape and movements of my mouth. *Good lord,* I thought to myself at long last, *she is my real mother.*

Maybe I don't back the car quite like an old lady, but I started growing my beard back that same day.

***

When I first started dating Stephanie, a black woman, my mother asked me if I cared what other people thought about our interracial relationship.

"Not really," I told her. "But I am interested in what you think."

"Well," she said, studying the floor, "I guess if you're in love and happy, that's what's important."

Five years later, I picked my mother up at the Columbus, Ohio, airport. I was twenty-eight years old and about to marry Stephanie. We drove ninety minutes to Stephanie's parents' home in rural Ohio where the wedding would take place. Mom was talkative as we drove through the darkness on unfamiliar country roads.

"Does Stephanie's family have many white friends?" she asked.

"Sure," I replied. "It's a mostly white town, so they have lots of white friends."

"I just was worried that I'd be out of place at the wedding," she said.

I laughed. "Well, if you're out of place sitting in the audience, imagine how I'll feel up in front of everybody."

"Is it strange to be marrying someone so different?"

"Stephanie isn't really that different," I said. "We're a lot more alike than different. She grew up outside a small town and went to a small high school, just like I did. Her parents worked, just like you and Dad. Their family wasn't rich or poor. She has lots of the same interests as I do. Race is about the only difference, but we're both human."

"I guess," Mom said, and then she was thoughtful for a moment. Then she asked, "Do you remember your cousin Danielle?"

"The one who's a kindergarten teacher?"

"She bought a house," Mom said. She was always fond of telling me mundane information about people I hadn't seen in at least a decade.

"Uh-huh," I said.

"She's not married," Mom continued.

"Uh-huh," I repeated.

"She bought the house with a *friend* of hers who works at another school," Mom said.

"Her boyfriend?" I asked.

"That's the funny thing," Mom said. "It's another woman. They're both in their thirties, never been married, no kids."

I remembered Danielle fondly. She was a great athlete even as an adolescent. We played basketball when she came to visit, and she always beat me even though I was already taller than she was by the time I was nine and she was thirteen.

"Do you think they're a couple?" I asked.

Mom turned toward me. "What do you mean?"

"You know," I said. "Are they gay?"

"No!" Mom said, pushing her back against the passenger door. "That's just gross. I can't understand that whole thing. It just makes me sick."

"What?" I asked.

"Two women together–that's just sickening," she said.

"Well," I continued, "there are people who think it's sickening that Stephanie and I are together."

Mom was quiet.

"In fact, it used to be against the law for me to marry Stephanie. And there are still people in the world who would kill us if they could get away with it, just because we love each other."

"But they're two women," Mom said. "It's unnatural."

"There are plenty of men and women together who aren't very 'natural.' Men who hit their wives, women who scream at their husbands–that doesn't sound very 'natural.' "

"What kind of lives can they have together?" Mom asked. "What do they *do* with each other?"

I chuckled. "I imagine they do pretty much what every couple does. They worry about the bills and watch TV, sit on the porch at sunset. They argue about stupid little things. When one of them is sick, the other one takes care of her. They go to weddings. They complain about their bosses. Pay the mortgage. Gossip about relatives. They love each other."

"But when I think about them in bed," Mom said with a shudder, "it's sickening."

I laughed again. "Then don't think about them in bed. Besides, there are plenty of things that straight couples do in bed that a lot of people think are sickening. But those couples are allowed to do what they want. Suppose somebody told you and Dad that the love you felt for each other and the way you expressed that love was 'sickening.' Suppose they told you that you shouldn't be together, that your love was wrong and evil. How would you feel about that?"

"Grandma felt that way about us," Mom said.

My dad's mother had objected to the fact that Mom had a child from her first marriage when she and Dad got married. It didn't matter to Grandma that Mom was a young widow. To her, it was still a scandal. Mom and Grandma didn't really become friends until after Dad died.

"How did that make you feel?" I asked.

"I didn't like it," Mom said.

We drove a few miles in silence. The wipers ticked away a steady drizzle. After a while, I started wondering about something. "Is she nice?"

"Who?" Mom asked.

"Danielle's girlfriend."

Mom laughed. "You know what? She is. She's funny and smart, and she likes to tease Danielle about her short hair. They seem really happy together."

The next evening, after the wedding, Mom sat at the kitchen table with Stephanie's mother and her relatives and friends, all of them women between fifty and seventy-five, half of them black, half white. Mom happily joined in the discussion of pride and disappointment in all their many kids, some of whom were within earshot and rolled their eyes each time their name came up–me included.

Nobody felt out of place at all.

***

From a very early age, I thought Mom had trouble remembering my name–especially if I did something that got on her nerves. When she tried to yell at me, she went through every male name in our family to get to mine: "Bill, er, Norman, I mean, Ronnie, ohhh . . . *John*. I know your name is John! I'm not crazy!" She'd call out, laughing, forgetting what annoyed her in the first place. I started calling these little incidents, "stuttering mothering."

The last time I visited my sister Tam, she had several episodes of Mom's "stuttering mothering," calling me by the names of both her husband and son before she got to mine. As we sat around the dinner table, she looked straight at me and said, "Dale, ahhh, Andrew, oh crap! *John*."

I may have inherited some of Mom's qualities that I hide behind my beard, but Tam got a few of Mom's quirks as well.

***

After I went to college, I sometimes felt awkward around Mom. She had seen me as her "baby" for so many years that I got defensive around her. I wanted to be a full-grown adult from age twelve, and I resented being thought of as her "little boy." So I didn't come to visit her as much as she wanted. I even stayed at college to take extra classes and work each summer instead of coming home.

During my senior year, I had reconstructive ankle surgery. Mom came to "take care of me" during my three days in the hospital. She wouldn't even stay in the motel across the street–she stayed in my room, telling the nurses who objected that she had to take care of her "baby boy." They looked at her, then at me (the bearded six-footer stretched out in the bed), then shrugged. How could they argue with a woman who thought of a twenty-one-year-old man as a "baby"? Seven years later when I had gall bladder surgery, I didn't call her until after the operation for fear that she would come and stay in my room again. Once was more than enough.

I never completely shut Mom out of my life, but I didn't come to visit her as often as she wanted. I only called her once a month or so, not every week as my sisters did. Each time I called, she inevitably asked, "When you coming to see me?" then followed up the question with words that prickled the hair on my neck and made me invent excuses to stay away: "I miss my little baby boy."

***

Throughout the week after I visited Mom in the hospital that second time, I half expected Tam's call to tell me that Mom had died. She did call on Thursday afternoon, surprising me with the news that Mom had improved enough to be released to a nursing home. In fact, Tam was calling from Mom's room at the nursing home, and she said Mom wanted to talk to me. I was flabbergasted because the last time I saw Mom, she couldn't talk at all.

"John?" her voice came strong and almost clear through the phone.

"Mom?" I asked. "How are you feeling?"

"When you coming to see me?" Mom asked, the same question I had heard so many times with slight measures of guilt and dread. This time, however, the answer was easy.

"How's Saturday? Can you squeeze me into your social calendar?"

"Good," she replied.

So Stephanie and I packed our overnight bags on Friday and prepared to drive six hours southwest the next morning.

Tam called at about seven Saturday morning to tell us that Mom had died Friday night. The antibiotics that were making her so weak were also keeping her alive. Without them, she had a temporary upswing, but the cancer was then free to run its final, rapid course. In a daze, we added a few extra items to our bags and changed our destination from Watsontown to Madley for Mom's funeral.

***

Chapter 4
Learning to Swear

When I tell rich city people that I grew up in the country, sometimes they ask me really ignorant things–like whether or not I had sex with farm animals or if I'm an inbred mountain man like the guys in the movie *Deliverance*.

Although I had a mostly normal rural childhood, the region did contain some very isolated hillbilly areas. People in these places bought cheap house trailers, tore out and sold the oil or gas furnaces, and then built campfires inside. Roving bands of wild dogs were rumored to carry away livestock and disobedient children. And some people were related to one another in a few too many ways–for example, one particular character known as "Uncle Myself."

At a gas station in central Pennsylvania, I see a set of twin boys who really are dead ringers for the banjo-playing hillbilly kid in *Deliverance*. I'm reminded that Pennsylvania is a very complex state, with some big, sophisticated cities, as well as lots of farmland and isolated hills that have more in common with the rural American southeast than with nearby New England.

During graduate school at Indiana University of Pennsylvania (in the *town* Indiana, in the *state* Pennsylvania), I met the wife of one of my new professors, a high school teacher originally from upstate New York. When she and her husband moved here, she rationalized that Pennsylvania would be okay because it was "next to New York." But after a few months of teaching Pennsylvania kids, she changed her mind. "Pennsylvania isn't next to New York," she lamented. "It's next to West Virginia."

As rural Pennsylvanians, the most popular target for our jokes were West Virginians. Even Dad occasionally teased Mom good-naturedly because she was born there, calling her a "hoopie." But most of the jokes I heard from other people were pretty mean. I guess we felt the need to validate our own sophistication by putting down people we saw as even more deprived than ourselves.

One joke I remember clearly from those days went like this: How can you tell a rich West Virginian from a poor West Virginian? The rich West Virginian has *two* cars up on blocks outside his trailer. Another one posed this question: Why did the West Virginians build a bridge across the Ohio River? In case it rained, they could swim across under it and not get wet. Despite their nasty tone, those two are just silly. This one is horrible: How do you define a West Virginia virgin? A ten-year-old girl who can outrun her brothers.

Ironically, when I went to college in West Virginia, my first visit home surprised me with how run-down and depressed our farm and the surrounding area looked. West Virginia may not have been exactly cosmopolitan, but we weren't the center of any universe either.

***

When I came home from college for a family reunion, one of my cousins asked me what I was studying.

"Sociology," I said.

"Well," he replied, "that there must be some goddamned important shit 'cause I don't even know what the hell it is." He slapped me on the back and grabbed another burger from the grill.

Another cousin asked, "Where's that college you go to?"

"Buckhannon," I answered.

"Is that anyplace near Fairmont?" he asked.

"About half an hour away," I replied.

"I spent a week in jail in Fairmont once," he told me.

What does someone say to something like that?

"Was it a nice jail?" I asked.

"Wasn't the worst one I stayed in," he said.

***

I hardly uttered a swear word before I went to college, and I still don't swear nearly as often as most people I know. But when I turned fifteen, I decided my time had come to say bad words. On the way to becoming a grown-up, I thought I should sound like one.

For privacy, I walked down to our barn and climbed up into the hayloft. To be sure no one could hear me, I situated myself way back in the corner farthest away from our house and from the church just beyond the hill.

I started small, using some words that weren't really swears but were the closest I came in my everyday language.

"Darn," I whispered. "Darn it," I continued, a little louder. Then, in a voice about half my normal volume, "Darn it all to heck!"

At the sound of my voice, a group of crows took off from a rafter and flew out a high window. They startled me so much I said, "Shoot!"

Darn? Heck? Shoot? Was I a toddler?

"Damn," I said. This one didn't really count because I had heard it in church, but it still sounded pretty harsh in my own voice.

"Hell," I continued, but this was just another church word. I had to try a real curse word to see if I could do it.

"Sh*t," I spat out quickly, and then looked around. No birds flew, and my parents didn't burst through the barn door telling me I had said something horrible. I repeated the word a few times, saying it louder and more drawn out each time. After a few tries, I sounded just like one of my older cousins when he swore and spat a stream of tobacco juice. "She-yit."

I tried the few other swears I could think of that day. First, the basic insults: "bit*h" and "basta*d." Then the general anatomical terms: "a*s" and "a*s ho*e." Then some gender specific bad words: "di*k," "co*k," "t*t," and "pus*y." I went back to my religious roots and expanded on them: "go to he*l," "da*n you," and "g*d da*n it."

Finally, I went for the big one . . . the "f" word. To make it a really well-rounded experience, I even practiced giving the finger to some "a*s ho*e basta*d kid on the g*d da*n school bus who threw fu*king chewing gum in my hair."

After a while, I got bored with saying swear words. They rang dull in my ears after a few tries. So I left the barn, walked to our vegetable garden, and pulled some carrots for a snack.

They tasted livelier than any curse.

***

"What's brown and yellow and screams?" my cousin Gene asked for the second time, not hiding the grin that spilled into a cackle. This was a joke, I assumed.

My father stared at the floor, as did Gloria, joke-teller Gene's wife. I was twelve years old and had just picked a bushel of sweet corn from our garden in the dwindling summer dusk. We always gave relatives vegetables, even though most of them had gardens of their own. We may have been poor in money, but we were rich in vegetables.

"I give up," my mother said politely, breaking the silence. She and I looked expectantly at Gene because we were the only ones in the kitchen that evening who had not heard this joke before. My father and Gloria continued to study the pattern in the linoleum.

"A school bus load of nigger kids going over a cliff!" Gene hollered before breaking into a spitting fit of laughter.

My mother, ever polite, shook her head. "Good one," she said before turning her attention to something in the vicinity of the stove. I think her sarcasm was lost on Gene.

Out of a general subservience I felt when around adults, I coughed out a half-laugh, then quickly cut it off as I made a mental image of the joke: screaming schoolchildren plunging to their deaths . . . horrifying.

Gene slapped both his knees with both his hands, then clapped me across a shoulder blade, clearly mistaking my deference for appreciation, perhaps even approval.

There were no black people in Hyndman where I went to school. In fact, only a few dozen black people lived in all of Bedford County. I didn't actually see a black person up close until I was in junior high and went on a class trip to Washington, D.C. At the Smithsonian, a black tour guide smiled at me and asked a group of my friends what we thought of the Apollo spacecraft exhibit. We stared at him like he was from the moon. He just chucked, probably thinking to himself, *Okay, another busload of hillbilly white kids from the sticks.* He would have been at least partly right.

One summer, I rode my bike to Hyndman to play basketball at the high school courts. An older guy who was maybe twenty told us between games that he had played basketball with some "darkies" in the big city where he had found a factory job.

"Some of them are kind of okay," he said. "But most of them smell funny and will cut you up for the change in your pocket."

"How many did you meet," I asked.

"Three or four," he said. "That's enough to know."

Most white people I knew growing up had what I later called "TV Negro Disorder." The only black people they had ever seen were on television, so they thought the whole race consisted of drug dealers, athletes, and Huxtables. Some of these white people would say things like, "They're just too lazy and dumb to get jobs or make something of themselves." Then these same white people would cash their welfare checks and use their foodstamps to buy cigarettes.

Even at the mostly white college I attended after leaving the farm, I met dark-skinned people from Africa, Jamaica, South America, Australia–even exotic places such as Ohio and New Jersey. I discovered that I needed to meet a lot more than three or four to be "enough to know" about them. My ex-wife is African-American, and I loved getting to know her wonderful family. Racial differences had no effect on our marriage or divorce. I've now had the pleasure of meeting thousands of black people as my life has opened up, and I know that they are as diverse as I am different from my cousin Gene.

The other day I saw a television show about racist jokes. One of the ones examined went like this: "Question: What's worse than a bus load of niggers going over a cliff? Answer: One seat being empty."

As evil as this joke is, there's an ugly, mean intelligence behind it. You have to think for a fraction of a second to get it. The sense of negation and lost opportunity to do away with one more hated black person who could have been in that empty seat shows a mind at work–twisted and sick, but reasonably intelligent. Such an intelligence is rare among bigots. Cousin Gene's black-and-yellow-and-screams joke–that's just dumb.

I was an ignorant country kid. I grew up not knowing anything about people of different races because of geographical and cultural isolation. But my brain worked well enough to understand that people have differences–but people are people. Most bigots are a lot like my cousin Gene was that day in my kitchen all those years ago–not only ignorant, but too stupid even to tell their racist jokes correctly.

***

As I drive, I notice those little zones on the highway where the radio fades out for a few seconds. I've always wondered: If your house is within one of those zones, can you listen to the radio at home?

I'm lucky to be driving on Monday instead of Sunday when the rural Pennsylvania radio dial would be filled with hell-fire preachers. Because this is Monday, there's a healthy fifty-fifty split between country music and hell-fire preachers.

I really enjoyed listening to the radio as a kid. Our television reception may have been limited, but I could get a lot on my little red, ball-shaped radio. When it came to music, I hardly ever missed American Top 40 with Casey Kasem on Saturday mornings. For three hours while doing chores or shooting baskets or lying in my tent, I listened to all forty songs and the music trivia and long-distance dedications. I used to predict the number-one hit in the nation each week, guessing right more often than not.

Sports also dominated my radio back in the days before nearly every game was televised. I listened to more Steelers football and Pirates baseball games than I ever saw on TV. Many enjoyable evenings involved nothing more than sitting on the porch with Dad listening to baseball games on the radio as lightning bugs pincushioned the gathering dusk. We could have been living in the thirties and forties rather than the sixties and seventies.

I even heard the "immaculate reception" on the radio while sitting in my bedroom one winter afternoon. When Terry Bradshaw's last-second pass bounced from Frenchy Fuqua's hands, I was crestfallen because I thought my Steelers had just lost their 1972 playoff game to the hated Oakland Raiders. But a few seconds later, my radio shouted out that Franco Harris had somehow scored the winning touchdown. I stayed up until eleven that night to see the television replay and figure out exactly what the hell had happened.

Most nights, I could even tune in Cleveland Cavalier basketball games. I'd never seen them play on television and didn't have any idea what they looked like. I didn't know that Austin Carr was black and Dick Snyder was white, and I didn't care because they played for *my team*–the only team I could find on my radio.

***

On a bridge abutment in central Pennsylvania, I see a mysterious spray-painted graffiti message: "Trust Jes 08." After a moment, I realize that someone named Jessica from the class of 2008 has tempted eternal damnation by profanely altering a "Trust Jesus" message to flout her own name and graduation year instead.

I just hope the radio evangelists don't see this sight. It would fuel their sermons for years to come.

***

After a few hours of Route 80's disturbing rhythms, I turn southwest on Route 220, slipping through the Allegheny Mountain ranges that stripe central Pennsylvania. For the first half hour on Route 220, I drive on a two-lane road in what's labeled a "targeted enforcement area." Bright orange signs posted every half mile or so advise me to wear my seatbelt, slow down, and watch out for aggressive drivers.

I'm going the standard ten miles over the fifty miles-per-hour speed limit when I notice a middle-aged woman tailgating me. At the first opportunity, she whips around and passes me. Two minutes later, a tractor-trailer does the same. A mile down the highway, a car driven by a scruffy teenager with his back end jacked up (the car, not the teenager) passes me in a no-passing zone around a curve in an area with several homes and a craft shop less than fifteen feet from the road.

This stretch of road features large white dots painted in each lane, spaced at even intervals of about fifty feet. A sign advises me to keep a minimum safe driving distance of two dots between my car and the car ahead. I notice that I'm following behind the next car by a dot and a half–not bad considering how traffic experts always exaggerate the safe-driving standards, erring on the side of caution. I look in my rearview mirror to see a car about two dots back. Unfortunately, two other cars are between that one and mine, each weaving around and looking for a place to pass.

I'm fond of complaining about the crazy drivers in New England and rhapsodizing nostalgically about the calm and polite driving in Pennsylvania. But there are as many tractor-trailers and scruffy teenagers here as anywhere else. Pennsylvania drivers may not be as off-the-scale crazy as those in New England, but the contrast is not as great as I remembered. Maybe drivers here have changed, or maybe my memory is foggy.

Then again, maybe I'm thinking of Ohio.

***

Route 220 eventually widens again into four-lane traffic. In an hour or so, I've gone by Altoona and am approaching Bedford, the county seat of Bedford County, roughly half an hour northeast of the farm where I grew up. Wills Mountain begins around Bedford and goes on to Cumberland, Maryland, some twenty-five miles to the south.

Bedford occupies an interesting place in my personal history. It's a small town of about 45,000, but I grew up seeing it as urban. A trip from the farm to Bedford was an event. To me, street signs and banks and businesses and a church ten times the size of ours made it a big city.

Bedford High School was Hyndman's biggest basketball rival. With so many more students to draw on for their athletic program, they usually won, especially in their enormous gym. But in the best game of my junior year, we beat them on our tiny court. I scored five points in the fourth quarter and drew an offensive foul from their best player as he missed the winning basket.

I went to Lutheran catechism classes at the huge and gaudy (to my eyes) Trinity Lutheran Church in Bedford, under the guidance of pastor Dick D. Dick (not a made-up name). Mom worked for a while as a tour guide at the Fort Bedford Museum, so I sometimes rode to work with her and walked around town during her four-hour shift. After my initial fear of "city people" wore off, I even did some shopping in the local stores–the first time I ever bought anything more than a candy bar and a soda without Mom looking over my shoulder. Sometimes, I walked to the park near the Raystown Branch of the Juniata River and sat on a bench reading the *Bedford Gazette*. I felt so mature that I could almost hear people thinking, *Why, look at that young man with the newspaper. He looks so grown up.*

***

As a teenager, I had very few paying jobs. With so much work in the fields, gardens, and woods, I couldn't pursue frivolous jobs like fast food cook, gas pumper, or house painter.

But I did spend two weeks one summer working at the Bedford County Fair. The first week, I worked from two in the afternoon until ten at night as a fence guard. My task, along with a dozen or so other teenagers, was to patrol the fence around the fairgrounds and make sure no one broke in to avoid paying the three-dollar admission fee. For most of the afternoon and early evening, this job was pretty much a walk in the park–literally. I strolled around the wooded area behind the fairgrounds, enjoying the scenery and earning two dollars an hour–big money in those days.

After the sun went down, however, things got complicated. We were given flashlights and sent off alone to sit quietly at the fence's weak points and wait for juvenile delinquents to storm the gates. When they tried to break in, we were supposed to shine our flashlights in their eyes and growl in our deepest voices, "Hey, you kids! Get the hell away from there!"

My station was pretty quiet, and I actually thwarted a couple of break-in attempts during the first four nights. My deep growl, to my great surprise, sent most would-be gatecrashers scurrying into the woods.

The last night of the fair, however, my flashlight burned out with about an hour left in my shift. Naturally, that was when a dozen rowdy teenagers rushed the gate, their leader calling out, "We're coming through! Try to stop us if you want, but it ain't gonna work!" I sat motionless in the dark and didn't say a word as they stormed by less than five feet from me, their beer-and-cigarette breath filling the air around them.

When I reported to my supervisor that night, I told him a couple of little kids came by, but I scared them off.

The second week, after the fair closed, I worked the day shift cleaning out the livestock barns rather than hiding in the dark with a dead flashlight. In the time it took everyone else to pitchfork out one stall, I did four–and they were clean enough to spread out a tablecloth and have a picnic. At fifteen, one of the youngest kids there, I was promoted to unofficial crew chief on the second day.

All that farm work at home had finally paid off in the "real world."

***

I get lost driving through Bedford, of course. I'm still a country boy and Bedford is still the big city. When I finally make it through town to Route 31 heading south, I'm delighted to know that I'm less than half an hour from the farm. In only a few minutes, I make it to Manns Choice, a town whose name made it the mailing address for a men's magazine called *True* that featured photos of topless women back in the 1960s and 70s. Getting my hands on a *True* magazine was quite a thrill at age fourteen.

Manns Choice is also the home of Coral Caverns, a cave where I took several thrilling tours as a kid. The most electrifying moment came when the tour reached its greatest depth, and the guides turned off all the lights, plunging us all into the blackest darkness imaginable. I held my breath for the entire thirty seconds they kept us in the dark, my head swimming from claustrophobia mixed with oxygen deprivation mixed with plain old terror that a cave monster would tiptoe up and bite my head right off.

Route 31 connects with Route 96 in Manns Choice. This is a big moment in my trip because Route 96 goes right to my childhood home, running along the base of Wills Mountain. Growing up, we called it, "the main road" or just, "the road." In no time, I pass through Buffalo Mills and Bard, and then I get my first look at the quarry cutting across the top of Wills Mountain.

***

The bumper-sticker market here is pretty thin. I see an occasional "United We Stand" and "God Bless America"–and I notice one at a convenience store with a muscled-up cartoon Uncle Sam urinating on a cowering caricature of Osama Bin Laden. I wonder how popular I'd be around here if I got a bumper sticker that read, "Peace is Patriotic" or "Re-Elect President Gore in 2004"?

***

Not far south of Bard, I see a bus stop shelter, a structure barely large enough for a few kids to stand inside as they wait for the big yellow ride to school. These shelters are provided free by insurance companies with company name and logo plastered on the sides for advertising.

I have no idea why some bus stops had shelters while others didn't, but I felt jealous of the kids who had a shelter back when I waited for the school bus. Our bus stop was at the intersection of Route 96 and Madley Hollow Road, a quarter mile from our house. Not only did we have to hike to the bus stop, but we also had to wait there through all kinds of weather.

The actual process of catching the bus was complicated to begin with. We got out of bed, cleaned up, got dressed, ate breakfast, did any chores that needed done, then watched out the window for our bus to go by. It turned around a few miles north on Route 96, and then started back south to pick up kids on the way to school in Hyndman six miles away. When we spied the bus going north, we yelled, "Bus!" at the top of our lungs, and then hustled up to Route 96 to be there and waiting when the bus returned a few minutes later.

We took turns watching for the bus, a job somewhat like air traffic controller in terms of stress and responsibility. Through a tiny gap in the trees, we could catch a fleeting glimpse of yellow as the bus went north. And we couldn't be fooled by the *other* bus that turned west on Madley Hollow Road to pick up all the hillbilly children who lived back there. If the designated bus watcher happened to glance down at the exact instant the bus went by, we were sunk.

On the few occasions when we didn't see the bus going northbound, we saw it slow to a stop looking for us on its southbound swing. If that happened, my job was to sprint up the road and hold the bus until my slower sisters got there. My success rate was about fifty-fifty, depending on the bus driver. Mrs. Rondell (our kind and wonderful regular driver) would wait long enough to for me to burst into view, then gladly wait for my sisters. But if the driver was a dreaded substitute, I had no chance.

If we missed it, Mom rushed us out to her car and raced down the road to catch the bus a few miles to the south, angry that we had delayed her from the countless household chores she struggled with each day. During the entire drive, she chewed us out for our incompetence at a task as simple as watching for a bus.

"It's a *bus*," she growled. "It's bright yellow and five hundred feet long. How could you miss it?" I was usually wise enough not to burden Mom with the actual measurements of a typical school bus on those mornings.

She'd close the gap and pull over behind the bus a few stops down the road, and we'd pile out of the car and into the bus, hoping that no one had taken our regular seats.

I brought up the possibility of getting a bus shelter a few times, but Mom wasn't interested. She believed that spending the time in the harsh elements was good for us. Occasionally, however, on too-cold-to-stand-outside December mornings, we managed to convince Mom to drive us to the bus stop. Mom chose one of those rare mornings, sitting in the car with the heater blasting away wonderfully, to inform us that Santa Claus didn't really exist. She was kind and gentle in telling us, but I felt devastated anyway. I guess I should have seen it coming, considering that an older boy on the bus had been bragging for weeks that he knew Santa was a fake.

I still detest that evil boy.

***

Up the hill from our bus stop is the church I attended as a child. The original church was called Lybarger Lutheran Church, named for an Irish immigrant family that settled in this area in the early 1800s. The old church still stands in very good condition–except for the missing stained glass windows that were stolen a few months before the church closed. I remember wondering what kind of person would steal stained glass from a country church–a city jerk, I figured.

The "new" church just up the road, built nearly twenty years ago, is called Christ Lutheran Church, named, apparently, for the founder of the Christian religion. It's surprising that a foreigner like Christ superseded a local like Lybarger.

***

Instead of going directly to the cabin, I decide to drive around for a while. One of my favorite places to walk and jog as a teenager was the road leading to the old Lybarger Lutheran Church. The church and its extensive graveyard sit on a steep hill with a terrific view of Wills Mountain and part of the valley below. The route to the top of that hill, however, is a gravel road that hasn't been plowed recently and is rutted with snow and ice. I could do the wise thing–get out of the Tracker and turn the hubs to engage the four-wheel drive–but for some reason, I decide against wisdom and gun the engine, trying for the top with two-wheel drive.

Thirty feet up the road, the Tracker slides back and left into a ditch. All I can do is laugh, knowing that I'm in no danger but that I'm also helpless when it comes to making the car go where I want it to go.

Within seconds, I'm leaning at a forty-five degree angle on my driver's side door and smashed up against a snowbank. I have to climb up and out of the car on the passenger side. I engage the right side hub for the four-wheel drive pretty easily, but then I have to get down on my knees and dig through the hard-packed snow to reach the driver's side hub. Then I climb back in through the wrong door, wriggle into the driver's seat, put the car in reverse, and slowly back my way down onto the level road again.

On the second try, the four-wheel drive pulls me along, and I make it to the top without even a slip.

I had another strange driving experience on this hill fifteen years ago. I was a poverty-stricken graduate student when Grandma died. To get to her funeral, I borrowed a neighbor's car with a dreaded manual transmission. Dad tried several times to teach me to drive his truck, but I couldn't get the hang of it.

I would lift my clutch foot slowly and smoothly–just the way Dad said to do it–but every time, the truck lurched violently and then stalled. One lurch pushed Dad's face to within an inch of the windshield. I can still remember his look of frustration and disappointment at learning that his teenaged son wasn't manly enough to drive a pickup truck. I've avoided manual transmissions as much as possible since then.

In Grandma's funeral procession, I shifted into second, held my breath, and turned up the steep church hill road, following the line of cars ahead of me. Of course, I stalled right away and took three tries to get myself moving up the annoying road. Thankfully, the cousin driving behind me had given me lots of room and patiently waited as I finally got the car up the hill. I saw him chuckling in my rearview mirror even as I saw Dad's pained expression in my memory.

My bad driving was pretty embarrassing, but it did provide a welcome touch of comic relief during the otherwise somber ceremony. I didn't script the scene as well as Shakespeare's graveyard, but it served the same purpose.

***

After my adventure on the church hill, I head out on Madley Hollow Road. "Private Property" and "No Trespassing" signs are everywhere. My first thought is, *No trespassing? Who would want to? There's nothing here. This is the middle of nowhere.* But my second thought is, *I would want to trespass–that's who.* I want to get out of the car right now and see what's back here in the woods. Of course, the woods here are the same as everywhere–trees, shrubs, rocks, birds, squirrels–but I can't shake the thrill of new discovery. That thrill led me to walk everywhere I could as a kid, and I'm happy to still feel it after all these years.

Madley Hollow Road winds westward beyond our old bus stop and along Wolf Camp Run, the little stream that flows by our house and joins Little Wills Creek at the base of Wills Mountain. As a teenager, my favorite route for summer walking and bike riding began with three miles on Madley Hollow, then turned south and around Lybarger Hill, then cut east back toward Route 96 at Gravelpit, and then returned north toward home. The whole trip was about seven miles through a series of steep, curvy hills and switchbacks on roads that were once wagon paths. Before that, they were most likely Indian footpaths, deer paths before that.

One Sunday afternoon at age sixteen, I took my usual walk down Madley Hollow, a route I had walked many times before without seeing anyone. But this time, as I turned uphill onto the road that circled Lybarger Hill and wound back toward home, I saw a group of people at a house about thirty yards farther along Madley Hollow. It didn't escape my teenager's notice that several of these people were girls near my own age.

As I watched them, one of the girls waved to me–not the casual lifting of a hand that everyone around here used to greet a passing stranger. She stepped away from the group, looked purposefully in my direction, and waved with real warmth and openness that I could sense from thirty yards. She was too far away for a detailed look, but even at that distance, I could see she was slender and pretty.

I waved back with as much feeling as she had, but I kept walking. This girl intrigued me, but my shyness kept me from going over to introduce myself. I knew all the teenagers in the area, but I definitely didn't recognize her. So I let inertia make my decision. Already moving in a different direction, I kept going up the hill and away from her.

But I didn't stop thinking about her. For the rest of my walk, I kept wishing I had been walking closer to her house so that I could have gotten a better look at her and stopped to say hello rather than waving from a distance. I also kept revisiting her wave in my memory. Was it really as friendly and inviting as I thought? Or did I simply want an attractive girl to wave at me so much that I had imagined it?

By the time I got home, I had all but talked myself into believing the wave had been nothing more than a gesture. This girl had no way of knowing what I might be like. She must just be a friendly person who waves at everyone, so I decided to forget her. And that's exactly what I did–until I went to bed that night.

As soon as I turned out the light and shut my eyes, she returned to my thoughts. I lay awake for hours wondering about her. This time, I didn't try to convince myself that the wave had been just a casual greeting. She must have meant something important by it and felt the same charge of connection that I had experienced at that moment. She had wanted me to change direction and come over to see her. This wave was a serious invitation, and she must be lying awake in her own bed right then wondering why I didn't accept.

The following week crawled by as my resolve to meet her grew. I could hardly wait for Sunday to walk up Madley Hollow Road and meet my mystery woman. In fact, I didn't wait for Sunday. I got up early Saturday morning and did a full day's worth of work around the farm by noon, splitting firewood for the following winter, weeding the garden, and shelling enough field corn to feed the chickens for a month. When I asked Dad if I could take a walk in the afternoon, he was happy to reward my good works.

I covered the three miles to the house in record time, pumping my arms almost like a speed walker. As I approached this time, I didn't see anyone outside the house, but a car sat in the driveway. I walked by slowly, trying to look casual, but no one stirred. After going a few hundred yards up the road and around the bend, I sat on the guardrail for about ten minutes, then started back toward the house.

On this pass, I saw a man and woman packing a few boxes into the car. Their faces lit up as I approached, and they stopped loading.

"Hello," the man said, extending his hand. He had a full salt-and-pepper beard and a firm handshake.

"Hi there," the woman said as she walked toward me. She had long dark hair streaked with gray and the brightest eyes and smile I'd ever seen. "We just bought this old place for a weekend getaway. Do you live around here?"

I had just met the Ellsworth parents. We talked for ten minutes, and I found them to be two of the nicest adults I'd ever met. The woman smiled and laughed easily, and the man talked to me as if I were an adult and not a little kid. They lived in Ellerslie, Maryland, about twenty miles away, and had four daughters, the oldest three near my own age.

As we said our good-byes, Mrs. Ellsworth asked me, "By the way, did you walk by here and wave to my daughter last weekend?"

"I think so," I replied. "I mean, I waved at a girl."

"Oh good," she continued. "That was Sarah. She told me if I saw you to invite you to a picnic here tomorrow afternoon."

"Me?" I asked.

"Well, she said she waved to a tall boy with dark hair and glasses walking along the road. I guess that's you. She thought you looked friendly." Mrs. Ellsworth narrowed her eyes and studied me for a moment, then smiled. "I think she was right."

I walked home that afternoon with three thoughts in my mind. First, her name was Sarah. Second, she had remembered me and must have felt at least some of what I sensed when we waved. And third, I would meet her tomorrow.

"Well, aren't you the ladies man," Mom joked when I told her what happened and asked if I could go to the Ellsworth's house for a picnic the next day.

"Do you know how to behave like a gentleman around girls?" Dad asked me.

Dad clearly had a subtext to the question that I didn't fully understand, but I answered as honestly as I could. "I'll be nice."

I didn't know if that was exactly the answer Dad was looking for, but he said, "That's good enough for me."

The next day, I met not only Sarah Ellsworth, but her sisters Naomi, Vivianne, and Cassandra as well. Seventeen-year-old Cassandra seemed very grown-up and was already engaged. Fifteen-year-old Vivianne already had full breasts and a sexuality that frightened and attracted me simultaneously. Naomi was twelve and a smart, sweet little girl who had a wonderful and sophisticated sense of humor. Sarah was my own age, and I quickly felt drawn to her even more than I had when she first waved.

She had short dark hair and dark eyes, a deep voice, an adorable lopsided smile that was both cute and beautiful, and a not-quite-tomboy casual way of carrying herself that showed strength and confidence. Sarah had a boyfriend at home, and I was far too shy to express romantic feelings for her, so we became instant best friends–but with something more.

For the rest of that summer and the next two, I made as many weekend trips to the Ellsworth house as I could. We didn't do anything extraordinary during my visits–just walks in the woods and games of touch football. When it rained, we played cards or board games. If the girls had weekend activities and couldn't come to the house, I visited with their parents, who always welcomed my company. Mrs. Ellsworth was a grown-up version of her daughters, so we shared many laughs as well. Even though I usually felt somewhat uncomfortable around adult men, I enjoyed my time with Mr. Ellsworth, like me a quiet person who didn't mind silence as I helped him with chores around the house.

The Ellsworths' getaway house became my escape too. The girls broke into wide smiles when I arrived. They hugged me when I left and made me promise to come back the following weekend. They even cried when their parents closed up the house at the end of each September.

This was all such a contrast to my life at home and school where I had been the same person my whole life. I didn't really know what it meant to be taken for granted, but I could definitely sense that the Ellsworths treated me differently. This family saw me as someone new, someone special, someone whose company mattered.

I quickly fell in love with Sarah, of course. No girl had yet showed me such friendship, kindness, interest, or affection. Her boyfriends at her own school came and went, but she always held my hand when we went walking alone, and we exchanged letters all winter. "You're my summer-weekend-sort-of boyfriend," she told me. Because she emphasized the word "boyfriend" and not "sort of," I didn't feel at all slighted.

The Ellsworths met my family once when they stopped at my house on their way home. My sisters seemed wary of this group of females who took their place as the primary women in my life on summer weekends. Mom was charmed by Mrs. Ellsworth, and Dad later told me that he thought Sarah seemed like "a very nice young woman . . . pretty too."

Each winter, our basketball team played at the Ellsworths' school. My senior year, I sat with three of the sisters during the junior varsity game, and my teammates were stunned to see me in the company of pretty girls. They teased me and wanted to know how I knew them. Our little towns were all pretty isolated, so knowing anyone at another school was rare. I just smiled and told my teammates that we'd been friends a long time. I loved having a touch of mystery in my life for a change.

Of course, they wanted to know if I'd slept with any of them. I told them to mind their own business, which they correctly interpreted as meaning I hadn't. My nickname in high school could have been "Olive Oil"–extra virgin. Sarah and I often flirted, but she told me about the boyfriends she dumped because they wanted to go too far with her. I didn't know exactly how far "too far" was for her, and I never asked. Sarah seemed only slightly more experienced than I was, for which I'm grateful. If she had tried to seduce me or suggested that I seduce her, my head probably would have exploded.

My time with the Ellsworths came to an end when I went off to college. My last Sunday at home, I rode my bike to their house, only to find a note from Sarah saying they had been there yesterday and missed seeing me. Sarah was also going to college that fall, and she promised to write. We did exchange a few letters, but within a few months, we both discovered the wonders of being away from home. She met lots of other boys, and I met lots of other girls.

I tacked up a photo of the Ellsworth girls on the wall of my first college dorm room. My roommate asked me which one was my girlfriend, and I almost pointed to Sarah. At the end of that first year, I took the photo down to add to my growing shoebox full of family and college snapshots.

Before I put the picture away, I looked at it closely, seeing a detail I hadn't really noticed before. The photo showed the four Ellsworth girls standing in a row with me kneeling in front. Madley Hollow Road tapers away into the distance behind us.

Just out of frame in the lower right-hand corner, Sarah's hand is touching my arm.

***

Chapter 5
Between the Eyes

Although the creation of Route 96 in the 1930s cut our farm in half, we still owned one hilly chunk of woods on the western side of the highway that we called "the pines," several acres of pine trees planted in long, straight rows across the hillside for some future timber project. I loved walking there as a kid because the whole place seemed like a hauntingly beautiful outdoor cathedral. The trees grew perfectly straight and had very few branches below about thirty feet, and the fallen needles made a soft carpet. I even fantasized about someday having my wedding in that beautiful place.

The first and only time I "ran away from home," I went to the pines. I was thirteen and left a note in my bedroom telling my parents that I needed to "be by myself," my great getaway covering about a ten-minute walk from the house. I guess I had been feeling crowded with all my sisters around, so I made a sandwich and walked to the pines, sitting and thinking among the rows of beautiful trees until well after dark. By eleven o'clock, I got cold and a little scared, so I walked home. Mom and Dad were only annoyed with me, but my sisters had actually been crying, perhaps even missing their irritating little brother.

The rest of the pines was not as uniform as the planted section but just as wonderful. I helped clear an old overgrown logging road that twisted through the hills with Dad and two uncles when I was barely ten years old. Seeing Dad interact with his brothers Glenn and Harvey was a pleasure. I got a kick out of how they treated him as the "baby" of the family–just like me. When Dad's chainsaw stalled in the middle of a log, his brothers laughed and said, "He's young. He'll learn."

Once we cleared the road, Dad and I often took his truck up into the pines to get firewood for burning in our coal furnace. I used the road up into the pines for walking, jogging, and even bike riding. I'm amazed now as a slightly chubby man in my forties with bad joints that as a skinny teenager, I could run the two miles from our house to the highest elevation in the pines in about eighteen minutes. And long before mountain biking was popular, I rode my junky little bicycle up into the woods. I especially loved the thrill of riding down the steep, bumpy hills.

One such bike ride, however, alerted me to the dangers of going too far in my pursuit of a thrill. Coming down the pines road on my bike at a pretty good clip, I hit a bump and flew over the handlebars. I remember slamming into the ground, but everything went blank after that until I found myself pushing my bike into the shed at our house. I must have given myself a concussion and lost the memory of the half hour after the accident. If I had broken my neck or fractured my skull, I might have been up there for days before anyone found me. By then, the buzzards might have visited–not a happy thought.

***

Last summer, when Jenny and I came to stay in the cabin for the first time, we got quite a surprise as we turned onto the gravel road that goes by my childhood home and continues to the cabin. When I lived there, it was officially Township Road 363, but we called it the "old road" or the "log road," a reference to long-ago logging on Wills Mountain. I learned to ride a bike on this road and later used it as the first and last legs of my jogging route when I ran a few miles down Route 96 most evenings during my teenage summers.

As Jenny and I pulled off Route 96, I saw a new street sign at the corner. When we got close, I laughed for nearly a full minute before I could point out the sign that read "Sheirer Road" to Jenny. Not only had it never occurred to me that anyone would feel the need to give this little road a name, but I certainly didn't expect it to be named after my family.

But if the road had to have a name, I suppose Sheirer Road makes as much sense as anything else. Our farm originally came into the family in 1913 when my paternal grandparents, William Wesley Sheirer and Annie Katherine Stuby Sheirer, bought 575 acres of the valley and mountain from the Francis Miller family for $7,000. This purchase included the family farmhouse, built in 1884 by George Hilderbrandt, the landowner at the time. The Sheirer family lived on this road for seventy-two years until 1985. My grandfather was a prominent man in the area until his early death in 1932, and my grandmother was one of the most well-known family matriarchs in the county. Dad and Mom were also well known and well liked, and people still recognize my sisters' names (and even my own) two decades after we all moved away.

It's a shame no Sheirer lives on this road now.

***

My house seemed rather ordinary to me when I lived in it. Ours was a basic old-style two-story farmhouse with a pitched attic roof and two porches: a concrete one on the side parallel to Sheirer Road, and a wooden one on the side nearest the driveway. These porches were primarily the territory of the many cats who took up residence on our farm. The basement (which we called the cellar) had a cement floor and housed the furnace, canned goods, and–eventually–a shower.

The shower Dad installed in the basement changed my life for the better. Our bathtub was in the primary bathroom of the house, so the minute I settled down in the hot water, someone would inevitably knock on the door needing to pee right that second. Taking a shower, on the other hand, made for far fewer interruptions. The only person who came down into the cellar with any regularity was Dad when he tended the furnace. After particularly hard days in the field or at basketball practice, I would bring an old wooden chair into the shower with me and sit in the steaming spray for half an hour until Mom yelled down to stop wasting so much water.

Putting the shower in the dirty cellar always struck me as ironic. Even with a cement floor layers of mud, coal, and wood fragments formed everywhere after a heavy rain, and cobwebs hung from the five-and-a-half-feet-high ceiling. No matter how clean I felt after my shower, the twenty-step walk through that filth always made me feel instantly covered with several layers of grit.

**

Snow fell here a few days ago, and everything looks post-card lovely. I remember many long and snow-filled seasons during my youth with seven or eight big snowstorms that paralyzed the entire state. One year, school was canceled so many times from October to March that we had to keep going until after Independence Day. Often we trudged off to school no matter how deep the snow because there were no more summer days left for make-ups.

Mom would wake me up an hour earlier than usual after a snowy night, and I became close friends with the snow shovel. First I slogged the hundred yards to our mailbox near the highway and cleared the snow away so that mail could be delivered. Then I made a path from the back door to the cars, cleared them off, then continued shoveling to the chicken house so that I could feed the chickens and add boiling water to thaw their frozen drinking supply. Finally, I finished my work by shoveling a path from Grandma's front porch to the road–a particularly useless task because no one ever walked that way. But Mom insisted so that Grandma wouldn't give her grief over the unshoveled path.

When I got home from school these afternoons after a long, dangerous bus ride over poorly plowed roads, I usually had to do all of the shoveling a second time to clear the snow that fell while I fought off sleep at school. If the snow happened to be deeper than usual, Dad sent me up to shovel the roof. He worried about it collapsing under the snow's weight, creating an unthinkable repair job in the middle of a frigid winter.

I secretly loved roof shoveling. The roof was one of my favorite places to be anyway, and I often crept out there at night to watch the stars and enjoy the open air, an act forbidden in normal circumstances. Being *required* to climb out my bedroom window was a dream come true. I took my time, partly because of the danger of falling, but mostly because I enjoyed the isolation and the view.

Dad occasionally peeked out a window to watch me work. I could tell he was proud of me for happily taking on this job that he dreaded doing himself. It must have been gratifying for him to see me growing into a tall, hard-working young man who shared many of his values. This pride was quite a contrast to his disappointment at my inability to master the clutch in his old pick-up truck.

He also got quite a kick when I would send a shovelful of snow down onto the unsuspecting heads of a cat or a dog–or, with luck, a sister or two. Once I hit the trifecta, getting all three sisters with one shot as they walked to the car. They screamed and yelled for Mom while feebly flinging snowballs that fell short of my perch. Dad tried to give me a reproachful look from the window, but I saw him fighting back a mischievous grin.

***

About a quarter of the first floor in our house was called "Grandma's side," dominated by an adjoining kitchen as large as our own with a full complement of appliances. Grandma cooked her own meals and largely ate by herself–with the exception of Sunday afternoon "dinner" (our term for lunch). Mom and Grandma shared cooking duties on Sunday, and they seemed to get along well, despite the fact that each had her own way of doing things, and each was massively stubborn. They simply learned to divide tasks over the years, not actually working together on a meal, but working on parallel, non-intersecting paths to keep from bumping into each other.

Grandma's living room, bathroom, and bedroom were all contained in a narrow area of the house that made for a very unusual "mother-in-law" apartment. Her living room was barely eight feet wide and twenty feet long, with a TV at one end, a couch along the wall, and two large chairs at the other end. The truly unusual feature was hidden behind a partition. In a space about six by ten feet, Grandma had a twin bed. And near the head of the bed, where she could simply slip out from under the sheets and sit down without taking a full step–was her toilet.

As convenient as this must have been for her, I had a hard time imagining what it would be like to sleep with your face three feet from a toilet. But her bathroom came in very handy on many occasions. With three sisters who seemed to spend inordinately long stretches in our only other bathroom upstairs, I often slipped back to Grandma's toilet for a quick pee while she sliced carrots or boiled potatoes in her kitchen.

***

Having three sisters near my age also gave me a slightly better than average knowledge of teenage female body functions. Unfortunately, this knowledge came slowly and with a price. My sisters wrote their names on different dates on the kitchen calendar, confusing me, so at age fourteen, I asked Mom for clarification.

I pointed to the tenth of the month where my sister June had written her name. Mom said, "Oh, let's just call that 'Be-Nice-to-June Day.' "

I felt jealous because I wanted my day too. So I picked the fifteenth day of the following month and wrote my name along with the words, "Be-Nice-to-John Day," expecting that I might get a special meal or not have to help clear the dishes.

All I got that day was a lot of silly laughter from my sisters, so I never wrote my name on the calendar again.

***

We had an interesting series of outbuildings clustered around the house. The barn was the dominant structure. It stood majestically out in the field halfway to the cabin. The barn had hanging track doors that slid open to reveal a main floor big enough to park four hay wagons. We kept cows and large stores of hay and oats in the barn, but I appreciated it as a place to get away and hide. I even put up a basketball hoop inside, making it my own private gymnasium.

Near the house was a building that we called the shed, although it probably qualified as a small barn. Dad kept our garden tractor and lawn mower there, along with a variety of tools and "junk" that he had collected over the years. I built my first "clubhouse" in an alcove above the main part of this building, even using several old tires and boards to fashion an uncomfortable couch.

Next to the shed was the chicken house, which we used for storing junk that should have been thrown away–until one day when Dad cleared it out and brought home a dozen chickens and two ducks. I carried food and water to these birds every morning before going to school. They rewarded us with lots of eggs, but I saw them mainly as pets, fun to observe as they went about their eccentric daily activities.

Halfway to the barn was a building we called the garage–but we never kept a car there, just Dad's junk, sometimes crammed so full that no one could walk in more than five feet before running out of floor space. Beside the garage was an outhouse, convenient during the summer months when our farm work or gardening made us too dirty to go inside for the bathroom.

As the only boy in a house full of sisters, I craved time by myself. Having my own little room helped, but I still felt the press of my family all around me. During warm weather, my quest for solitude expanded. For several preteen summers, I spent as much time as possible in a tiny canvas pup tent, sweating in the greenhouse-like heat and listening to the radio. Mom wouldn't let me sleep in the tent because she thought the bears would smell my body odor, come down off the mountain, and carry me away for their dinner. At least that's what she told me, perhaps thinking it would scare me back into the house each evening.

At age fourteen, I put a cot in a wooden out-building with a concrete floor and slept there until the first frost. We called it the "milk house" because that's where the milk was kept long ago when the farm had real milk cows instead of the ones we kept mostly for pets. The milk house had the advantage of a solid door that I could close, so Mom couldn't convince me that the bears would find my scent and break in. The disadvantages were many: no electricity, no heat, dampness, a leaky roof, dirt everywhere, and barely fifty square feet of space. But I loved it anyway because it was all mine.

My dreams came true the following summer when Dad bought an ancient house trailer from a distant cousin. He paid $50 and parked it next to the cow pasture about fifty yards from the house. Dad planned to use it as his own getaway, but I beat him to it. He kept some of his tools in the front part, but I put an old black-and-white television next to the cot in the back and ran wires from the antenna atop the house so that I could get as many stations in the trailer as we could in the house: four.

I spent four summers in that trailer practicing for adulthood. Dad's tools got shoved farther and farther out of my way until they were out of sight in a closet or shuttled off to the shed under cover of darkness. I eventually figured out how to work the propane stove without worrying that I would die in my sleep from fumes or explosion. Nearly every night, I made popcorn or pancakes to eat while I watched television or read. The place became so much my own that I even got to keep it locked with the key tucked in my pocket. This, of course, meant that I could hide a couple dirty magazines under the mattress, making it all the home a teenaged boy could ever need.

When I finally went away to West Virginia Wesleyan College at the end of that fourth summer, I did most of my packing in the trailer. My bedroom back in the house held only my winter clothes, coats, and a few books. Those summers in the trailer probably explain why I was the only guy in my freshman dorm who knew how to cook, do dishes and laundry, and even make minor sewing repairs. Living like a bachelor every summer for so long put me way ahead of my classmates.

In fact, that crowded dorm was sometimes too much like the crowded farmhouse of my youth. If only I could have convinced Dad to let me drag the trailer to college, I would have parked it in an isolated lot and escaped to my own happy version of solitary adult life.

***

I made my share of minor trouble as a kid sometimes playing pranks on classmates at school or teasing my sisters at home. Mom called me a "brat" more than once, and my report cards bore the phrases "poor deportment" and "discipline problem" a few times. I had a brief phase when I experimented with my parents' matches, but I didn't burn the house down. All in all, I wasn't exactly a juvenile delinquent–usually.

One summer day when I was fourteen, my parents and sisters were all out of the house. Mom and Dad were off on some errand, and my sisters had been dropped off for a friend's birthday party (girls only). So Grandma and I were alone in the house. When she told me she was going to take a nap, I felt like I had the world all to myself.

Instead of doing something productive like cleaning the bathroom or weeding the garden, I immediately went to Dad's gun cabinet, grabbed his .22 rifle and a box of bullets, and ran through the field to the cabin, holding the gun under my shirt to conceal it from anyone who might happen to drive along the road at that moment.

At the cabin, I set up a few chunks of wood for targets and spent about ten minutes shooting at them. The cabin itself blocked the view from our house in case the shots woke Grandma. If she looked in my direction, she would blame hunters on the mountain. After my brief target practice, I returned to the house with the gun hidden under my shirt, then replaced it in the cabinet. I redistributed a few bullets from several other boxes to replace the ones I'd used, then spent an hour or so shooting hoops until the rest of my family got home.

What compelled me to swipe Dad's gun? The whole incident was very out of character for a kid who asked his parents' permission to use the bathroom until age ten. While I liked shooting the gun, I wasn't obsessed like many boys my age. Dad had taught me to shoot the gun a couple years before, and I'm sure he would have been happy to oblige if I'd asked him to do some target practice with me.

I guess I did it because I had so little unsupervised time and so much burning desire to be an adult. I wanted to live without anyone watching over me and telling me what to do, what time to go to bed, what days to go to school, what foods to eat at dinner. My parents would never have allowed me to take the gun off on my own, so I thought the most forbidden thing I could think of would be the most "grown-up" thing to do.

No one ever discovered my shooting spree. There would be more afternoons during the coming years when I stayed home alone, and I read or took walks or played basketball by myself. Once I actually did clean the bathroom, pleasing Mom but spurring my sisters to call me a "goodie-goodie brown-nose."

They clearly had no idea what an outlaw I could be.

***

On the first morning of our visit here a few weeks ago, Jenny found the light brown carcass of a dead deer half-submerged in Little Wills Creek near the cabin. The deer couldn't have been dead long and looked at first glance like it was simply lounging in the creek. When we got closer, however, we could see that its neck was twisted at an impossible angle, possibly from a fall along the steep creek bank upstream.

I saw plenty of dead deer close up when I was young. Our family had a permit to shoot them out of season for crop damage. A group of eight or ten deer (very common where we lived) could bed down in a hayfield at night and easily ruin hundreds of square feet. Dad was a hunter, of course, and we often ate more venison than beef.

As strange as it may seem, my sister Pam even once shot a deer from the window of our house. This was my brother-in-law-to-be Dale's first visit to our home, and he must have thought we were some kind of stump-jumping, possum-eating, bark-chewing, chicken-for-pets hillbilly family. In a way we were ... but we certainly never ate possum. It's just too tough and flavorless.

***

As a growing farm boy, I ate as much meat as anyone else. Beef and venison were my favorites–but butchering was not. The strongest person in our family from about age fifteen, I was also the most sensitive. I hated butchering more than any other farm task. I simply couldn't bring myself to cut into an animal carcass, so my job was limited to heavy lifting. I hoisted the dead-weight animal up to a hook and hung it there by notches Dad had carved between the bones of its lower hind legs. Then I went away and waited to be called when more lifting needed to be done. Dad recognized all of the other hard work I did on the farm as a kid, and I felt grateful to him for respecting my wishes not to be a full participant in the butchering.

We butchered one of our cows every other year or so. Our cousin Blaine, a butcher, came to help us in exchange for a quarter of the beef. Blaine thought a normal, healthy boy like me should be interested in cutting chunks out of livestock. Each time I hoisted part of the cow up to a hook, then walked away, the way Blaine rolled his eyes showed that he thought I was kind of a sissy, but he was too polite to say so in front of Dad.

My last summer at home before college, I decided to show Blaine that I was more of a man than he thought.

We were preparing to butcher the largest bull we had ever owned. Despite his size, he was gentle enough for children to pet his enormous snout. Mom had christened him "Suzie" for his calm nature. Blaine arrived at seven one cool Saturday morning in early summer, and he and Dad sipped coffee and chatted on the porch for half an hour while I listened to their country banter. Then Blaine reached into his truck window and pulled out his rifle.

"I guess I'd better go shoot this big fella so we can get started on him," he said.

I stood and spoke my first words of the morning. "How about if I do it?"

Blaine looked surprised. "I thought you didn't go for this kind of thing."

"I'd like to give it a try," I said.

Blaine turned the stock of the gun my way. "Okay, young man. It's already loaded for the job. Just put one right between the eyes."

I took the gun and walked the fifty yards or so toward the field where Suzie was contentedly chewing dewy grass and swishing his tail to fend off the flies that were already out that early in the morning. I didn't want to shoot this fine animal whose company I had enjoyed while feeding him cornstalks and green apples for two years. But today would be his last morning on earth–that was certain–and at least this way, he would die in the company of a familiar face rather than Blaine, a stranger to him. Besides, I was eighteen and wanted Blaine to stop thinking of me as a little softhearted boy.

Suzie glanced up at my approach, and I spoke quietly to him while raising the gun. As I sighted on the middle of his forehead, I kept talking, telling him that he was a good bull, the best bull we'd ever had. Then I squeezed the trigger.

The gun jerked a little, but I didn't really hear the shot until it echoed off the mountain a second later. Suzie didn't even flinch. For a confused second, I thought I must have missed–but I couldn't have missed from six feet away. Then I noticed a small red circle and a trickle of blood forming right where I had aimed at his forehead. The bull snorted twice and shook his head, as if shaking off an annoying fly.

With my heart hammering and my ears ringing, I pulled the bolt back, ejected the shell, and brought the gun back up to aim at the same spot. This time, when I pulled the trigger, Suzie's legs crumpled so quickly that they seemed to disappear. He landed with a meaty thump.

By then, Dad and Blaine had walked up behind me.

"What the hell happened?" Dad asked.

"It took two shots," I said, sounding calmer than I felt.

"I'll be damned," Blaine whispered. "I ain't never seen that before."

He took the gun from me and picked up the ejected shell casings.

"You hit him with the first one?" Dad wondered aloud, still puzzled.

"He sure as hell did," Blaine said. "Boy, you are one steady son of a gun. You shot him twice like you been doing it for years."

The rest of the morning was a blur. We tied the bull to the back of the truck and dragged him to the barn for butchering. I did my lifting when called, and this time Blaine didn't chuckle when I walked back to the house. The rest of the time I sat on the porch and looked at the spot where the bull had fallen.

That was twenty-five years ago. I haven't touched a gun since.

Chapter 6
New Millennium

Janet and Fred have a brochure for the cabin with a couple of nice photos and some well-written, adjective-filled text. Part of it reads, "Enjoy a country-style getaway in this rustic retreat, situated on a private forty-acre working farm. Located at the foot of Wills Mountain along Little Wills Creek, the Mansion Log Home provides visitors with a comfortable, casual atmosphere in a quiet country setting."

I had no idea as a child that part of our farm would ever be the subject of a brochure, let alone be referred to as a "mansion."

Henry Lybarger, of the same Lybarger family that the old Lutheran Church just over the hill was named for, built the cabin in 1812. Being two stories high made it unusually large for its time. Classic stripes of log and cement cover every outside wall, broken only by a one-foot square of cement in one of the logs just above the front porch. Family legend has it that the cement fills a hole long-ago occupants once poked their rifles through to shoot at hostile natives. In fact, records show that some of the early settlers here had to retreat to the fort in Cumberland for protection from the Indians.

***

Wills Mountain takes its name from a Native American, probably a Shawnee, referred to as "Indian Will" who lived in the area in the 1700s. Indian Will was something of a local legend in his time, and he even was credited with original "ownership" of the mountain. Records indicate settlers knew the area for a while as "Wills Town." Much like the famous purchase of Manhattan for a handful of beads, early settlers gave Will some sort of trinkets whenever they built a new home or established a new farm in the area.

Like many stories of contact between natives and settlers in our nation's history, the story of Indian Will has a violent and tragic end. Will was friendly with the settlers and well liked by them. But in the late 1700s, another group of natives from the north raided the homes of some settlers encroaching on Indian land. A number of the whites were killed, and several women and children were taken hostage. Some settlers believed Will had been part of the raiding party–very much in contrast to Will's reputation.

The raiders made their way south to the Cumberland area and blended into a large native council gathering there. By the time a posse was organized, the large group of natives had begun moving westward. Only Indian Will remained in the area, believing he had no reason to leave his lifetime home.

One member of the posse had lost his wife in the raid and vowed revenge. Because there was no way for him to follow the large group west, he focused on the one native who stayed behind. He tracked Indian Will across Wills Mountain, found him, and shot him to death. When he realized he had killed a man much respected in the area, he buried him on the mountain just south of Bedford. There is no record of any trial or punishment for this murder because it was considered partly justified revenge and partly an accident of mistaken identity.

The story doesn't end there, however. More than fifty years after the killing, a group of men from Baltimore came to Wills Mountain, located Will's grave, and dug up his remains. Supposedly, they passed themselves off as some sort of early anthropologists who were making a scientific study, but no record of any such study exists.

Unfortunately, the story of the man whose name lives on in this mountain has become just another account of the countless natives whose land and lives–and even their bones–were taken from them.

***

The porch stretches across the entire front of the cabin. It's a concrete slab with a brown wooden railing. A porch swing hangs here, and motion sensor lights have been added for security. We could have used those lights years ago to deter the occasional firewood thieves or the teenagers who once broke into the cabin for a beer and pot party.

Walking in the door, the first noticeable item is the cook stove on the left, the only major "authentic" appliance left although I have no idea how old it is (definitely older than I am). Further to the left is the living room with some nice old couches and chairs, a new futon, and the TV-VCR. The floor downstairs is beautifully refinished hardwood. Very bad wallpaper used to hang in here, but Janet and Fred did a great job stripping down to the actual logs themselves. It looks as beautiful as it must have in 1945 when the walls were re-cemented. A dining table is just beyond the cook stove, then the modern kitchen addition with a stainless steel sink, roomy counters, a refrigerator-freezer, and a gas stove. A wall hanging reads, "I don't mind if you smoke, but please don't exhale." I'm grateful to see this, considering Mom died of lung cancer and Dad of smoking-related heart disease.

Just beyond the kitchen is a luxurious bathroom with shower, hot tub, and flush toilet—with the cabin's old "slop jar" sitting beside the toilet. (An outhouse stands in the backyard, but with the new indoor plumbing, it probably doesn't get as much use as the one Dad and I built years ago.) Over the tub is a Keenan Ward photo of a brown bear rising from a Rocky Mountain lake. The placement is great because it looks like the bear is on his way out of the tub itself.

To reach the upstairs, there's a very narrow, steep stairway that turns ninety degrees halfway up. It has hard wooden steps that have hurt my stocking feet on previous visits. No handrail makes for a some-times-difficult passage. At the top of the stairs is a small open area where the slop jar used to be kept for late-night peeing when the outhouse was too far in the cold darkness.

There are three upstairs bedrooms. The one on the left is largest, with double and twin beds. Straight on is a smaller bedroom with two twin beds, and to the right is the smallest bedroom with one twin bed. The same beds have been in here for decades, at least fifty years. The floor is made of rough planks with the same heavy coat of deep red paint that I remember from thirty years ago.

Strangely, no electrical outlets can be found up here, and single bare bulbs hang from fixtures in the middle of each room's ceiling. There are no heaters up here either—just a vent in the floor of one bedroom that allows heat to pass up from the living room. In a mild fit of mischief, Jenny and I dropped pennies down through this vent onto Rob and Jim before they went to sleep on the living room futon and couch during our last visit.

All in all, the downstairs is fairly contemporary, except for the cook stove (and the log walls, of course). The upstairs is very much like when my family stayed here occasionally on warm summer nights. Probably, the upstairs looked much the same for decades before that. The wallpaper is even the same as it used to be, still peeling away in glacial slow motion to reveal layers of wallpaper beneath.

Janet told me that one of the regular renters compared the trip up the stairs to a time machine going back a century or two. That's accurate. When I stand very still, I can almost sense the people dead for nearly two centuries. I'd love to bring them all back to life for one night so that we could share stories of their lives in this place.

Maybe we could even walk downstairs and watch a reality TV show. That would probably make them happy they didn't live to see the twenty-first century.

***

Back in fifth grade math class, we did an activity to figure out how old we would be when the new millennium began. We took the year of our birth (1961 for me and most of my classmates) and subtracted it from the year 2000. I was amazed to learn that I'd be thirty-nine years old on May 17, 2000.

Thinking of myself as that ancient was harder to imagine than any technological advances that I thought might arrive with the twenty-first century. Rockets to Mars, palm pilots, and cloned sheep probably wouldn't have surprised me back in fifth grade, but the idea that I would someday be as old as my teachers was real science fiction.

***

Settling into the cabin is not complete until I put a book by the toilet to read later. My ex-wife often gave me grief about my bathroom reading. "Just a few pages–I mean a few more minutes," I'd call when she chided me.

I generally read three books at once. One is in the shoulder bag that I haul pretty much everywhere I go. I often pull that book out at home for some afternoon or bedtime reading, and it's available at the office when I have some downtime between classes or meetings (sometimes *at* meetings if they're boring). That book also comes in handy for bathroom trips at the college. Another book is on tape in my car, perfect for long trips or just five minutes to the grocery store and back. And the third book is, of course, in my bathroom at home, usually a hardback to protect against the shower's humidity.

I inherited my habit of reading in the bathroom from Dad. By the toilet in my boyhood home, we had a stack of *Reader's Digest* for him and *Boy's Life* for me. Sometimes, I felt very grown up reading Dad's *Reader's Digest*–especially "Drama in Real Life." I wonder if he read any of my *Boy's Life*?

My youthful reading was somewhat limited in variety. In addition to those two bathroom magazines, we subscribed to the big city *Pittsburgh Post Gazette* (always delivered a day late) and the more local *Bedford Gazette*. I gobbled up the sports section and the funnies, and sometimes, as I grew older, I ventured deeper into the paper to discover the national and local news as well.

My sisters had many *Nancy Drew* mysteries on their shelves, as well as a subscription to *Teen Magazine*. I devoured the magazine articles in an attempt to understand (at a safe distance) those mysterious and alluring creatures known as "girls." And I read all of the *Nancy*

Drew books before I even knew about the corresponding *Hardy Boys*. It didn't bother me that Nancy was a girl. I identified with her intelligence and sense of adventure that transcended gender.

Believe it or not, a traveling salesperson changed my reading life. My parents paid a small fortune for the 1968 edition of the *World Book Encyclopedia*, and I read each volume cover to cover over the years. I loved digging through this huge set of books, even long after they were clearly out of date. Half the useless trivia in my head today comes from going to college, the other half from a youth spent reading the *World Book* on rainy afternoons.

I also read a set of old 1950s books originally owned by my older brothers. These were thematic story collections about teenage boys. My favorites were the science fiction tales and the sports stories–lots of robot-like aliens whose world-takeover plans were foiled by the same country boys who became basketball stars by slinging hook shots at a peach basket nailed to the barn.

In school, we were forced to read lots of stuff that was more intended for adult consumption; consequently, I remember very little of it. Only a few works stand out. Carl Sandburg's poem "The Fog" was the first one I ever enjoyed reading because of the simple and playful language. Several Edgar Allen Poe poems, most notably "Israfel" and "Annabelle Lee," were difficult, but I loved the rhythms and the dark tone. I memorized e.e. cummings's quirky "buffalo bill's defunct" although I had little idea what it really meant. And Alexandre Dumas's *The Count of Monte Cristo* hooked me one spring, a book selected to appeal to the adventurous, action-oriented boys in the class.

That was the only novel I completed before age twenty, and the first of only about ten that I read before going to graduate school to study, among other things, novels. Now I'm making up for lost time. Counting books on tape, I read about one hundred books each year. I subscribe to a dozen magazines and journals, and have bookmarked fifty e-zines, my literary reading on the Internet. The most boring moments of my life are being caught in a restroom, waiting room, or restaurant without at least the *USA Today* sports section.

The book I put in the cabin bathroom is *Me Talk Pretty One Day*, by David Sedaris, a collection of hilarious essays that are better than anything I could ever hope to write. Just for fun, I've turned to my favorite essay in the book, "Big Boy," possibly the best two and a half pages ever written. Appropriately enough for the setting, the essay is about visiting the bathroom during a dinner party and finding a huge, unflushable turd in the toilet.

Rereading the essay makes me glad I'm here alone. I'm unlikely to discover anything of mysterious origin in the toilet, and no one will hear my laughter through the bathroom door.

***

Unlike my last two trips here, this time I'm alone with a digital camera, hand-held tape recorder, and laptop computer. These tools are my props to perpetuate the long-term illusion that I'm a writer.

This illusion got its start around age twelve, when, for reasons I can't remember, I began narrating my life. I might walk through the field near our house and think to myself, *The lone graceful young man walked gracefully through the field of gracefully blowing clover in the lonely field, alone. If anyone saw that lone young man that day, they would think he was a graceful young man from the graceful way he walked alone.* I enjoyed trying out different words. (In this case, I was quite enamored with "graceful." "Lone" caught my fancy as well.) I even imagined someone someday reading (while alone) my (no-doubt graceful) writing, being quite impressed with my sophistication rather than thinking of me as a nerdy, brainy, awkward, back-woods kid.

As an adolescent, I dabbled in writing a few love poems that had no capital letters or punctuation. My thoughts and emotions weren't limited by such conventions, I told myself at the time. I also once decided to write a science fiction novel entitled, *Journey to the Stars*. It would be an account of a young starship inventor's graceful journey to, well, to the stars … alone, of course. I drew an elaborate cover for this novel, then never wrote a word. What did I know about going to the stars–or about writing for that matter?

In high school, I tinkered with essay writing–not voluntarily, but because my senior English teacher required one "composition" each week. I wrote about my pre-basketball game rituals, my farm chores, and my walks through the woods on the weekends. Of course, I wrote one composition about all the things I did to waste time while putting off writing the required essay.

My best essay recalled making cider with Dad. I wrote about climbing the wild apple trees on our farm and jumping up and down on the limbs to make the hard little apples fall to the ground … stuffing dozens of burlap bags with apples and hoisting them into the back of Dad's pick-up … getting up at 4 a.m. with Dad and driving to the cider mill in the frosty early-fall morning to get a place near the front of the line with dozens of other pick-up trucks loaded with apples ... pouring the apples into the press and being stung by the countless bees that hovered around the freshly crushed apples ... filling our wooden barrels with the most delicious cider imaginable, cider that we gave to relatives and friends, sold to passing tourists, and drank for weeks until it fermented. I concluded the composition by noting how making cider brought Dad and me closer together, a daring display of emotion for the reserved males of our family.

This was the only composition I ever asked Dad to read. I watched expectantly as he sat in his recliner and slowly made his way through the three handwritten pages with interest but without comment. When he finished, he nodded a few times and handed the pages back to me.

"What do you think?" I asked him.

"It's kind of sloppy," he said.

Sloppy? I was confused. Then I realized he meant my *handwriting*.

"But what do you think of the ideas?" I asked. "What do you think of the ending?"

"Oh, I like that part," he replied as he settled back to watch the evening news. "Yeah, that's good, real good."

As I headed up to bed a few hours later, Dad said, "Hey, John. Just a few more months."

I didn't know what he meant. When he saw my quizzical look, he continued. "A few more months before the apples will be ready for cider again."

***

I did almost all of my writing with pencils because they were cheaper than pens. We didn't even have a sharpener at home, so I tore the wood off with my thumbnail until enough lead poked out and blood oozed from under the nail. Although teachers always criticized my poor handwriting, I penciled all of my assignments in longhand until high school. I took a typing class my senior year, and I did my first academic research paper on a school typewriter. The topic was whether Hamlet was crazy or pretending. My position then, articulated in exactly three typewritten pages, was that he was pretending. Now, I'm not so sure.

A week before I left for college, my parents gave me a $50 bill as a belated high school graduation gift. This represented a major investment for them, especially considering they gave the same amount to my twin sister June. As soon as I saw the money, I knew what I would use it for. Mom drove me to the new mall in Cumberland, and I bought an electric typewriter. After pounding on the keys of the ancient manuals at school, I loved the easy-touch keys, the powerful automatic return, and the soothing hum of my new machine.

Although I continued to use a pencil to write first drafts of my papers in college, I loved cranking out the beautiful final versions on my electric typewriter. I even began typing papers for other people in my dorm–only fifty cents per page, a dollar if they wanted me to fix their grammar. Some nights, I stayed up until dawn in the dorm lobby with my electric typewriter and made thirty bucks from desperate guys with a variety of freshman composition assignments.

During my senior year, to expand my horizons, I took a class called Computer Programming for the Social Sciences. The class worked with ponderous programs like Basic and Minitab–some of which I fear people still use today. Despite my limited math and technical background, I managed to grasp the concepts well enough to do okay in the class. And I had an unexpected glimpse into the future while finishing my final class project.

At about seven in the morning, I sat down at the terminal in the college computer lab, a room filled floor to ceiling with enormous machines that did the actual computations. The place looked like something out of a 1950s science fiction movie. The only other people in the lab were bleary-eyed, pale-skinned computer science majors who had been there all night working on final projects for their "real" computer classes. They gave me semi-dirty looks as if I stole precious computer power from their legitimate scientific projects for my sociology fluff.

But their dirty looks went up to another level of disgust when my friend Andy walked into the lab. He was a history major, but he went right up to a terminal and began using it like he belonged there.

Intrigued, I walked over to his chair and asked, "What are you working on?"

He replied with four words that would change my life forever: "I'm typing a paper."

"What do you mean?" I asked.

"Well," he said, taking on the tone of someone explaining where clouds come from to a child, "I use the computer to type my paper. It stores it, and I can come back and make changes. When I'm done, I can print it."

I just stared. "Like this," Andy said. He touched a few buttons, then half a minute later, the printer across the room came to life. All the computer people glared at us, but Andy walked confidently to the printer and pulled off a sheet of green-and-white striped paper with letters, words, sentences, paragraphs–all written with a computer.

"Is this legal?" I asked.

Andy laughed. "Of course."

"And your professors think it's okay?"

"They say it's how writers will do things in the future."

Andy was right. I left the computer lab that morning with a hint of what was to come in my life. Two years later in graduate school, I took a word processing workshop taught by some computer guys. They used so much jargon and smirked at my ignorance so often that it took me two hours to produce one sentence–thirty minutes just to underline one word in that sentence. The only two words I remember from that workshop are "format" and "command." I still don't know exactly what those words mean.

A year later, a fellow graduate student showed me a funny looking machine hidden in a locked closet on the third floor of the English department building at Ohio University. He had slipped ten dollars to a janitor for a key to the little room. The machine was called a Macintosh, named for apples too sophisticated for the cider Dad and I made all those years before. I sat down in front of it and emerged an hour later with five pages of a research paper. No jargon, no commands, no smirks–but an actual paper that was stored on a little computer disk.

I slept soundly that night, dreaming of apples. Soon the university had a whole lab full of Macintosh computers, and I did all of my writing on them. Eventually, I even became a lab supervisor and taught some of my writing classes in the lab, one computer per student.

At this moment, I am writing these words on another Macintosh, a Powerbook G3 laptop the college issued me so that I could write our reaccreditation report a few years ago. And I have my own Macintosh at home called an iMac. It sits on a little cart in its own room in my house, surrounded by its own printer, scanner, Internet connection, and CD and DVD drives. I even know how to use most of these accessories.

People tell me that my laptop is already outdated, but I love it. I once saw it fall off the edge of my desk and ran to it like I would to an injured child, cradling it in my arms until it came back to life. I carry it with me in a shoulder bag everywhere I go. My favorite weekday afternoon activity is taking my laptop to lunch at about three when the restaurant is nearly empty. I sit alone, eating pasta and drinking Diet Coke, working on class planning, college reports, or my own writing for a couple of hours before going back to the college to teach my night classes. I usually order an extra Diet Coke for my laptop, but it doesn't like diet soft drinks, so I drink it.

A few weeks ago, I received a memo about the college's policy concerning computer use. Apparently, I am not allowed to do anything on the computer that isn't specifically work-related, so the writing that I'm doing on my laptop at this moment is somehow against the rules. I'm grateful to the college for this computer, but I use my iMac at home to do college work, so I also do personal work on the laptop. Besides, every computer at the college has solitaire installed on it, so what exactly is my crime? When I take my laptop to lunch, am I violating the college's sexual harassment policy?

Back in the days of ruining my thumbnail to sharpen a pencil, the thought that I would have twenty-four-hour computer access for my writing ... well, I would never have believed that I could be so rich or lucky. Sometimes, my students ask me what writing was like back before computers. They sound like me as a kid asking adults what they did before TV. I pull out my pencil and launch into stories that seem remarkably similar to Grandma's stories about walking ten miles through the snow to get to school each day. It was uphill–both ways.

All in all, I feel the same way about my laptop that Dad felt about his truck. He once put his hand gently on the fender of his 1962 Dodge Power Wagon Pick-up and said, "How did I ever live without it?"

***

Chapter 7
Lord Land

Alongside the field behind the cabin is a hill that we simply called "the hill"—a ridge that rises a hundred feet or so above the former tracks of the Penn Central railroad. This stretch of the railroad stopped operating in the mid-1970s after extensive damage from Hurricane Agnes and is now a very pleasant raised footpath connecting the north and south sections of Sheirer Road.

One of the highlights of my youth was hearing the train coming in the middle of a dull summer afternoon, then running alongside through our field as fast as I could to see if I could outrun it. I couldn't, of course, but the engineers occasionally threw candy. Today, no parent would allow a child to eat candy thrown from a train by a stranger without first subjecting it to a metal-detector, x-rays, and chemical analysis to find the razor blades and heroin.

I used to walk to the hill almost every day as a kid. From the southern portion of Sheirer Road, I climbed the steep end of the ridge and walked all the way to the north end. In my memory, I found hundreds of fossils there, but I didn't save a single one. Most of the ones I remember finding had shells or ferns in them, but some had little fish and even tiny creatures with legs and claws.

I'm probably making up my fossil memories and spinning so much yarn in my head that it comes out as a complete sweater. Most likely, I found one or two simple fossils that progressively became hundreds in my mind. But I recently talked with a geologist who told me that southern Pennsylvania is rich in fossils. Who knows? Maybe there's an old box hidden in the barn full of the best fossil collection in the northeast.

***

One morning when I was a teenager, as my sisters put on their best dresses and Mom called me for the fifth time to get ready for church, I sat on my bed and decided not to go. Finally, as everyone was heading to the car, I walked out in my jeans and t-shirt and announced my intention to stay home. Mom was upset, but she knew I could be extremely stubborn on those rare occasions when I defied her.

As she drove off, I walked onto the hill. I could see our house on one side and the church on the other. Families drove up to the church, parked, unloaded, and staggered up the concrete steps to the front door.

They felt so far away. To me, God was more present on this beautiful hill–in the trees and soil and rocks and fossils–than in the stale and dull church service across the highway.

From then on, I returned to the hill many Sundays, but I seldom went back to any church.

***

Uncle Glenn planted pine trees in the field beyond the wooded area of the hill. This field was hard to farm because it was hilly, so he had the brainstorm to plant pine trees. Of course, not long after the seedlings were planted, more than half of them died. They're a bit scattered and spotty, but the ones that remain today are tall and healthy and growing in straight rows.

Uncle Glenn was something of the black sheep of his generation. Most of his brothers and sisters remained in the area and lived "normal" lives, but Uncle Glenn lived in Texas and occasionally spent time in exotic places like Malaysia for his work with an aircraft manufacturing company. He even divorced and remarried, a rarity in our family.

For about five consecutive summers in my youth, Uncle Glenn came to visit us for several weeks with his second wife, Mary Lynn, and her two teenaged duaghters from a first marriage, Jamie and Linnae. Jamie was prettier and more talkative, but Linnae was kinder. I was thrilled to share the house with attractive girls who liked my company. Aunt Mary Lynn, a native Texan, was a bright, funny woman who laughed frequently and told dirty jokes with a southern drawl that kept us all blushing and giggling.

Because I was also "different," I got along well with Uncle Glenn, a talker and one of my best sources of intellectual conversation as a kid. Dad was fond of complaining about Uncle Glenn, so I once asked Dad why he didn't like him. "Oh, I love him, I guess," he said. "He's the only brother I have left alive." Then Dad laughed. "But he sure gets on my nerves more often than my dead brothers do." The only thing that annoyed me about Uncle Glenn was that he introduced himself as Glenn "Sheer-er." I've often been called that when people don't know how to say my name, but I will never give up the *real* pronunciation: "Shy-er."

Uncle Glenn once told me about his plan to put in an underground house on the hill. It sounded silly. *What view would he have from the windows?* I thought. *Dirt?* Of course, now when I look in that direction from the back window of the cabin, I can't help but think how wonderful it would be to live in a house dug into the side of the hill. If the house were designed correctly, the cabin and quarry would be part of the fantastic view.

Uncle Glenn was ahead of his time. He lived out the rest of his life far away in Texas (staying married to Aunt Mary Lynn but eventually living in neighboring houses to keep from driving each other crazy), and his vision for an underground house died with him in 1997.

***

Uncle Glenn was not the first person to tinker with our family's last name. Much confusion has surrounded the name "Sheirer" during the last two centuries. The family origin in Europe is generally considered to be southern Germany or, less likely, northern Switzerland. In the historical record of our family, the name has many different spellings (often even within the same nuclear family), including "Scheirer," "Scheurer," "Shirer," "Shirrar," "Shearer," and even "Shirey." In fact, on the web site for the Mansion Log Home, the address is incorrectly noted as "Shirey Road."

My earliest recorded ancestor in the area was Adam Sheirer (possibly Scheirer) who is known to have lived in Somerset County in the late 1700 and early 1800s. The Sheirer family may have even been an early contributor to the weird names of towns in this area. One town in southern Somerset County (probably present-day Salisbury) about thirty miles west of our farm was reported to have originally been named "Shiretown" after our ancestors.

Three aspects of the issue of my name were as clear to me as a kid as they are now: "Sheirer" is correctly pronounced "Shy-er," not "Sheer-er"; the spelling "S-h-e-i-r-e-r" is the only acceptable form; and "Shirey" is a hayseed backwoods hillbilly name that I want nothing to do with.

***

Uncle Glenn and Aunt Mary Lynn once invited my eleventh-grade Spanish teacher, Miss Elias, to dinner at our house. Because he lived in Texas, Uncle Glenn had picked up a little Spanish and was anxious to try it out on her. Of course, no one bothered to tell *me* that Miss Elias was coming to dinner.

Like every other boy in Spanish class, I worshiped her. About twenty-five, barely five feet tall, dark complexioned, she was (to our teenagers' eyes) far more beautiful than any teacher should be allowed to be. So I nearly fainted one evening when Miss Elias followed the school bus to our house and pulled into the driveway.

All through dinner that night, I did my best not to stare at Miss Elias as Uncle Glenn flirted with her in broken Spanish that wasn't even as good as my own. At one point, he told her, *"Tu es bonito ojos."* She giggled, and Aunt Mary Lynn kicked his shin for telling her, roughly translated, "You are boy's eyes beautiful."

Miss Elias had brought a bottle of Spanish wine and insisted I have a drink. I could barely swallow it without coughing. I had the sense to know that Miss Elias, like the wine, was way too much for me. The following year, she married and moved to teach in another state.

Our next Spanish teacher was about sixty and lost control of the rowdy kids in class after about fifteen minutes on the first day. I didn't learn much more Spanish that year. My only clear memory of that class was when she tried to teach us to make *Ojos de Dios* ("God's Eyes") from yarn and sticks. People threw so much yarn up into the hanging florescent lights that it looked like a huge spider had spun a multi-colored web. But, as Uncle Glenn might have said, some of our completed God's Eyes certainly were "boy's eyes beautiful."

***

Uncle Glenn was the first person I knew who climbed up to the quarry. He showed me the pictures he had taken from the top, and I couldn't believe how beautiful the view was. From the valley where I spent so much of my early life, everything looked ordinary. Uncle Glenn's photos showed that our farm was just one small patch of a landscape quilt that looked as lovely as a postcard.

Most of the nearby section of Wills Mountain was and still is owned by the Lord family–"Lord Land," we called it, as much for the irony as acknowledgment of ownership. The Lords were obsessive about keeping people off their property, so Uncle Glenn's climb to the quarry was even more appealing because it was so forbidden. At one time, the Lords probably had good reasons to discourage trespassers. They had valuable equipment that could be stolen or vandalized. But by the time I came along, the quarry had been shut down for so long that their stuff had little more than museum value.

I always wanted to climb Wills Mountain as a kid, but I never did–not out of fear of getting into trouble. In fact, Dad might have been proud of me for defying the overly property-conscious Lords. I didn't climb the mountain because I just didn't–there was no real reason. The words "No Trespassing" had been imprinted on my brain from such an early age that they stuck.

***

Grandma's husband William (my paternal grandfather) died in 1932, nearly three decades before my birth. When their children were all grown in 1946, Grandma sold most of the family land on Wills Mountain to the Lords. She always had a suspicious relationship with the Lords and actually said that they forced the sale by illegally logging some of her land. Decades later, she still carried bitter feelings. She even told a story about one of them moving a surveyor's tool during measurements for the land sale.

I don't know if any of Grandma's stories about the Lords are true, but I do know that Dad shared her sense of being cheated. We piped our drinking water from a spring about one-fourth of the way up the mountain in the only section that we still owned. Every couple of months, we took a family hike to clear the leaves and dirt out of the spring to ensure good water flow. When we climbed the mountain to the spring, Dad pointed to "Lord Land" only a hundred yards uphill and shook his head. "That should be ours," he repeated on every trip.

When I described the Lords to a friend of mine a few years ago, he suggested that maybe they grew pot over there. That would explain their behavior, but, of course, they weren't growing pot. The Lords were just mildly antisocial, small-scale xenophobes who couldn't imagine someone might simply enjoy walking on the mountain without having theft or vandalism in mind.

The Lords once even called Dad to enlist his help in stopping a carload of people they suspected of trespassing. He reluctantly agreed and blocked the road with his old pick-up truck. It turned out that the "trespassers" were a city family from Cumberland who saw the quarry along the road and were curious to explore it. They didn't even make it halfway to the top when they got tired and turned around. When Dad heard their story, he let them go with his apologies. A couple of Lords showed up a few minutes later, and Dad told them never to bother him with their "foolishness" again, then walked back into the house without another word.

***

At age thirteen, I took an evening walk down the road by the cabin. I stepped out on the railroad bridge, hoisted myself up onto the side, and let my feet dangle over the water of Little Wills Creek. Something about the sound of the clear water flowing and the colors of the rocks rippling beneath in the dusky light left me feeling peaceful and content. I wasn't thinking about why girls didn't like me as much as I liked them, or if I would be a major league baseball player when I grew up, or why Mom insisted on making beef liver for dinner once a month. For a change, my mind was nearly blank.

I was close to a meditative state, immersed in the connection with nature, when a voice called out, "What the hell are you doing?" I nearly fell into the water.

Roger Lord, a twenty-year-old grandson of the family patriarch, walked to the edge of the railroad bridge and stared at me. I stared back, not understanding why he had yelled. Then I noticed the rifle he held across his chest, not quite pointed at me–but not down at his side either.

"I'm just sitting here," I said.

"What do you mean, 'just sitting'?" he asked, looking suspicious.

"Just sitting," I repeated. "Thinking. Looking at the water. Sitting."

"You were on our property," he said, less accusation than what he considered fact.

"No," I replied.

"You weren't over there?" he said, gesturing with the barrel of his rifle.

"No," I said. "I never go over there. That's your property. I'm sitting on the bridge. It belongs to the railroad."

Roger puzzled over this for a minute. Then he lowered the rifle and walked out to where I sat in the middle of the bridge. He peered down into the water.

"How long you been sitting here?" he asked.

"I don't know," I said. "Half an hour maybe."

"Your parents know where you are?" he asked, trying to sound grown up even though he had fewer whiskers on his chin at twenty than I had at thirteen.

"They know I'm out for a walk," I replied. "I'm not a baby."

"You know anybody who's been over on our property?" Roger asked.

"No," I said, a white lie. A school friend who lived two miles down the road told me he kept animal traps on Lord property.

"It's nice up here on the bridge," he said, noticing the hypnotic water below. "You just sit here thinking, do you?"

"Yeah."

"What do you think about?" he asked.

"Nothing, I guess." This was a hard question to answer.

"Nothing," he repeated. "You're a deep little guy, aren't you?"

I shrugged my shoulders. We shared a few moments of quiet, listening to the creek and looking out into the woods.

"If you hear of anybody being on our property, you'll tell me, won't you?" he said.

"Sure," I replied.

"You take it easy then, Mr. Thinker." That was the longest conversation I'd ever had with a Lord. He walked off the bridge to where his car was parked. As he drove away without a wave, gravel flew out behind his spinning tires.

***

As an adult, I've had a few decades to lose the "No Trespassing" imprint, so last August, when I came to Pennsylvania with Jenny, we climbed Wills Mountain. On our second day here, after a wonderful night relaxing in the cabin, we felt like taking a walk. The day was sunny and pleasant, and we had no specific idea where we might go. We just started walking about mid-morning, wearing somewhat flimsy sneakers and carrying no packs with food or water. We crossed the creek at the base of the mountain on stones that rose an inch or two above the shallow water and started up.

After the creek bank, which is pretty steep in some places where the water has cut its way back into the mountain's base, the land rose gently. The hike on the first half of the mountain was a leisurely uphill stroll, invigorating, as always, to be in the woods on a beautiful day with a great walking partner. I turned to Jenny and asked, "Wanna try for the quarry?" She saw my enthusiasm and was just as game to keep climbing despite our lack of preparation, so our purposeless walk quickly became one with a very specific goal in mind–the top, the quarry.

A little farther along, however, the mountain angled sharply upward. After some steep climbing, we came to a thick band of mountain laurel. In one way, these shrubs helped with the climb by acting as handholds. Of course, they also scratched at our faces and grabbed at our feet. Between the rocks, the laurel, and the steepness, that nice uphill walk had definitely turned into a hike.

After an hour or so, Jenny and I began to wonder aloud if we were near the top. We both wished we had our hiking boots, water bottles, and some chocolate or beef jerky. But half the fun of any hike is how tired you get, the sense of accomplishment you earn at reaching your goal, and how wonderful it feels to lean back in a soft chair when you get home. Jenny had her plant-identification book, thrilled to find a few species she hadn't seen in New England, and I basked in the childhood memories these woods brought back.

We kept slogging ahead and soon found an old logging road angling its way across and up the steep slope. The road had been unused for decades and made a comfortable walking surface, covered with soft topsoil and thin sod, protecting our feet from the rock chunks beneath. After a few steps on the road, we both looked up through the treetops and saw a pale beige wall of rock illuminated by the near-noon sunlight.

"There it is!" I shouted. Without thinking about my bad knees and ankles, I ran the last hundred yards or so to the quarry. Fatigue vanished in my excitement at being about to set foot in a place that I had seen throughout my youth, a place that had been a symbol of where I lived–not just a house, but a family and way of life on our small valley farm that somehow made me unique, the person I was at age ten, fourteen, eighteen, even now at forty-one.

When I made it to the top and emerged into the clearing at the base of the quarry, the scale of it was almost overwhelming. Viewed from our farm, the quarry looked big, no doubt, but with very little detail beyond a few wrinkles and ridges. Here, though, only a few hundred feet away, those ridges were breaks in the rock face dozens of yards across, and the wrinkles were cracks so deep a person could slip into one and disappear.

As a child, I imagined the quarry to be as tall as our house, but from this close perspective, I saw that our house could be stacked on four or five other big houses and barely reach the top, easily one hundred feet high in some places. The trees that grew precariously on its top edge looked like tiny shrubs but were as tall as the huge shade trees in the valley below.

While the vertical qualities of the quarry were impressive enough, I had a harder time taking in the horizontal scale. We must have emerged somewhere near the middle because I couldn't see either end. When I stared at the cliff face and let my eyes slip out of focus, I felt surrounded by rock as the quarry enfolded me and filled the periphery of my vision.

At the quarry's base were countless boulders–some as much as ten feet high and wide–piled nearly one-fourth of the way to the top. I assumed they had tumbled off the quarry's face during the decades since the limestone mining ended. For fun, I picked up a rock about the size of a baseball and prepared to test my throwing arm. I figured I could hit a target about a third of the way to the top. But when I let the rock fly, it landed well short of the quarry. The thing was so off-the-scale big that I had lost my ability to measure my surroundings in any meaningful way.

Jenny arrived beside me and took my hand in hers. She looked up and down and side to side for a moment at this landmark that represented so much of the first half of my life–the sentinel that had watched over my youth from the top of this mountain.

She said only one soft word: "Wow."

***

When we were packing the car to leave that weekend, a truck pulled up to the cabin and a guy in his mid-thirties got out. As we chatted, I realized that he looked familiar, so I asked him his name. He turned out to be a former neighbor who grew up a few houses up the road. I hadn't seen him since he was about fourteen. I told him that I climbed the mountain for the first time that weekend.

"You never climbed it as a kid?" he asked.

"No," I replied. "I didn't want to trespass."

"Well, I climbed it about ten times back then," he said. "Everybody did. You must have been the only kid around here who didn't."

***

Two weeks ago, Jenny and I came back to the cabin with her sons, Rob and Jim. On our first morning here, the weather was a little cold and overcast, but Jim and I took a walk down the road. Just beyond the railroad bridge, we got a pretty good view up the ridge of Wills Mountain. I pointed up to the quarry where it peeked out through the morning fog.

"Hey, Jim," I said. "Wanna climb up there?"

His eyes lit up. "Yeah," he said, striding toward the mountain.

"Wait," I said with a laugh. "Not yet."

He stopped short, sighed, and drooped his head exactly as I would have at his age when someone said we were going to do something fun and then said *"not yet."* For a kid, "not yet" is as bad as "never." I assured him we'd go back to the cabin, get his mother and brother, go out for breakfast, and then come back and climb the mountain together in the early afternoon.

Three times on the thirty-minute drive to Bedford for breakfast, Jim asked when we were going to climb the mountain. Jenny and I took turns answering, "When we get back to the cabin." Twice at breakfast, Jim asked when we were going to climb the mountain. Rob took over the task of saying, "When we get back to the cabin." Four times on the drive home, Jim asked when we were going to climb the mountain. Jenny, Rob, and I said in unison each time, *"When we get back to the cabin."*

When we got back to the cabin, we used the bathroom, changed our clothes, and packed water and snacks for the hike. Jim sighed loudly and asked, "Are we ever gonna go?" so many times that I could almost hear my own Mom saying, "We're not going at all unless you stop complaining, young man." I bit my tongue to keep from saying it myself.

We crossed Little Wills Creek at the railroad bridge because the water was too high from snowmelt to ford it near the cabin. The wooden railroad ties and steel rails had long ago been removed for scrap, so all that remained was the cast iron framework. We had to walk across beams six inches wide, a feat made more difficult by one-inch rounded rivets that stuck up every few inches, playing games with our balance. Jenny and I took our time crossing, but both Rob and Jim raced across with no fear, just as Jenny and I would have at their age. Maybe we're getting old, but we both had visions of them sprinting right off the side of the bridge and floating away in the icy water while we stared helplessly after them.

The walk up the mountain that day was very different from the previous climb with Jenny in August. Having the boys along made it fun in a different way, seeing their excitement at some sights–abandoned buildings, ancient rail cars–along with their inexplicable boredom at some of the things Jenny and I found fascinating–trees, moss, animal tracks. Both boys were disgusted with me when I picked up some deer turds to show them. But both of them, especially Jim, loved throwing rocks down the mountain to see how far they would fly, bounce, and roll. Even Rob–despite the teenagers' code of behavior forbidding enthusiasm–smiled and mimicked crashing sounds with each rock hurled into the air.

As soon as we crossed, we noticed something unusual on the other side of the creek. The buildings there had once been the loading and processing station for the quarry stones but had been unused for decades. Some of them had even collapsed. But the abandoned roadway had a new layer of gravel. After we walked along the road for a while and started uphill, we saw many downed branches and fresh stumps. The ground itself had been trampled and torn up by heavy machinery. Only small trees were left standing, and many of these had been damaged by equipment and larger trees falling on them. The whole place looked awful, even nightmarish, especially compared with the graceful natural beauty of the woods that Jenny and I had climbed through a few months earlier. We quickly realized that someone was harvesting the mountain's timber for the first time since long before my birth.

A short way up the mountain, we found several bulldozers, logging trucks, and large stacks of cut timber. Beyond these, we found more of the same downed and damaged trees. Roads cut across the hillside, probably the same ones that had been used many years before by the quarry workers, now torn apart by the bulldozer treads.

At their best, these roads had become little more than loose rocks and dirt turned over by the machines and were very difficult to walk on without stumbling. At worst, they were muddy bogs–as I soon discovered when my foot sank to the top of my boots. I stepped quickly to try to keep reasonably clean, but the mud sucked so hard that it almost pulled my boot right off my foot.

***

I have nothing against logging, but I've just rediscovered this area after so many years away. I wish I had more time to enjoy it before the trees are taken.

Besides the rough way that the land is being treated, two things strike me immediately as problems with this logging operation. All the larger trees are being cut, leaving only a scattering of small ones to provide a transition to the next phase of forest growth. And a great deal of brush is being left on the ground. The brush makes good habitat for small animals and much of it will eventually rot into the soil, but this much is too much. Without shade from large trees, the brush could create a fire hazard during the hot, dry periods of the coming summer.

In a way, the timing seems to be good. Late fall is the best part of the year to begin logging because the ground is getting colder and dryer, so it's less likely to be damaged by erosion than it would be in warmer, wetter months. Even with all the mud we're wading through this afternoon, things would be worse in April or May. Rains would wash away essential topsoil leaving bare rock in many places, making life difficult for plants.

Jenny is as upset with how the mountain looks today as I am because she saw how beautiful it was last August. But Jenny has worked as a naturalist and knows a lot more than I do about how the woods will recover from an assault like logging. She tells me that the logging, despite its immediate devastation, will eventually infuse the mountain with a diversity of plants and wildlife. Her knowledge is a real comfort.

To my surprise, forests adapt well to properly done logging because they are designed to react to natural disasters that have roughly the same effects. Fires and hurricanes, for example, can destroy a large wooded area much faster and more completely than even clear-cut logging. I'm grateful that this is not a clear-cut operation–at least not yet. They may come through after the large trees are gone and start on the small ones. The mountain would certainly recover from clear-cutting, but I don't want to come here this summer and hike a bald mountain.

After the logging is completed, wild annuals will be the first plants to grow. They will live for only a season, but their numerous seeds are light and wind-blown, carried by the air to the cleared forest. The dandelion in the valley below, for example, will turn from bright yellow flowers to snow-white seeds that will float up onto the mountain, grow for a year, then die, only to be reborn from their seeds.

Perennial wildflowers will come next. The cleared mountain will experience a rebirth of color in the growth of flowers that previously didn't thrive here because the trees blocked too much sunlight. In a few years, Wills Mountain might be dappled with purple Ironweed and Spiderwort, white Allegheny Foamflower and Hen's Toes, yellow Goldenrod and Black-Eyed Susans, red Queen of the Meadow and Fire Pink.

Shrubs come back soon as well. Blueberry and Sumac bushes could be everywhere in a few years. Birds and animals relish their seed-bearing fruit as a food source, which are transported widely in scat droppings. The increased presence of these shrubs will also attract more wildlife to the mountain. As many birds and animals as there have been here over the years, there will be even more while the trees grow back. The downed branches and smaller fallen trees will provide shelter for small animals like rabbits, squirrels, chipmunks, and turkeys, making them even more plentiful. The increase in small prey animals will attract more predators (foxes, coyotes, and hawks) and scavengers (turkey vultures, raccoons, and possums) to feed on them.

The first trees to return will be Cherry, White Pine, and Birch, fast-growing but short-lived smaller trees that thrive in the open sunlight of the cleared areas. Within five years, the mountain won't looks quite so bare as it will in a few months when the logging is completed. And after a decade, the woods will be leafy and beautiful again. It will certainly look different from the years when I grew up admiring its beauty, but nature will once again give the residents of our valley a lovely place to rest their eyes.

The smaller trees will mostly die off in approximately forty years, making way for Maples and Hickories, the larger, slower-growing trees that thrive in moderate shade and will eventually take over the forest once again. But the canopy created when these large trees mature will shade the ground so fully that their own seeds will not be able to grow. Beeches and especially Hemlocks will then grow slowly but steadily in the heavy shade. Without a natural disaster or another session of logging, Wills Mountain will probably be a thick Hemlock forest sometime around my one-hundredth birthday.

I'd be thrilled to live to see it.

***

The first few hundred yards of our climb was a preview of the rest of the day. With so much mud and so many fallen branches to navigate around, the climb took nearly twice as long as it should have. Several times, with the four of us mud-covered, grimy, and tired of the disturbing scenery, Jenny asked me if I wanted to turn around and go back to the cabin. I think she was worried about me more than wanting to go back herself, so I said I wanted to keep going.

Near the top, we cleared the logging area, but the snow got deeper and the angle of our ascent steepened considerably. When we finally crested to the base of the quarry, I felt more relief than exhilaration. But then the clouds unexpectedly parted, and the sun hit the quarry as we drew near, making us all grateful that we had kept climbing to the top. We quickly forgot our muddy and disquieting trip up through the heavily logged woods to soak in the beauty of the quarry.

We spent nearly an hour there, with each of the boys scampering over the boulders to go right up to the face of the cliff. We passed the camera around and took pictures until the light began to fade. Then we made our way down the mountain to the cabin–where Jenny immediately started the shower for the filthy boys as I packed our muddy clothes into a garbage bag to deal with later when we get back to New England.

That evening, we watched TV for half an hour before bedtime, our heads bobbing forward as we fought off sleep. I asked Jim if he wanted to climb the mountain again tomorrow.

"Maybe next year," he replied.

***

The whole time we were on the mountain, I kept an eye out for the Lords or their loggers. I half expected two or three of them to jump out from behind a tree and yell at us, rifles clutched in their hands. We didn't see anyone, but if we had, and they had told us to get off their land, I would have calmly explained who I was, who my parents were, that my grandparents had sold them this land, that I had grown up at the foot of the mountain, that I had never trespassed here as a kid, and that my family and I were taking a leisurely hike on a pleasant winter day. If they still insisted that we leave, I would have told them not to bother me with their foolishness, then kept walking.

I'm not thirteen years old anymore.

***

Chapter 8
Last Words

I plan to get an early start up the mountain on Tuesday, the last day of 2002. The previous night's weather reports called for heavy rain later in the day. When it comes to snow, I tend to doubt the predictions. I've listened to weather forecasters winter after winter, and it occurs to me that they're a lot like insecure men. They talk and talk about eight to ten inches, but it usually turns out to be three or four. But they're talking about rain today, so I put a little more faith in them.

I can hear the loggers already at work by seven in the morning. To locate them, I drive to the old Lybarger Church on the opposite hillside. I want to avoid them during my climb today, but when I get to the top of the graveyard and look over at the mountain, I can't make out anything but trees and snow.

I decide to take a path where I'll cross Wolf Camp Run and Little Wills Creek at the bend in Sheirer Road halfway between the cabin and the house. I'll cross both streams just before they meet because they're each smaller by themselves than when they join. I brought no waterproof boots, so I improvise by putting garbage bags over my boots for the short passage across the shallow water. My ingenuity works pretty well. Just a few drops of chilly water leak in, and I slip only twice, not coming close to falling in.

Judging by the sound of their chainsaws, the loggers seem to be working almost directly across from the cabin, only a few hundred yards up the mountain, so they shouldn't be hard to avoid. I stash the trash bags under a rock at the base of a tree for the return crossing, walk north along the base of the mountain for a quarter mile, and then angle uphill and to the south, keeping just off the area that's already logged. This way, I'll stay mostly in the still preserved woods, avoiding the depressing sight of the harshly logged landscape.

***

The deer tracks are everywhere in the snow and soft ground around the water runoffs. Literally thousands of them criss-cross in every direction, and I can't go ten steps without seeing another pile of deer droppings. I recognize raccoon, wild turkey, and even fox tracks. As a child who spent many hours in the woods, I naturally learned to recognize some animal signs. The raccoon tracks are easy to identify because of their small size and the little claws at the end of each digit pad. The wild turkey is one of the only birds that would leave such large tracks around here. And the fox is a guess, but what else could it be? No wild cats roam here, and a wolf, wild dog, or coyote would be out of place as well.

After listening to Bill Bryson ramble about his fear of bears on the Appalachian Trail, I confess I'm thinking about bears–although I never saw one here as a youth. Newspapers sometimes reported bear sightings back then. I remember one story about a bear attacking a house trailer. For reasons unknown, the enraged creature beat the trailer around with the owner inside for an hour or so before the game warden shot it. I don't know if that story was true, but it had an effect on me because I, too, slept in a house trailer.

Last summer, Jenny and I spotted a bear track in the firm mud at the base of the quarry. We stared at it for a few minutes, trying to figure out what else it could be. After eliminating other possibilities, we felt awed. The print was deep and smooth, pretty recent. I touched it, half expecting it to be warm.

I'm scanning for bear tracks on my way up the mountain today, but with the noise of the logging, I don't have much hope of seeing such a shy creature. Then I remember a basic lesson learned in elementary school science class: bears hibernate in the winter. Even if a bear is on this mountain today, it must be sleeping peacefully in a hidden lair to conserve energy for spring–not eagerly waiting to bite my silly head off.

***

Twice on the way up, I venture into the newly logged territory. Almost halfway to the top, I see one of the logging trucks fifty yards away laboring in low gear down a mountain road toward me, so I turn quickly upward and northward to avoid it. I half walk, half run for about five minutes, making great time despite the rocks and steepness, covering a good distance to make sure the loggers don't see me.

When I slow, I see a deer hunters' lookout right in front of me, a small platform nailed fifteen feet high in a tree with ladder-like rungs for access. Hunters must have built it thirty years ago for a dry, concealed place to wait quietly for deer to come into view. Most people imagine deer hunting as a woodland safari, but it involves sitting in silence for long periods, hoping a deer walks into your rifle's range.

I found it too sedentary, but hunting can be a peaceful, contemplative activity that is, unfortunately, sometimes interrupted by deafening, lethal gunshots.

I grab one of the rungs and give a tug. After all these years, it's still solid. I make a vow to return here with Jenny and sit in the lookout until the deer come by. Instead of guns, we'll bring binoculars and cameras.

***

The weather has turned absolutely tropical for mid-winter, sunny and forty-five degrees with no sign of the predicted rain, but I watch the sky just in case. I'm prepared to hurry down the mountain if the weather gets bad and then try for the top tomorrow. For now, I keep climbing and avoiding the loggers.

The snow gets deeper the farther up I go. Soon I get to the familiar steepening of the ascent, then move into the mountain laurel. After that, I'm in the dreaded felsenmeer rocks that jut straight up like footballs planted in the earth. The deep snow makes climbing easier by dulling the sharp rocks, but it's also harder because the snow conceals the crevasses between the rocks. Many times, I put my foot somewhere that looks fairly solid, only to sink into a gap two feet deep.

I'm going very slowly and being as careful as possible. I wish I had bought those $100 collapsible hiking poles I saw at EMS–or better yet, the $15 ones at Target. I'd love to pull them out of my pack and strap one onto each hand to aid my climb and keep me from lurching along the incline. Instead, I improvise with two fallen branches. I keep one in each hand to help my ascent. They're a little rickety, but so am I. At least they're free.

Last August, I tried to climb above the quarry along the southern side, but the rise was too steep and rocky for my sneakers, so I gave up halfway there and retreated. Today's climb up the steep northern portion of the ridge is easier than last summer's aborted attempt to the south–but still difficult for a guy with two weak ankles, a bad knee, and a screwed-together pinkie finger. So I take it slowly and carefully. I'm in no hurry. Today's job is to climb this mountain, and, as long as the weather holds, I've got all day to do it.

When I finally see the top edge, very rocky and steep in the distance, I feel unsure what to expect. I don't know if there will be a flat wooded area or if the mountain immediately descends down the eastern side. Part of me thinks that I might emerge into someone's backyard with a swing set and swimming pool. Maybe those UFOs I wished for as a child are up here, finally getting my message. But now I'm committed to this world. I've got a wonderful girlfriend, a great job, a comfortable place to live, basic cable, a gym membership, and car payments. I no longer want to leave with the aliens.

After half an hour of very steep, rocky climbing, I pull myself up to the top of Wills Mountain. I'm on the ridge above the northern end of the quarry, and the trail here looks like it may have been a utility road at one time. To my left is a wildlife preserve sign–preserved for hunting, that is. At least it's public land that people can hike through safely outside of hunting season. Of course, one of the first things I notice to the south is a "No Trespassing" sign. I'm not surprised. I'm either still on "Lord Land," or the urge to claim ownership of the earth infected more than one strange family of neighbors.

I've never been all the way up here before, not even on the last two visits when I climbed to the quarry base. Unlike the leafy foliage of August, here on the top on the last day of the year, only a scattering of bare branches blocks my vision. The view is everything I'd hoped it would be.

To the west far down in the valley below, I see the house where I grew up, looking like a tiny toy. My eyes are drawn directly to the house itself, and then I glance to the left and see the barn with the snow melting in a graceful oval across the middle of its roof. The western portion of Sheirer Road is the darkest feature in my view, cutting a short stripe by our house and intersecting with Route 96. The bulge of Wills Mountain itself hides the eastern part of the road and the cabin. Madley Hollow Road winds a graceful path through snowy fields and beyond the hills, disappearing into a cove not far from the Ellsworth's summer house.

A two-second glance encompasses what had been almost my whole world for much of my life.

***

Last summer, Jenny and I climbed Mount Monadnock in southern New Hampshire, the most frequently climbed peak in the Western Hemisphere–second only in the world to Japan's Mount Fuji. The climb was beautiful, and we encountered only a few other people on our way up. But when we reached the summit, at least one hundred people crowded among the bare rocks. We snapped photos for three other couples before we found a spot to sit down for lunch.

The summit of Monadnock is well over 3,000 feet above sea level and 2,000 feet above the land below, twice the elevation gain of Wills

Mountain, and I felt so high that I had a hard time standing in the breeze without feeling dizzy. The views were wonderful and dramatic, of course, but they didn't compare to what I'm seeing now as I look down from the quarry.

I had no personal connection with the Monadnock landscape, other than the connection any human being naturally feels with the earth. But here, I know what I'm looking at. Every prominent feature is a place I knew intimately in my youth, a place where I stood and looked up at the quarry and wondered what the view was like up there.

Now I know.

***

When I look to the east, toward that mythical "other side," I can see land that lies about two miles from my homestead "as the crow flies." But I've never laid eyes on it before today. For me, this land didn't exist except as a legend until this moment when I look out over it.

In my teenage fantasies, there may have been a girl my age living over here. She may have been a person like me–slightly outcast, thoughtful, kind, delighted to say or hear something funny. She could have been someone I might have fallen in love with as a teenager. She could have been right there all that time, but because this small mountain separated us, we wouldn't have gone to the same church, the same stores, or the same school. Those UFOs that I dreamed would come for me might as well have carried her off.

No one has cut any lumber on the other side recently, so it still looks beautiful and clean. I can see a farm in the distance and hear what sounds like a tractor far off. If I were a prehistoric human standing atop a mountain at the edge of my familiar territory eons ago, I might have felt something like what I'm feeling now. *What strange things do those people down there do?* I might have wondered. Odd as it would have seemed to me, they probably do pretty much the same stuff on that side that we did on our side.

***

Now that I'm up here on top of the mountain, it's time to do something I've planned since deciding to take this trip. I'm going to call Jenny on my cell phone. I miss her, and this is the place she would most enjoy if she were here with me. It's about two o'clock, and Jenny should be home from work now, so I dial and press send.

As I wait for her phone to ring, I'm struck once again by how the world has changed since I left this home. Standing atop a mountain and calling someone almost five hundred miles away never would have occurred to me as a child. Only Captain Kirk could do that when he wanted Scotty to beam him up. Since then, we've gone through Captains Picard, Sisko, Janeway, and Archer–not to mention cell phones as big as combat radios that evolved into ones the size of a credit card.

Jenny's phone is busy on my first two attempts, but I get through on the third try. I'm so happy to hear her voice that I practically gush. For a moment, I wonder if the altitude is making me giddy, but this isn't exactly Mount Everest–I'm only a hair more than 2,000 feet above sea level.

She's also thrilled to hear from me. I tell her about the view first, then about the climb, then the drive here. Soon, we're having an everyday conversation about how we slept, how her work was today, when the kids will come home from their father's house, what we watched on TV last night–all the topics we'd cover if we were sitting in the living room together rather than being as far apart as we've been since we started dating.

The combination of ordinary talk with a loved one and this extraordinary location seems perfectly natural. Of course, if other hikers walk by and hear me prattling on about how few times I stopped to use the rest room while driving here, they might consider this a strange mountain-top conversation.

***

The deer have been running the ridge, and there are even more tracks up here than on the mountainside below. To my surprise, I also notice a set of human bootprints as big as my size twelves that look like they were made within the last forty-eight hours. I hunker down and look closely to see another type of print along with the deer and human tracks. It takes me a moment to recognize what is probably the most common animal print I've seen in my life. I wasn't expecting to see it here in the "wilderness." Whatever human was up here before me was walking a big dog.

The person who made these bootprints might be very unhappy to see me trespassing on his land–or he might be a trespasser like I am who may even duck behind the trees if he sees me coming. Either way, it's comforting to know that someone else has been here doing something as casual as walking a dog. That knowledge helps ease the minor fear in the back of my mind that I could take a wrong step and fall off the mountain, rolling and rolling to the bottom, waving at the loggers as I tumble by, then landing with a splash in the cold waters of Little Wills Creek–not a comforting thought.

***

My plan is to walk above the quarry southward on the ridge trail like the bear in the children's song, "to see what I can see." I'll eventually switch back down the mountain and come out at the base of the quarry, then find my way down from there, probably somewhere near the route I followed on the way up. After the steep climb up to the ridge, this trail is a pleasant relief. Snow still covers the ground, but it's melting in the steady sunshine. Lots of limestone chunks are scattered around the trail, and I put a couple in my pack to take home, feeling a guilty pleasure stealing from the Lords.

The only real problem with walking up here is the thorns. Every thirty feet, a thicket of bushes with thorns as sharp as hypodermics. I can usually work my way around them, but in several cases, I'm forced to plunge through. No matter how careful I am, I end up with a thorn digging into a leg or going through a thin glove. A few even stab me in the face. As soon as I feel one, my reflex is to pull away, which, of course, only draws the thorn in deeper and tears at the skin. At one point, I wrap my hand around a small tree to help pull me over a slight rise, and I end up with a shark-tooth thorn from the tree half an inch into my palm. This is not a pleasant moment for me–or the tree for that matter because I give it a couple of hard kicks that knock off a few chunks of bark. Thorn *bushes* I've always been familiar with, but down in the valley we had no thorn *trees*.

As I'm extricating myself from another thicket, I hear crashing about ten yards down the mountain on the west side, trespassing on Lord Land. When I look quickly in that direction, I see a group of five white-tailed deer running along a path from the north. I can't tell if they see me or not, but they are so close that I see steam exiting their nostrils and the articulation of muscle rippling in their shoulders and haunches. I reach for my camera, but the deer are veering downhill in unison like synchronized swimmers, gone before I get the camera out of my pocket. From here on, I vow to keep it powered up with my finger on the button.

***

I sense that I'm near the middle of the quarry by now, but I can't be sure. As I've aged, my fear of heights has intensified. I loved climbing trees as a kid and even jumped off the high-dive into a pool. Now I can barely step off the dock into water two feet below. Jenny laughs at the noises I make when we go on carnival rides that rise higher than six feet.

So I've surprised myself by daring to come off the trail and walking downhill about fifty feet to stand near the upper edge of the quarry.

The closer I get to the edge, the shorter my steps get and the tighter I grip the trees that I can reach. Now that I'm standing here about three feet from the point where solid ground becomes thin air, I can't believe how exhilarated I feel. I'm not scared at all as I look out on a nearly unobstructed view of the valley floor stretching miles and miles off to the west. I can even look down to the base of the quarry with only a twinge of anxiety. Directly below me are abandoned ore cars and iced-over pools of snowmelt and even one of the monstrous rusting cranes that I marveled at on my previous visits. From here, the crane looks like a toddler's forgotten beach toy rusting on the shore. I'm not about to get any closer to the edge or unhook my left arm from a nearby tree, but I am enjoying myself. Jenny would be proud.

For fun, I decide to toss a rock down over the face of the quarry–something Jenny's sons would do if they were here. Part of me is still a little boy who wants to see what happens when I do things like that, and no grown-ups are here to tell me I can't. I pick up a rock about four inches square and underhand it over the lip of the cliff. Less than a second after it disappears, I hear it bounce against other rocks, but then I don't hear anything for three seconds . . . four, five, six . . . then another cracking bounce far below. After another few seconds, I hear two more quick muffled cracks . . . then silence.

I hold tighter onto the tree, grab another rock, and overhand it out as far as I can without risking tossing myself over with it. It arcs out and down and disappears into a silence that seems to last for a minute before I hear a series of muffled bounces near the bottom. This is fun. I want to try more rocks from different angles to see how they sound.

As I'm looking for a third rock, a movement catches my eye. I glance about fifteen feet to my right and see what looks like a small animal scurrying–but then I realize that a couple of stones are rolling toward the quarry edge. They gain momentum and tumble over, cracking again and again for a very long moment before falling silent.

It's one thing to toss rocks off the edge voluntarily but another to see them rolling off under their own power–or, more accurately, the power of gravity. Then I hear more rocks rolling and falling about fifty feet to my left. These are bigger, heavier rocks that bang and crack so loud that I'm sure someone could hear them from the valley below. For a moment, the ground under my feet doesn't feel as firm as it once did, so I turn back and climb quickly toward the trail, my heart thumping harder than it did a moment ago.

Back on the trail, I continue walking south, avoiding the thorns, enjoying the view, reflecting on my life and all the choices and forces that took me away from this place so many years ago and brought me back today. Quite suddenly, about one hundred paces from where I inched down to the edge, my reverie is interrupted as I walk directly to a point where the trail drops off over the quarry into nothingness. I had been walking with my head down for a moment to avoid stepping on loose rocks when, for no reason, I looked up to find myself two steps from the edge.

When I inched down to the quarry a few minutes ago, each move was voluntary, planned, and carefully executed. This time, I'm utterly terrified for a moment and frozen in place. Slowly, as if I'm inching away from an angry dog or a coiled rattlesnake, I take a few steps backward, keeping my eyes glued on the edge. I back right into a tree and lean back against its solid bulk, allowing myself to breathe for the first time in a while.

I suppose I had very little chance of falling off, but I walked uphill to this edge, coming over a slight rise with strong steps. Could I have been distracted enough to propel myself into space, only to think as I fell, *Oh my goodness, what just happened?* I pick up a rock and toss it over the edge here where the cliff face seems closer to vertical than my last stop, and I don't hear it hit anything, as impossible as that seems. This silence is more frightening than all the bouncing and crashing I heard before.

After a moment, I move very carefully to a few feet from the edge and look down. Everyone tells me not to look down when I'm up high, but I have to look down. *Down* is where my feet are, and I get a great deal of comfort seeing my feet on firm earth. If I look up, I imagine my feet sliding toward open space, and I get fuzzy-headed. From this edge of the quarry, I have my first unobstructed view of the valley, not even a few stray branches in front of me. The view is absolutely amazing, so I squeeze off several pictures to make sure I have at least one that does justice to the panorama below.

I'm tempted to get down on my belly, shimmy to the drop off, hold my camera an arm's length over the edge, and point it down to get a picture of the quarry face from above. The ground is dirty and wet, and I decide not to get my pants messed up. Of course, that's not the full truth. I don't get down on my belly because I'm not about to angle the soles of my feet away from solid ground this close to the edge.

I remember the pilfered limestone samples in my pack, however, and plan a story for Jenny and the boys. I'll hand them the rocks when I get home and tell them that I crawled out to the edge of the cliff, reached over, and pried them from the quarry face. When I have everybody wide-eyed with amazement at my daring feat, I'll break out laughing and admit the truth.

***

After soaking up the view for ten minutes, I start back along the trail. I soon discover the reason reception was strong when I called Jenny earlier: a cell phone tower on the ridge at the south end of the quarry. This artificial feature looked so unnatural from down in the valley that I must have blocked it from my mind until it popped into my view fifty feet ahead of me.

As I approach, I look down to the east and see a road leading all the way up here from the other side, probably an access road to the cell tower and the source of the human and dog footprints. I have to laugh at the fact that I could have put my Tracker into four-wheel drive and motored in comfort to this exact spot in a few minutes instead of getting here in a couple hours of fairly strenuous hiking. I file this information away for future visits.

A ladder goes all the way up the tower. This strikes me as a crazy idea–climbing to the top of this mountain, feeling a palpable sense of vertigo just walking along the ridge, then climbing another hundred feet higher to the top of a fragile looking tower.

Climbing that thing in this place is almost literally beyond my imagination. About the only thing I *can* imagine is that if I climbed it, I'd probably get to the top just as a historically powerful gust of wind blows the whole thing over the edge–me included. How much longer would I fall if I were at the top of the tower compared to simply stepping off the edge of the quarry? How much more of my life would flash before my eyes? How many more endless seconds would I have to call out my last words? Would they be, *"Ooooohhhhh, Ssssshhhhhiiiiittttt!!!!!"*?

Seeing the cell tower brings me back to reality. I reached the ridge around two o'clock, so I estimate that it must be three by now. I pull out my watch and find that it's nearly half past four. Where did the time go? I have only forty-five minutes of daylight to make my way off the mountain.

I hike downhill from the trail and cut back to the north toward the face of the quarry. When I pause to scout my route, I'm surprised to notice a pick-up truck idling toward me on the ridge a hundred yards to the south. I can barely see it through the trees, but I can hear the engine and make out a muffled conversation between two men in the truck. This is well above where the Lords are logging, and I have no idea who would be on this part of the mountain now.

I have no interest in meeting strangers up here, so I scurry quickly but carefully down the very steep ridge until I'm hidden by the thick mountain laurel. On a future visit, I plan to continue walking out the ridge trail to see where this pick-up came from. For now, I'm going to slip away and leave the idling truck far behind me.

The rocks are plentiful and sharp, and the deep snow and steepness make for slow and tedious going, but I eventually make it to a spot about fifty feet below the quarry. I have to make another short but difficult climb to get up there, but this is my last climb of the day. From there, it's all downhill to the cabin.

When I reach the base of the quarry, I'm once again amazed by the place. I take a few photos and wish I could stay, but the light is leaving. I promise myself that I'll be back again. I find one of the logging roads near the center of the quarry and start downhill, relieved not to hear any chainsaws. The loggers started work early this morning and must be home for New Year's Eve by now. I'm also relieved that the logging roads are no longer mud pits, but the loose rocks still keep me alert with every step. Rolling one of my weak ankles up here with darkness approaching would be bad. I want to spend the night nodding off on the futon in the cabin with the TV remote in my hand, not scrunched in a fetal position on a cold mountainside.

Eventually, I make my way out of the logging area, and the road turns back into the solid path that I remember from my childhood and the visit in August. To my delight, I come upon my own footprints from this morning. The sun has been shining all day, and the temperature rose to well above freezing, so my snow tracks have melted so much that they look a week old. I pass the deer lookout again and make another promise to return. As darkness begins to close in around me, I arrive at the foot of the mountain, find my garbage bags, and ford the streams. The water level has risen from the snowmelt, and the bags have developed small tears. When I step out of the creek, I feel the shocking cold water soaking through my right boot, and I'm relieved to be only a five-minute walk from the cabin.

I reach the porch just as the last light fades. My timing was good enough to allow me every possible moment of afternoon light on the mountain, but I chide myself for cutting things so closely. A mountain, even one as small as Wills, is not a good place to be at night in the winter with a light jacket and no flashlight.

When I go inside and pull off my boots and clothes, I realize that I haven't eaten the snacks I packed for the hike. As soon as this knowledge hits me, it goes directly from my brain to my stomach, which unleashes an inhuman belly growl that rumbles for thirty seconds. I want to sit down in the big comfy chair in the corner of the living room and pull out my laptop to start writing about this day, but I need a hot shower and warm food before I can do anything else.

***

Chapter 9
First Hoop

Because I lived outside of town and would have needed countless rides to practice and games, I didn't play organized sports until eighth-grade basketball–and only then because I arranged rides with my teammates and coaches as often as I could so that Mom and Dad didn't have to go out of their way. I played very little basketball with other kids before then, but I took to it well, earning a starting spot and developing the rebounding and defensive skills that would be my trademark through high school.

Much as I enjoyed the eighth-grade team, my worst moment in sports came in one of those games. I got spun around and elbowed in the head while going for a rebound, and the ball fell into my hands under the basket. On instinct, I jumped up and laid it off the backboard into the hoop. When I turned and started running to the other end of the court, I saw all nine players, teammates and opponents, standing still and staring at me. None of the fifty or so people scattered through the stands made a sound. Finally, our coach waved me over, put his arm around my shoulders, and said, "John, that was the wrong basket."

I came home that day and struggled for the right words when Dad asked me, "How was the game?"

***

From an early age, I spent as many hours as possible shooting hoops in our yard. The first hoop was on a light pole about twenty yards from the house. I inherited it from my much-older brothers, a crooked rim and a rotting backboard only eight feet high. But then Dad and I replaced the original backboard with a broad sheet of plywood and hung the rim a standard ten feet from the ground. We took Dad's old pick-up into the woods and got three loads of sandy clay that I spread over the ground around the hoop to form a playing surface. For hours that afternoon, I bounced my basketball and stomped my feet to smooth and harden the clay.

Eventually, it made a nice court, and I must have shot ten million baskets there, rain or shine. I even played at night when Mom would let me. The light at the top of the pole illuminated the court, but the arc of my shot took the ball above the light and into darkness. I watched the flight of my shot until it disappeared, then magically reappeared, either swishing through the net or clanking off the rim. I even played there in the winter, pounding down the snow, much as I had the clay, until the ball bounced on the hard-packed ice. Then I cut the fingertips out of an old pair of work gloves so that I could control the ball. My fingers froze, but I had *control*.

To beat the weather, I decided to put a hoop inside our barn. It's traditional to nail a hoop outside the barn, but it rains and snows outside. I wanted a year-round dry place to play–sort of my own personal gym. So I built my own backboard and nailed it to one of the beams. All I needed was a hoop.

In the spring of my junior year, construction began on a new gym at our high school. The tiny old gym was gutted and the baskets taken down. One day when Dad picked me up at the school after baseball practice, I asked him to wait for a moment while I got something. I ducked back into the school and slipped under the yellow construction tape blocking the old gym, waded through the debris, and spotted one of the old basketball hoops that had been unbolted from its backboard. With a quick look around for witnesses, I grabbed it and went back out to the car.

Dad gave me a funny look as I jumped into the front seat and tossed the hoop into the back.

"They're just going to throw it away," I announced. "I don't want it to go to waste."

What could he say? For years, Dad had come home from work sites with old tools, hard hats, work gloves–once even a paint-stained and slightly dented aluminum ladder. He always told Mom that they were going to throw these treasures away, and he couldn't stand to see them go to waste.

Were they really going to throw that hoop away? I don't know. Was Dad's ladder actually bound for the junk pile? I don't know that either, but we made excellent use of both our acquisitions. I used the ladder to hang the hoop inside the barn where no school officials could ever see it.

***

Our new high school gym was finished by Christmas 1978 during my senior year, but not before we played our first five games on the road and practiced at a tiny church gymnasium fifteen miles away. The church was unheated, so we practiced with long underwear beneath our gym shorts. We were such bumpkins that the idea of wearing sweat pants hadn't occurred to us. The gym was in terrible condition. Once, as I dragged my right hand against the backboard while making a lay-up an exposed nail opened a three-inch gash on the back of my hand.

The team felt excited and relieved when we finally moved into our spacious new gym–and I had plans of my own for the new venue. Because Dad had hit the first home run at the town's baseball field nearly forty years before, I had the brilliant idea that I would make the first basket in the new gym. In my imagination, I could see Dad and me smiling for the cameras as the newspaper ran a father-and-son story recounting our historic "firsts."

Despite my sad experience scoring a basket for the wrong team a few years earlier, I kept playing and was a varsity starter by my senior year, making me one of ten players with a chance for that first basket. Unfortunately, scoring wasn't my strength. I set picks, rebounded, and played defense. None of our plays were designed to get me the ball in scoring position. Most of my points came from offensive rebounds, moving relentlessly without the ball to get open around the basket, and running like a maniac on the fast break.

Strangely enough, in the pre-season newspaper write-up about our team, the coach didn't mention anything about my rebounding, defense, or speed on the fast break. But he called me a "pure shooter." When had he noticed? I couldn't help developing a good shot during the long hours of practice at the hoops in our yard and barn, but I let my teammates do most of the shooting. The coach was probably feeding misinformation to our opponents' coaches, wanting them to waste a good defender on me, the only guy on the team who could happily play an entire game without taking a shot.

But I still wanted that first hoop in the new gym, so I made a vow to shoot the ball as soon as I touched it. Our first trip down court, a teammate took a long set-shot completely out of the flow of the game. Apparently, I wasn't the only one who wanted that first basket. He missed, and I jumped over three guys (two from my own team) pursuing the rebound, but I knocked it into the stands.

The second time down court, I cut through the lane without the ball and was wide open under the basket. I held my hands up and called for the ball, something I rarely did. The pass came high and hard but just beyond my fingertips as it sailed out of bounds.

The third time down court, one of my teammates made a beautiful fake and dribble move, perfectly in tune with our offensive plans, and hit a ten-foot bank shot. He earned the first basket fair and square. Visions of Dad and me in the newspaper vanished. The next time we had the ball, I tipped in a teammate's missed shot for the second basket in the new gym.

Later that night, as I lay in bed reliving the game in my mind, it occurred to me that I had scored the last basket in the old gym the previous season, a meaningless lay-up in the fourth quarter of a blowout victory. Last basket at the old court, second at the new court–that sums up my athletic career.

***

During my senior year, I averaged about six points and six rebounds per game. My high scoring game was thirteen, and I had double-figure rebounds several times (not bad for being a shade under six feet tall). In the newspaper write-ups, I was occasionally singled out for rebounding or defense–never for scoring. My picture even made the paper once, showing me snagging a rebound. My crazy hair flopped everywhere, and I looked rail thin, but I seemed to know what I was doing. I even appeared on television once. My parents told me they saw me in the highlights of a playoff game at the end of the season. We lost, but all I remember of that game was taking an elbow in the ribs from a muscular player named Jeff Hosteller, who would later quarterback the New York Giants to a Super Bowl victory.

I missed very few games although I got hurt pretty often–never in the games when the fans could see, but at practice when only my coaches and teammates were around. And I always seemed to get the same injury, a sprained left ankle. That ankle had been a problem since second grade when a flap of my shoe came loose, tripping me on the playground and breaking my ankle. During my high school basketball career, I turned that ankle at least ten times.

Strangely enough, my teammates enjoyed making fun of me for getting hurt. Once in practice when I lay on the floor holding my leg after twisting my ankle, the coach asked me what happened. The pain was so intense, I could only moan, "Ankle." The next day when I arrived at school on crutches, several of my teammates fell on the floor and grasped their feet, moaning, "Ankle! Ankle!" then burst out in laughter.

As the years went by, several of those teammates had the pleasure of spraining their own ankles, writhing on the floor, and crying like babies. They each apologized because they had no idea a twisted ankle could hurt that much. "What did you think it felt like?" I asked them. Four years after graduating from high school, I had two operations to reconstruct that ankle. The surgeon said it had the worst damage he had ever seen in a sports injury.

It still hurts–both the ankle and the way my teammates laughed.

***

In my mid-teens, I became fascinated with dunking. I could get half of my palm above the rim when I jumped, not quite enough for a clean dunk, but I wanted to do what I'd seen the pros doing on television. So I devised several ways to add those crucial last few inches.

At school, I could dunk on one of the side baskets in the new gym by running behind the backboard, planting my foot about three feet up on the cinder-block wall, and jumping up and back toward the rim. The first time I tried it, I was so amazed that it worked that I fell flat on my butt. My teammates loved my discovery and started imitating me. We had our own slam-dunk contests–of course, only when the coaches were nowhere in sight.

At home, I put a plastic milk crate about three feet from the basket, ran up, and leaped from the crate. I even devised a way to dunk at the hoop in the barn. I planted my foot on a diagonal crossbeam to get the extra lift. Of course, on about the five hundredth dunk of my barn career, I came up short of the crossbeam and tore every inch of skin off my shin. I wore long pants for a month that summer to keep Mom from seeing what I'd done.

By my senior year, I could dunk without any extra launching pads–but only one time out of five. If I timed my jump and jammed the ball against the rim just right, I could use the hoop for extra leverage and muscle my body up the inch or so I needed to shove the ball over the rim and down through the basket. This remains one of the greatest thrills of my athletic life. Of course, I would never try this in a game. If I got anywhere near the basket with the ball, I gently banked it off the backboard for a boring, normal two points.

I did dunk in uniform once–my baseball uniform. I was at home waiting for Mom to drive me to Hyndman for a game. As a benchwarmer throughout my baseball career, the chances of playing that evening were slim. So to get some exercise, I was shooting baskets in the yard, and I discovered that I could jump pretty well in my baseball spikes. I even got high enough to do my jam-the-ball-against-the-rim dunk on the first try. But when I landed, my left ankle rolled so far that my toes nearly touched the back of my calf. My face immediately broke into a cold sweat from the pain. Of course, I couldn't admit this accident to Mom because she wouldn't take me to the baseball game.

So when she came out to the car and asked if I was ready, I smiled through the pain and said, "Sure!"

By the time we'd made the half-hour drive to town, I could barely walk, but I still wouldn't admit what happened. I waved good-bye to Mom and shuffled painfully out for fielding practice. The first time a ball was hit toward me, I fell to the ground and pretended I had hurt myself right at that moment. When the coach took my shoe and sock off, my ankle was already swollen and richly black and blue from toes to shin. Seeing this, my teammates all made pained faces and whistled through their teeth.

No one who saw my ankle that day made fun of me for hurting myself, but I'm sure they would have if they knew how it really happened.

***

I had the usual number of fights growing up, many in the school boy's room. Our high school housed grades seven through twelve, so I spent the first few years there holding my bladder all day to avoid running into older boys who liked to knock around smaller kids between classes. I got beaten up there once by a guy whose girlfriend told him that I said he had funny-looking hair. He did have funny-looking hair, but I would never have said so. Fortunately, by the time I got to tenth grade, I was big enough to visit the boy's room in relative safety.

I had three notable fights in elementary school. The first involved a kid hitting me three or four times before I knew we were fighting. We had been arguing over some game on the playground, and he decided to hit first and ask questions not at all. I ended up with a swollen lip, but no blood was drawn.

The second one happened in the middle of winter. We were all having a great time bombarding each other with snowballs one sunny afternoon during recess. No one was in any danger. A couple of kids (me included) got hit on the shoulders or the back, but we were all so bundled up that nothing really hurt. But on one throw, I reared back and launched a perfect strike directly into the face of a classmate. After wiping the slush away, he swore and started chasing me. He was a big kid but not very fast. I took off toward the athletic fields and stayed well ahead of him for quite some time and distance. Eventually, I got more tired of running than afraid of him beating me up, so I worked my way back to the playground and waited for him.

When he finally caught up, he was so winded that his fighting ability was seriously compromised. He rushed me, flailing his arms, but I stepped around him as he lurched forward and landed in the snow. Everyone who had watched our fox-and-hound chase through the athletic fields got a good laugh from his tumble, which, of course, made him mad enough to get up and run at me again. I jumped out of the way once more, and again he fell into a snowbank. More laughter made him swing again. By now, I felt too tired and bored to keep going, so I punched him in his unsuspecting nose–about the same spot my snowball hit.

He stood straight up and rock still for a moment with a blank look, and then blood began pouring from his nose into his open mouth, oozing into the gaps between his white teeth. As soon as he tasted it, he stuck a finger in his mouth, pulled it out, saw the blood, and started crying. I took his arm and led him to the school nurse where I told her that he had slipped on the ice and banged his face on the ground.

The third fight was one of my finest moments. A class bully had tied knots in the sleeves of his sweatshirt and was swinging it around to smack other kids in the head. He had hit a couple of my friends and was working his way over toward me. His henchmen laughed uproariously each time he hit somebody, causing the victim to run off in tears. My friends urged me to move on as the bully and his crew got closer, but I stayed put. These jerks wouldn't get the best of me this time.

When the bully swung his knotted sweatshirt at me, I caught it in mid-swing and yanked it from his hands. He and his buddies looked stunned, but not half as stunned as when I tossed the shirt in a mud puddle. The bully came at me with both fists up, but I managed to get him in a bear hug and wrestle him to the ground. Before he could get up, I rolled him into the same puddle where I had thrown his sweatshirt, staining the rest of his clothes as well. By this time, one of the teachers had grabbed me and pulled me off the playground toward the principal's office where I got a stern lecture, but my point was made.

All that afternoon, I was the subject of school gossip. Half of the buzz centered on how I had taken on the bully, and the other half speculated on his revenge. On the way to the bus at the end of the school day, the bully and his gang jumped me and tossed me into the hedge in front of the school. But I had won this encounter. I just brushed a few leaves and sticks off my jacket. Even bullies have mothers, and he had to go home and explain all those muddy clothes to his.

***

By the time I got to high school, I had pretty much outgrown fighting–with one exception. I had a fight with a kid a year younger than I named Dan Fay, who had a brother a year older than I named Don Fay. I had been feuding with the Fay boys for years.

The feud began in fifth grade. At lunch, we had been listening to my beloved Pittsburgh Pirates play the hated Cincinnati Reds on Don's radio. The radio had a long antenna that extended about three feet from the console. Somehow, my sleeve snagged the antenna and bent it slightly, and Don dropped it, knocking the batteries out and replacing the baseball game with silence. When I bent down and picked up the radio, Dan started yelling. "You busted my brother's radio!"

"It's not broken," I said. "Let me just get the batteries back in."

But Dan wouldn't listen. He kept yelling, "You busted it! You busted it!" I managed to get the batteries back in, and the game instantly resumed as clearly as before the mishap. I handed the radio back to Don, who bent the antenna back more-or-less straight. Dan fumed but didn't say anything else. He wanted to fight me right on the spot for "busting" his brother's radio, but I ignored him.

The next day, Don told me that the radio was indeed broken, and that I would have to pay him twenty dollars for it. I didn't have twenty cents in fifth grade, let alone twenty dollars, so I couldn't pay.

"It can't be broken," I said, stunned. "It worked yesterday."

He showed me the radio. The antenna was twisted nearly off, a couple of dials were missing, and a crack ran across the front.

"I didn't do that!" I said. "You know I didn't do that."

Just then Dan came over and said, "Yes you did! I saw you. As soon as the game was over, you got mad because the Reds won, and you smashed the radio!"

"You know I didn't do that," I repeated to Don, who just stared at the radio. Don and Dan lived a couple of miles up the road from me, and we rode the same bus to school. We hadn't exactly been friends, but we weren't enemies either. Finally, Don looked at me.

"You owe me twenty dollars," he said flatly. Then he and Dan walked away.

I avoided the Fay boys after that. I didn't understand what happened to the radio or why they had blamed me. After a few weeks, they stopped asking me to pay for the radio when it became clear that I wouldn't fork over twenty bucks even if I could get my hands on that kind of fortune.

Luckily, I never had to be in class with either one of them because of our age difference, but I played on the same sports teams with them for years. Don was a pretty good basketball player, but he shocked everybody by quitting the team in the middle of his junior year. He didn't seem up to the intensity of practice. Dan was a very talented baseball player, but he lacked the discipline and concentration to fulfill his potential. His brief pitching stint resulted in a school record for hit batters. Even when on the same teams, we kept our distance and spoke only when we had to.

By my junior year, I became a cafeteria monitor, a position that involved eating my lunch early, then watching over the other students as they ate, trying to keep ahead of food fights and other disruptions. Don was also a monitor, and toward the end of his senior year, we worked a couple of lunch shifts together. We ate quietly at the same table in the empty cafeteria, occasionally making meaningless small talk, then spent our shift leaning on the radiator and watching everyone.

On our last shift together, Don surprised me.

"I owe you an apology," he said, not looking at me.

"What for?" I asked.

"Remember the radio?" How could I forget? That's what started the whole feud years before. I nodded.

"You didn't break it," Don continued. "But when we got home that night, Dan told my dad a big story about how you had smashed it. My dad said that either I had to pay for it or get you to pay for it. I didn't have the money."

I thought for a moment. "How did it get smashed up so bad?"

Don looked at me. "One guess," he said.

"Dan?"

"He'll never admit to it," Don said. "He's a jerk, but he's my brother. But I feel bad about the whole thing. I have for a long time. I wanted you to know."

The peace I came to with Don unfortunately never filtered down to Dan. He remained a thorn in my side throughout high school, finding every opportunity to abuse me. He made fun of my hair, tossed chewing gum at me on the bus, even made up names for the girls I liked. I tried to ignore him, and he usually got bored quickly and moved on to terrorizing someone else.

By late in my senior year, Dan was a junior who had grown into a tough kid. He had tried to goad me into fighting many times. Although I had fantasized about it, I really didn't want to risk fighting him–but one day, I decided not to ignore him.

After one of his usual insults, I turned to him and said loud enough for everyone to hear, "You know, Danny-boy, you're the biggest dumb-ass I've ever met."

Everyone laughed, but Dan stared at me. I pointed at him and repeated the word "dumb-ass" to another chorus of laughter.

He tried to grab my finger, and I pushed him away. Before I knew what was happening, I hit him three times in the face, hard and fast. A nasty red welt started growing on his forehead above his surprised expression.

Someone had squealed to a teacher that a fight was breaking out, so we had only a few seconds to decide what to do. Neither one of us wanted to get into trouble, so we moved off in opposite directions. When the teacher came into the hallway, he saw no sign of a fight.

When I got home from school that night, Dad asked me to help him move some haybales in the barn. The first time I picked one up, pain shot through my right hand. I looked down to see the second knuckle on that hand swollen to three times its normal size.

"Where did you get that?" Dad asked.

I didn't really want to tell him, but I had to. "I had a fight today," I said.

"For God's sake, John, you're a senior," Dad scolded. "You're going to college in a few months. What the hell are you doing getting into a fight?"

He was right. I couldn't say anything to defend myself.

After a moment, Dad asked, "Well, did you win?" He was pleased to hear that I had.

I expected Dan to try for revenge, but he kept his distance after that. I don't think he was scared of me, so I have no idea why he left me alone. I'm glad he did because I didn't want to risk getting beaten up at the end of my senior year over a stupid feud that started because of a broken radio in fifth grade.

***

Six months ago, I almost got into a fight playing basketball. That's a pretty sad statement for a man in his forties.

I was guarding Kevin, a guy who I knew pretty well and had played with and against many times. We weren't exactly friends, but we always got along. Like a lot of guys I play with, the only place we ever see each other is at the gym. Once we had even teamed up to win an ad-hoc two-on-two tournament when not enough guys showed up to play full court. He was bigger and a better player but almost twenty years younger and not as experienced. When I guarded him, he often torched me with a combination of skill and superior athletic ability–although I usually got a few points on him as well.

But on this day, my experience was paying off. I scored more than my share of baskets with Kevin guarding me. At one point, I hit three top-of-the-key jumpers in a row with Kevin laying off of me, prompting one of his buddies on the sidelines to call out, "Somebody remind Kevin that John can make that shot." And I stole the ball from him a few times and even blocked one of his shots. But he kept calling fouls on me and went out of his way to bump into me every chance he got, telling me that I couldn't play him without fouling.

I usually keep a cool head when I'm playing. My goal is to have fun, get some exercise, make a few nice plays, and be able to walk the next day. But this guy was really getting on my nerves because he seemed to think the only way I could play him evenly was by resorting to intentional fouls. At one point, I told him that, yes, the old white guy with the knee brace was shutting him down–as close to trash-talking as I ever get.

The next time Kevin got the ball, he swung an elbow into my ribs when he turned toward the basket. I purposely hacked him across the arms as he shot and pushed him backward a few feet. We glared at each other, and he moved toward me. I watched his hands, waiting to see if he was going to swing a fist at me. If I saw his hands coming up, I was going to hit first and hit hard.

Before I knew what happened, he lunged forward and head-butted me in the face. His forehead walloped me hard just below the nose. My head rattled a bit, but I stood my ground. He took a step back, staring at me through eyes now more glassy than angry. Head-butts work better in the movies than in real life. Kevin staggered, nearly going down to one knee. I almost laughed at him.

A couple of guys stepped between us, but I hadn't even considered retaliating. Kevin took himself out of the game and sat on the sidelines with his head between his knees. Someone took his place, and I spent the rest of the game feeling around the front of my mouth with my tongue to make sure that my teeth hadn't been knocked loose.

After the game, I asked Kevin how his head was. "Sore," he replied. We had a civilized discussion about how he felt he was getting fouled on every play and about how I thought I was playing cleanly and hardly ever fouling him–certainly not on purpose. We finished the discussion with a handshake and an agreement to play the next game hard and fair.

About ten minutes later, he went in for a lay-up and got fouled hard by another guy on my team. Kevin immediately shoved the guy and yelled, "Goddamn it, John, that's a foul!" When he saw it wasn't me, but another guy my approximate size, shape, and color, he looked surprised.

When everyone realized his mistake, we all had a good laugh–including Kevin. Now when I play against him, we sometimes share a chuckle over the near fight. I think we've both learned a lesson. He learned that I don't foul him nearly as much as everyone else does, and I've learned to be thankful his head-butt didn't hit me an inch or so higher where it would have broken my nose.

***

I did act as peacemaker for a few fights. During my senior year, when things were not going well for the basketball team, I stopped a fight between our coach and one of my teammates at practice. The coach was yelling at one guy for not being in the right place and grabbed his arm to yank him into position. The guy pulled his arm back and swore, telling the coach not to touch him. Both of them balled up their fists and started moving toward each other with hate on their faces.

Without thinking, I stepped between them, stuck a hand in the middle of each of their chests, and held them apart. They both stared at me for a second, shocked that I had done something so assertive and that I was strong enough to stop them. I felt a bit surprised myself. To this day, I remember how hard I had to push to keep them apart.

I have no idea why I stepped in that day. It seemed like the right thing to do. Later, one teammate who didn't like how little playing time he got told me I should have let them fight to get the coach fired. But nothing good could come from a high school basketball coach fighting a player. Things could have gotten ugly in a hurry. I didn't want my teammate suspended from school or kicked off the team for hitting the coach, and I didn't want the coach's long and successful career to come to an end for hitting a player. Besides, I got most of the playing time that the complaining guy thought he deserved, and I wanted to keep it that way.

I managed to get myself squarely in the middle of another confrontation that year. The team bus was on its way to a game at Tussey Mountain in the northern part of Bedford County, one of our longest bus rides. The team had eight seniors that year, so we all sat two per seat at the back of the bus on the way to games.

My seat-mate in the next-to-the-last seat was a kid named Sam who had a bad reputation on the team. First, he was the coach's pet who got lots of praise and playing time that we didn't necessarily think he deserved. Behind his back, some of the players nicknamed him "Son" because they thought the coach saw him as the son he never had. Second, he was a little standoffish and didn't mix well with the other players. Third, and by far the worst, he sometimes got an erection in the shower after a practice.

Any hint that a guy might be gay in our backward little community was about the worst thing imaginable. I took lots of grief from other kids for being a good student who had very little interest in fixing cars or hunting–sure signs of being "queer." The only thing that saved me from full-time abuse was that I played sports and was usually in desperate love with at least one girl in school.

And I never got an erection in the shower surrounded by my teammates. In fact, I avoided showering with them as much as possible. They enjoyed snapping towels at each other and flushing the toilet to scald whichever unfortunate naked boy was under the water at that time. No one said anything to Sam's face about his boner, but everyone talked about it behind his back. Actual evidence that someone became excited in the presence of other boys, unlike the indirect evidence that led some people to think that I might be "that way," was too real for these kids to confront.

Sam's secret nickname quickly changed from "Son" to "Hardy Boy," in reference to his shower hard-on. I had no idea then or now if he was gay–and I don't care. Sympathetic to his situation because I took my share of abuse, I didn't do much of the behind-the-back teasing. I'm ashamed to confess, however, that I felt relieved to see someone other than me as the brunt of the jokes.

On the way to the Tussey Mountain game, Sam fell asleep in the seat beside me, and my fellow seniors encouraged me to write "Hardy Boy" on the steamed-covered window beside him. I did. We all got a big kick out of the words being right there not more than six inches from his dozing head. I felt guilty, but that didn't stop me from enjoying the admiration of my teammates for writing the nickname without waking him up.

Sam slept for quite a while, and I remember several times thinking that I should erase the window before he woke up. My teammates probably would have called me a "wuss," and I enjoyed their approval for a change, so I left the window alone.

When Sam awoke, we all pretended to be asleep. He glanced at the window, and I felt his shoulders stiffen. He slapped his palm against the window and erased the nickname, then turned toward me. I kept faking sleep, as much a coward as everyone else in those last two rows of seats. Sam stared daggers at me for a few seconds, then turned to the guys in the seat behind us.

One of them started snickering in his fake sleep, and then most of us were giggling. Before I knew what was happening, Sam reached back and punched one of them in the face, then flailed away in a frenzy. The guys put up their arms to protect their faces, and I managed to get my hands on both of Sam's upper arms and force him down into the seat. I desperately wanted to stop what was happening before the coach in the front of the bus noticed.

Sam broke my grip and started swinging at me and swearing at the top of his lungs. By then, the guys behind us started hitting him back, and, of course, the coach heard the commotion and turned around. He jumped out of his seat and headed toward us in less than a second, yelling the whole way back. By the time the coach got there, everybody had stopped throwing punches.

The coach pointed at Sam and called out, "You! Up front with me now!" Sam climbed over me and stomped up the aisle with everyone staring at him. The coach sat him down in a front seat, but Sam refused to say a word. Everyone in the back of the bus seethed. One kid growled, "Yeah, coach takes his son up to sit with him." When we arrived at Tussey Mountain High School about ten minutes later, Sam stormed off the bus and ran down the street out of sight.

As we watched the junior varsity game, many of my teammates were glad Sam was gone and didn't think he was coming back. The cheerleaders wanted to know what had caused the fight, but I kept my mouth shut. Most people thought Sam had over-reacted to some innocent, good-natured teasing, but I knew that he had gone nuts over us basically calling him a homosexual to his face–the worst insult any ignorant, small-town boy could hurl at another. Whether he reacted to our guessing the truth or misjudging him, I'll never know.

When we went back to the locker room near the end of the junior varsity game, Sam was seated on a bench in his uniform, his attention riveted on tying his shoes, not even glancing up at us. We got dressed quietly, with only a few mumbles about Sam's presence. The coach's pre-game talk focused on keeping our minds on the game, which was, of course, the last thing on our minds.

The game felt wrong from the beginning. Halfway through the first quarter, one of the Tussey players shoved me under the basket. That kind of thing happened ten times a game, and I usually just smiled and kept playing. This time, however, I turned to him and told him I'd "kick some ass" if he did it again. He looked surprised, then angry. A few minutes later, one of our players got tangled up with one of theirs while going for a rebound. If the referee hadn't stepped in, they would have started throwing punches.

At half time, we stared off into space as the coach yelled at us for losing focus. We were ahead by two, but we weren't playing well. In the second half, Tussey pulled ahead and stayed there. We still couldn't focus on the game. With only a few minutes to play, one of their players bumped one of ours as he drove to the basket. Our guy threw the ball at the Tussey guy, smacking him right in the face.

The whole gym froze for a second, and then Sam leaped out of nowhere and tackled a Tussey player. Suddenly, everybody was fighting everybody else. I wrestled briefly with a Tussey kid, pushed him away, then found Sam and grabbed him by the arms for the second time that night and tossed him off of a pile of people. An older guy in street clothes grabbed my arm, and I pulled away from him and yelled at him to go back to his seat. I thought a fan had charged in from the stands to pick a fight but later found out he was Tussey's assistant coach.

Eventually, the fight petered out. We played the last minutes like robots, then retreated to the locker room. We lost by eleven points, but it felt like fifty. The coach immediately dragged a bench to the corner and called the seniors over. We sat and stared at the floor.

"I'm not going to ask anybody to say what happened on the bus," he said, correctly assuming that we wouldn't tell him anyway. "But I am asking you to be men and take responsibility for what you did."

We all glanced around at each other, and I could tell nobody else knew what he expected. Finally, it dawned on me that he needed a gesture to tie this whole sorry evening together so that it wouldn't poison the rest of the season.

I stood up and walked over to Sam, holding out my hand.

"I'm sorry for my part in what happened," I said, and I meant it. But I made a point of saying "my part" so the coach would know I wasn't the only one responsible.

Sam half-heartedly shook my hand, and I sat down. My teammates stared at me, and I waited for one of them to do what I had done. Of course, no one did. They didn't need to. I had absorbed enough blame to keep them out of trouble.

After a moment, the coach said, "That's good enough for me." Then we all got dressed, avoided the shower, and made our way to the bus for the long ride home.

***

The basketball bus wasn't always as bad as it was on the trip to Tussey Mountain. On the way to games, the cheerleaders sat in the front while the players sat in the back. The theory was that mixing genders before the games would have destroyed everyone's concentration. If we had been allowed to sit together, the team would have lost by fifty points, and the cheerleaders' pyramids would have toppled before they were half finished. On the way home, however, we could sit anywhere we wanted. I had heard lots of rumors about what went on in the back of the bus where the players and their cheerleader girlfriends sat together. I never made it back that far, so I'm not sure exactly what was happening. I suspect, however, that every time the bus hit a bump, a few people were in danger of getting a bruised lip.

In ninth and tenth grade, I spent the return bus trips with one of the team managers because he was better at conversation than most of the players. In my junior year, I actually sat with one of the cheerleaders–not in the back, of course, but near the middle. I sat with Jan, the coach's daughter. She was a year older than I, an honor student whose company I enjoyed a great deal. The coach gave me a dirty look when he saw us sitting together, but then he smiled and winked. My teammates told me later they thought I had a lot of guts for going after the coach's daughter, but nothing romantic ever developed.

During my senior year, I spent half of the season riding back from games with Glenda Walters–again, nowhere near the back of the bus where all the wild sex was supposedly going on. I had carried a not-so-secret torch for Glenda since about seventh grade. I once told her that I loved her, but she said she didn't think of me that way. She emphasized, however, that she thought I was "really, really nice," and that she "really, really liked me." That really, really stung. But we had great conversations coming back from road games in that warm, dark bus.

Unfortunately, Glenda soon started dating an older guy, the son of our Spanish teacher from Cumberland, a guy I had always thought was a turd. I couldn't understand why a nice girl would want to be with a jerky guy. Once she started dating him, Glenda told me that he didn't want her sitting with me on the basketball bus, even though we were just friends. Her parents always liked me, and a few years later, they told me they wished she had married me instead of that creepy guy.

After that, I started sitting with a cheerleader named Amanda. If what I felt for Glenda was "young love," then what I felt for Amanda was more like "young lust." To be fair, that's not all I felt. I really liked her as a person, not simply as a sexy girl, and she responded to that. Amanda was far more experienced than I was, having ridden in the back of the bus with older guys in previous years. We made an odd pair, the beauty and the nerd, but I may have been the first guy who really listened to her and looked her in the eyes when she talked rather than staring at her breasts. (I did look now and then, of course, and they were lovely.) She was between boyfriends at the time, so we sat together and talked in the safe middle of the bus.

As we neared my stop on the ride home after the last game of my senior year, Amanda decided that she wanted to give me a goodnight kiss before I got off the bus. I quivered at the prospect of my first real kiss. When we stopped about a mile up the road from my house to let the first kid off, the bus lights were turned on. Every other trip that year, the driver turned the lights back off for the two or three minutes it took to get from that stop to mine. This was going to be the most exciting two or three minutes of my young life–considering all the kissing I envisioned once the lights went out. For some cruel reason beyond explanation, the driver kept the lights on. Amanda and I only stared at each other, too shy to kiss when everyone could see us.

As I walked the cold, dark, lonely road from the highway to my house, I couldn't decide whether to cry or scream. I'd have to wait until my first year in college for that first real kiss. And I was nearly twenty-two before I discovered all the wonderful things everyone else did in the backseat of the basketball bus.

***

Sometimes I wake at night not sure who's lying in bed with me. Back when I was married, my hand might have brushed against my wife's bare thigh, and the first woman I ever slept with would be fully alive right there beside me. My dream-sharpened memory would conjure her as real as the last time we shared a bed years and years before.

Then last month with Jenny warm and real beside me, I woke and was certain that I was breathing my ex-wife's scent, listening to her shallow middle-of-the-night breathing.

Sometimes an unfaithful guilt slides in with me under the covers. For all the troubles with my ex-wife, I can't help but remember many nights of delight and comfort beside her. Waking even to the *illusion* of her, the familiar presence of a woman I slept with for a decade–God help me, it felt good. When the illusion slipped away, I put my arms around the real woman beside me because I was happier to find myself with her–but also because I needed to still a minor vibration of shame at finding pleasure with another woman, even if only my ex-wife's sleep-fogged memory.

When I was a kid and shipped away to summer camp or sleeping at a relative's house, I sometimes opened my eyes to stare deep into the night at an unfamiliar corner or ceiling. When I blinked the sleep away and brought my eyes and brain back into focus, I remembered that I was at my uncle's farm for the weekend to help bring in the crops or in my sleeping bag in a rain-soaked tent with twelve other soggy camp kids.

That's kind of what it's like, waking next to a woman with one name, one face, one body, one lovely soul–yet thinking I'm with another. It's like waking in a cold, wet, smelly tent expecting a familiar bedroom.

I slept in a few strange beds growing up, and it was no big deal, just an occasional moment of confusion before drifting back to sleep. But how is it my adult self can trust one human being so completely to lie down with her and fall asleep, then eventually move on to another, then another, then another, then a dozen more across a lifetime–loving each one enough to share something as terrifying as a night of unconsciousness?

***

As a teenager, I would see married adults and marvel, "They've had sex. They know what it's like." So many of these ordinary people, some only a few years older than I was, had known the greatest mystery on earth. I sometimes studied them to see if this knowledge made them different in some way, but they seemed like regular people.

I didn't know it at the time, but at age sixteen, at least half of my classmates knew what "it" was like.

My parents never gave me a "birds-and-bees" talk, and I learned about sex from strange sources. In sixth grade, one kid told me that a boy peed on a girl to make her pregnant. That didn't seem very accurate, and, in fact, sounded really gross. I didn't want anything to do with sex if it involved peeing on someone.

A year after hearing the pee story, an older kid showed me a few dirty pictures. I felt intrigued but a bit queasy at what the couple in the pictures was doing. I wasn't exactly sure what was going on, but I knew the man wasn't peeing. Even at that young age, I knew you couldn't pee with it hard.

***

When I came home from college at age twenty-one for Dad's funeral, I sat dejectedly in our kitchen until a beautiful young woman walked in. I stared at her, stunned to see a woman this gorgeous in my modest childhood home. Her hair was short and dark and moved in a way that was energetic and seductive at the same time. Her eyes made me think of lines from bad poems, especially ones with phrases like "luminous orbs, "resplendent gems," "crystalline spheres," and "limpid pools."

To my great surprise, she ran up and hugged me as soon as she saw me, crying into my chest and telling me how sorry she felt about my dad. I managed to keep my wits, hug her in return, and thank her. We talked quietly for a moment before she hugged me again and left.

As soon as she walked out the door, I asked Mom, "Who the hell was that?" Mom laughed for the first time since Dad had died two days earlier. She told me the woman was Miranda, my sister Tam's best friend from high school. I hadn't seen Miranda in about five years. She had gone from a cute, skinny eighteen-year-old girl with braces to a young woman of twenty-three so beautiful I hadn't recognized her.

Miranda eventually got married and bought our house from Mom but sold it when she got divorced a few years later. Tam told me that Miranda hadn't remarried and was living in Bard, only a few miles from Madley. Tam showed me a recent photo, and she still looked great. I hadn't had a date in about six months at that point, so for a few minutes, I considered getting her phone number, driving down to the cabin, and inviting her to have dinner with me.

But then Tam told me that Miranda was a very conservative Republican. I felt as disillusioned as I had when I learned that Santa Claus didn't exist or that President Nixon really was a crook. I'm open to dating a pretty wide range of women, so I don't think anyone could call me overly picky. For me, however, a few things are deal-breakers in a relationship: smoking, heavy drug or alcohol use, really bad body odor, kisses that routinely draw blood, the inability to tell the difference between humor and sarcasm, and incompatible politics.

I love Miranda for comforting me with a lovely hug and for making Mom laugh on a very sad day many years ago–but I could never get seriously involved with a Republican.

***

Chapter 10
Tarpaper Goddess

I finally close the laptop well after midnight. My bones ache from the today's hike, but it's a good ache. Before I go to bed, I do about ten minutes of pilates exercises on the living room floor to slow down the soreness in my muscles that surely will develop tomorrow.

My ex-girlfriend Amy recently recruited me for the pilates class she teaches at the gym. These exercises involve using the abdominal muscles in intense ways to strengthen the body's "powerhouse," the stomach and lower back. I keep telling Amy that I'm working on my "powder-puff" and my "porterhouse," but I'm slowly getting the hang of it. I should be a natural at pilates because I've been sucking in my gut since it started getting a little chubby at age eighteen. Amy even wants to lead me through individual training sessions to make me her "poster boy" for how pilates can work for everybody–even a middle-aged, mildly pot-bellied body like mine.

Exercise and sports have always been a very important element of my life. Besides all the team sports I played in high school, I started jogging during my teen years, long before everyone owned ten pairs of Nikes. One summer, I cut up an old pair of canvas sneakers, lined them with lead, and wore them as ankle weights. I could see my calves growing and defining when I ran while wearing those homemade weights.

At my peak, I jogged past Gravelpit to Fossilville and back each evening during the summer (about seven miles when I included a muscle-burning run to the top of the cemetery hill behind the old church). Confused to see me running along Route 96, drivers often stopped to offer me a ride. If I said, "No thanks, I'm running," they replied, "I can see that. It looks tiring. That's why I'm offering you a ride."

***

I wake on New Year's Day morning at five. I want to go back to sleep, but I need to do something first. I fumble in the dark for the TV remote and quickly skim all seven channels to make sure no terrorist acts happened during the night.

This may be the place where I grew up, but it's a different world.

***

The first day of 2003 is gray and rainy, the weather forecast coming true one day late. After eating a bowl of oatmeal, I drive south on

Route 96 with no particular destination in mind. At Gravel Pit, I take a quick left onto Cove Road over a small bridge that crosses Little Wills Creek. I'm not sure why I'm drawn here–but then I remember Claire.

***

One morning, near the end of tenth grade, our school bus stopped a few miles down the road from our farm, and the most beautiful girl I'd ever seen climbed the steps into view.

She was dressed in jeans and a t-shirt, like almost everybody on the bus, but she stood out. She was tall and slender with light, honey-blonde hair cut well above her shoulders, feathered across the back. She also had bangs that set off her fine-boned features and blue eyes. All this was in sharp contrast to most of the girls in our little valley, who wore their dark hair long and flat and parted in the middle.

As the entire bus gawked in stunned silence, she smiled shyly, glided down the aisle to the nearest empty seat, and slid in next to the window. She leaned her head against the glass and gazed out at the passing scenery. Soon, curiosity overcame caution, and the other girls on the bus mustered up the courage to talk to her. Within minutes, they were leaning toward her, pulled into her orbit.

I found myself leaning too.

I watched with admiration as she fielded their seemingly endless questions, laughed when they teased her about her bangs, and charmed them with questions and compliments of her own. My friend Chris, who was sitting beside me, was impressed too. One moment we were talking about the Pirates' chances for success this season, the next we were staring, speechless.

New kids in school were a rare treat. People rarely moved to our rural valley because jobs were scarce. New arrivals were usually connected in some distant way to families already living in the area. Permanent residents like Chris and I were used to looking at each other day after day. We knew everything about one another–when someone got glasses, who had thrown up in the hallway last month, and who had peed his pants on the playground in first grade. New kids had no past. They were mysteries waiting to be solved.

By the time we got to school that morning, the buzz had filtered back to Chris and me that the new girl's name was Claire. I'd never known a real person with that name before. Only people in radio love songs and on TV were called Claire. To my inexperienced ears, her name sounded mature and exotic, mysterious and worldly. But that name was all anyone knew about her.

I admired Claire from a distance that day as she made friends with other girls. No boy could talk to a new girl, of course, and no new girl could talk to a boy for weeks–that would violate a strict rule in our unspoken awkward teenagers' code of behavior. But at one point in the middle of history class, Claire turned in her seat, saw me looking her way, and smiled. I nearly fell out of my chair but managed to smile back before looking away. For the rest of the day, I confined my admiration to corner-of-the-eye glances for fear she might see me watching her again.

Over dinner that night, Grandma asked me, "Did you see your cousin in school today?" Grandma was Dad's mother, nearly ninety, and the family matriarch. We were lucky to live in the house she had owned for more than sixty years. Her place atop the extended family meant we had a steady stream of visitors seeking her counsel and wisdom.

"Which cousin?" I asked, assuming she meant one of the dozen or so garden-variety cousins scattered through the school like weeds among the cornstalks.

"She just started school today," Grandma answered as she exchanged a look with Dad that I didn't understand. "Claire Schettler."

My mouth dropped to the floor. The most beautiful girl in the world was my cousin–third cousin to be exact–closer to being a sister than a stranger.

As I lay in bed that night, I realized that our family tie was a mixed blessing. Even for us country folks, the incest taboo included cousins. So I would never marry Claire or be her boyfriend–but so what? The chances of that happy happening weren't good even if we weren't related. In a way, knowing she was off-limits romantically let me think of her as a complete person, not only an object of my teenage desires. Most important, because we were family, I had a reason to march right up to her in school and say hello.

On the bus the following morning, I told Chris that I planned to talk to Claire at some point during the school day. He was skeptical, knowing my shyness with girls. So I bet him five dollars (money I didn't have) that I would talk with her before the bus took us home that afternoon. He took the bet instantly. Of course, I didn't tell him anything about discovering that Claire was my cousin.

When she saw me on the bus that morning, she smiled and waved before sitting with some new girlfriends near the front. Someone at her home must have asked her if she'd met any cousins in school. Chris stared at me and swore quietly. I calmly looked out the window as if beautiful new classmates waved at me every day.

Inside, I was blooming.

As lunch was winding to a close, I said to Chris, "Well, here goes." I walked from my boys-only table across the cafeteria to the girls-only table where Claire was finishing her lunch. The other girls glared at me, but Claire turned and beamed.

"Hi John!" she said with the warmest smile I'd ever seen. She patted the empty seat beside her, and I sat down. "My daddy told me we're cousins. I'm so happy to have family here." When the girls at the table realized I wasn't putting the "moves" on the new girl, they stopped throwing me the stink eye.

Chris and my other friends stared at me from their table, amazed that I had the guts to talk to the beautiful new girl. As I pointed out my sisters and other cousins to her, Claire and I talked like we were old friends. I wasn't used to a girl who enjoyed my company and didn't care what other kids would think. The way she leaned towards me, touched my arm, and laughed at my comments made the rest of the cafeteria fade away.

We walked back to class together with lots of eyes staring at us. We made quite a ripple through the hallways, even after people learned that we were related. I enjoyed knowing that my classmates saw me as someone other than the goofy farm kid who got good grades.

Chris approached me later and held out a five-dollar bill. He hadn't heard yet that Claire and I were cousins. I didn't often see that much money, but I told him that I couldn't take it. When I told him why, he said, "Your cousin? You lucky dog." He was right. I was lucky to have such an easy way to get to know Claire.

Claire and I became good friends during the final month of the school year. She was a deep thinker, so we talked about life and death, war and heartache, family and God. She was the first person I knew who loved figure skating and had even competed at her previous school.

"They make it look so easy on television," she told me the last day of school as we waited outside for our bus. "But it's as hard as any other sport. I trained for three hours every day, but there's no rink around here. I really miss it."

"That's as much as we practice basketball," I said, impressed that she would work as hard at her passion as I did at mine.

"I wish we'd moved here earlier so I could've seen you play," she said. "I bet you're good."

I laughed. "Well, I played junior varsity most of the year. I hardly ever got into the varsity games because I don't score much."

"But basketball is more than just scoring," she said. "I heard you defend and rebound really well."

I was amazed at her interest in my basketball career. My own sisters hardly noticed that I played, never mind that I could rebound.

"What's your favorite part of skating?" I asked her.

She looked off into the distance at the hills rising above our school building. "I feel so free when I'm on the ice. It's like I've got nothing holding me back, no one pulling me down, no past."

Her eyes grew watery and unfocused for a moment, and she gazed over my shoulder as if looking into a past that she couldn't share–but then she roused herself and laughed.

"Let's make a pact," she said. "I'll teach you to skate if you promise to wave to me from the court before every basketball game."

"I promise," I said, and held my hand out for her to shake. Instead she gave me a hug that drew a few stares from the kids around us.

A week into summer vacation, Claire and her parents came to our farm to visit Grandma. Claire and I sat on the porch swing for a while, then walked out to the garden where I picked sweet corn for her. She told me that she'd really like me to visit her house. Her parents were going away that weekend, and she wanted my company. She had pictures of herself ice skating to show me.

That Saturday morning, I set out on my bike for Claire's house. She lived beyond Cove Road, miles from the pavement, far up on the hillside along a deeply rutted dirt path that I couldn't imagine traversing in a car. Several times, I got off my bike and pushed it, afraid that I would fall off, flatten a tire, or break a wheel. When I finally reached her house, I thought I had made a mistake.

I'd heard the term "tarpaper shack" before, and I'd seen run-down houses plenty of times throughout our valley and up in the hills. But the building before me was literally made of tarpaper. The windows were empty holes covered with blankets. When I finally realized this was the right house, I knocked on the door. It rattled so much that I worried I might knock it off its hinges. When Claire opened the door, she had to lift and drag it inside to keep it from scraping against the dirt floor.

My parents were far from rich. In fact, I learned in college that we lived below the official poverty level for much of my childhood. But we had real floors, real windows, electricity, furniture, a television, and indoor plumbing.

Claire's family didn't.

She invited me in to sit down on a couch made of wooden crates padded with rugs. The house was one large room. Sheets had been hung to create separate living spaces. Claire must have seen the look in my eyes although I did everything I could to hide it. Before I knew what was happening, she rushed into my arms, crying and begging me not to tell any of her new friends about the way she lived.

Through her sobs, Claire told me how her father lost his job at a steel mill in Pittsburgh and her mother developed cancer. Her mother's health had eventually returned, but the family was deeply in debt from the medical bills. The bank had foreclosed on their home, their possessions were taken and sold, and they fled to the hills to escape creditors.

For a family like theirs, being in debt was as bad as being a criminal. Rather than face the humiliation of bankruptcy or accept charity, they had gone "underground" in these isolated hills. The owner of the shack home was another distant cousin who was letting them live rent-free and keeping their presence hidden from outsiders. Claire had begged her parents to let her finish the year at our school. She originally registered by promising to have her records sent from her old school. Those records would never arrive. Claire's parents were in another state that weekend, scouting out better job prospects and trying to convince another family of cousins to take them into their home.

We visited for a long time that day, talking about her situation for a while, and then purposely avoiding the subject. We talked about friends at school, the beauty of the woods, our hopes for the future, and which older boys had tried to get Claire to go to the prom with them. None had succeeded.

I asked if her parents would consider moving in with our family, but I knew the answer before I posed the question. "Your parents have enough to worry about," she said. "We could never impose like that." She quickly changed the subject by showing me her album of figure skating photos. I could have spent hours with these photos. In one of them, Claire was a goddess on the ice with one long leg lifted behind her, her arms extended like wings, her gaze fixed somewhere in the distance–more graceful and intense than I could have imagined. After a moment, she gently pulled the album from my hands.

I left as night was falling. Claire promised to write if her family moved away. This time I cried too, and we held each other for a long time. I'd only known her for a month, but I felt closer to her than I'd ever been to anyone but my parents. I walked my bike down the dirt road in near darkness, sad but thankful I'd been so close to such a wonderful person.

That was the last I heard from her. The following weekend I biked back to her house and found it deserted. Grandma had no idea where they went after they left our valley, and if my near-omniscient grandmother didn't know, no one would. The following school year, a few people asked me about Claire, but her memory faded as everyone moved on with their lives.

I never forgot Claire, even after twenty-five years. Surely her house has collapsed by now, the walls and roof rotted into the dirt floor. But each spring I send a wish for happiness to my beautiful cousin–the goddess who once lived in a tarpaper shack.

***

After a few miles, just plain Cove Road turns into Milligan's Cove Road, another nod to early Irish settlers. I realize that I've been bending around to the north and might be circling the quarry area of Wills Mountain. This is a particularly exciting revelation because I've never been on this road before. It's part of that mystery area I saw from the top of the ridge yesterday–so close to where I grew up but a world away.

This road must lead to the access road that goes up to the cell tower above the quarry. I look up to my left to try to find the tower, but the peak is shrouded in fog. Then I glance back at the road just as six deer bound across no more than fifteen feet in front of my car.

My heart immediately hammers against my chest as I stomp on the brake pedal. I didn't really come close to hitting them–still I'm rattled. No other cars are out here early on this holiday morning, so I sit in the middle of the road and watch the deer run through a field and towards the woods.

Near the trees, they stop in unison and turn back toward me. We stare at each other for some time before I remember my camera. I grab it quickly and squeeze off a picture of the tree line after the deer have disappeared into the woods.

***

Janet has assembled a binder with a couple of local newspaper articles about the cabin and twenty pages that look like they were done on an antique typewriter. It's a brief history of the farm and cabin, along with a more detailed history of the local area. My Great Uncle

Clarence Stuby (Uncle Caddy, as he was known, Grandma's brother) wrote these pages in 1934, and Grandma updated them in 1964, partly through dictation from her by-then blind brother and partly from her own rich memories and experiences.

Uncle Caddy was highly regarded as a schoolteacher and area historian. I don't remember meeting him, but my sister Tam recalls going to visit him on the farm where he and his wife Kathryn (Aunt Kate) lived when she was six years old–the same year as the 1964 updates to the historical papers. He was completely blind at the time, and Tam says he liked to feel her face to know what she looked like. Even though he did it out of curiosity and love, Tam remembers it as one of the creepiest experiences of her childhood.

***

Mom and Dad owned a house in Hagerstown, Maryland, where they had lived for years before moving to the farm and renting out the Hagerstown house. We visited the renters a few times, something I enjoyed because they had kids about my age, and I always liked having people to play with besides my sisters. As far as I could tell from my limited experience, the house seemed to be in a nice neighborhood in a nice town.

Around age twelve, I got it into my head that we might leave the farm and move to the house in Hagerstown. I probably misunderstood something I overheard my parents saying at the kitchen table one night. But I loved the idea of moving there–meeting new friends, living in an actual town where I could walk to school, and leaving behind most of the annoying people I had known to that point in my brief life.

Of course, we didn't move to Hagerstown, but we almost moved one other time. After Uncle Caddy died in the mid-1960s, and Aunt Kate followed him a few years later, Dad was interested in buying their very nice farm a few miles away on Tar Water Road. Possibly he had grown tired of living on the farm where he grew up, the farm that Grandma still owned.

But we didn't move to Tar Water Road either. Eventually, Mom and Dad bought our farm from Grandma, and Uncle Caddy and Aunt Kate's farm was purchased by a family who lived out of state and had big plans for their new property. That farm soon became the home of New Life Bible Camp, a place that gives me as many creepy memories as Tam has from Uncle Caddy touching her face.

***

Grandma knew so much about history because she had lived through more of it than most people. In her eighties and nineties, Grandma was not only one of the oldest people in the area, but one of the smartest. Anyone interested in local history came to Grandma first. Her revision and updating of her brother's historical documents carries a rich and charming voice to go with a strong sense of detail. She seems to know the name of all the people who ever lived in the area dating back to the late 1700s, and she writes almost as if she knew them personally.

Along with her detailed history of the area's residents and changes in land ownership, Grandma included charming and informative sections on pioneer life, early industry and implements, cemeteries and burial grounds, churches, and early mail paths. These sections aren't as fastidiously dated as the earlier parts, so I can't tell how much of this work is Grandma's and how much is her brother Caddy's. But I definitely get a sense of the quality of her writing in the post-1934 updates, and much of the later sections bear Grandma's distinctive voice and style.

These documents are in sharp contrast to the only other bits of her writing I've read. In my teens, I noticed that Grandma kept a diary. I was very curious about the kinds of things she might write in a diary. If age made a person wise, I figured Grandma's diary must be packed to the bindings with wisdom.

One day I simply asked if I could read hers. She seemed to appreciate both my boldness and my interest, so she handed me her current diary. I took it to my bedroom, prepared for enlightenment. To my great surprise, it contained countless entries that read something like this: "August 20, 1976. No rain today but no sunshine either. Bill says he'll make get one more cutting of hay. I'll take flowers to the cemetery this evening."

Where was the wisdom? Where was the meaning of life that only someone approaching a century on earth could comprehend? The next day when Grandma was outside in the garden, I slipped her diary back on the old sewing machine she used as a desk. Maybe the everyday things that Grandma wrote about–the rain, the crops, or the friends long-since dead and buried in the cemetery behind the church–hold the enlightenment.

***

"What did you learn in school today?" Grandma would ask every afternoon when my sisters and I came bounding into the house.

We'd have to think about it for a few seconds, then say in unison, "Nothing."

"Nothing?" Grandma would repeat in disbelief. "Well, then why are you going to school?"

Good question, Grandma.

***

Grandma was so concerned about not playing favorites that her will gave each of her six children a one-sixth share of her estate. Her surviving offspring each got their one-sixth, and the living children of her deceased offspring equally divided that one-sixth share. Because my father died before my grandmother, his one-sixth share was divided between my siblings and me.

When I was growing up, I assumed that Grandma was poor. She used to keep some change in a little cough-drop box to pay for milk or eggs, and I thought those coins were all the money she had in the world. So I didn't really think about her estate very much–until I got my share. It turned out that my one-sixth share of one-sixth of her estate was more money than I had ever seen. I used it for a down payment on a pick-up truck that I drove 150,000 miles during the next seven years.

I once told a friend that I felt guilty about Grandma's death being the only reason I had a nice new truck.

"Did you love your grandmother?" my friend asked.

I said that I did.

"Then your grandmother must be happy that you used her money to get that truck," my friend said. "Just think of her once in a while when you drive it."

And I did think of Grandma–every day for seven years of reliable transportation and a dozen jobs that I couldn't have gotten to and from without that truck. Her will may have been an odd piece of work, but the truck was a solid and long-lasting as Grandma herself.

***

After reading Grandma's historical documents for a while, I decide that I'd like to photocopy these pages and take them home with me. The it occurs to me that this is New Year's Day in the middle of rural southwest central Pennsylvania. Where can I find a copier on a holiday around here? The libraries and schools in Hyndman and Bedford are closed, so my best bet is probably finding a convenience store with a copier. Hyndman is a long shot but close and on the way to Cumberland, so I decide to head south.

Driving around here is strange. I did lots of riding with my parents, but I didn't drive as a teenager. Now, as an adult, the experience feels new. I've never seen these places from the perspective of the driver's seat, and the different angle makes everything appear just a bit off.

Distances between places seem different as well. I can't believe I thought the six-mile drive from the farm to Hyndman was a long one. I guess it seemed so long because I usually rode to town in the cramped backseat of our car bickering with my sisters or–even worse–in the hellish school bus, which could easily turn a twenty-minute ride into an hour-long horror show.

The most driving I did as a teenager involved farm equipment. When my classmates got their licenses and first cars, I drove a tractor along Route 96 to and from a family friend's farm ten miles south of us. I loved it. I sat proud and high on the tractor and waved to my classmates when they zoomed by. I didn't have a license or a car, but I felt mature and responsible chugging along the shoulder at twenty miles per hour.

I did a great deal of farm work for Dell, that family friend ten miles away on the other side of Hyndman. He and Dad knew each other from the local VFW (Veterans of Foreign Wars) the only "bar" in Hyndman, an otherwise dry town. Dad had a nice flat field to farm, and Dell had the equipment, so the two friends made a deal to share some farm work. Their agreement included Dad's hardworking teenage son– although no one bothered to consult me until after they struck the deal.

The last two summers that I lived at home, I rode my bike six miles to my custodian job at the high school. I spent from 6:30 a.m. to 3:30 p.m. there, painting, waxing floors, mowing the school lawns, and scraping gum from the underside of desks. Then I biked another four miles to Dell's farm and helped him for a few hours with making hay or cutting firewood or whatever else he needed done. When I finished at Dell's, I biked ten miles home, got there at dusk, ate something, did a few chores around our farm, then collapsed into my little bed at the back of the trailer so that I could get up at 5:30 the next morning and do it all again.

Although I had almost no free time during those summers, I didn't really mind helping Dell. I mostly thought of it as my way of paying Dad back for all the rides to basketball and baseball practice over the years. Whenever Dell mentioned that he would eventually pay me for all my work, I just shook my head.

At the end of the second summer, Dad and Dell took me to the VFW and bought me a beer. I appreciated that they saw me as a grown man–although I would have much preferred a cola. I managed a few sips of my beer and tried to keep from making faces at how bad it tasted. When we were getting ready to leave, Dell took out his wallet and handed me a bill.

"You've been a big help over the years, Johnny," he said as he shook my hand. "This'll come in handy at that fancy college you're going to." I refused the money the traditional three times, then reluctantly accepted it and thanked him, shoving the bill into my pocket without even a glance.

Later, when I got home, I pulled out the money–a ten dollar bill, my payment for two summers of work. Dell was right. That ten dollars came in handy at college. Back then, ten dollars bought a textbook.

***

The field behind the cabin is filled with those truck-sized haybales that can be found on every farm these days. Janet and Fred's llamas munch on one near the barn. In my youth, we made the old-style haybales that were about four feet by two feet by eighteen inches, held together with two strands of baling twine.

From an early age, I longed to join the "big boys" making hay in the fields. Because I was far too young to be any real help in bringing in the hay, I improvised by targeting one specific hay bale, wheeling my little red wagon over to it, and wrestling it onto the wagon. It took all my little-boy muscles to get it up even two feet to make it over the wagon's lip. Then I yanked on the handle and inched the wagon through the field to the barn. All of the grown men chuckled at my efforts, but they also praised me to no end when I finally managed to get the bale into the barn and started off after another one.

Over the years, my role in making hay advanced. When I got to be strong enough to hoist a bale onto a real hay wagon, I joined the men tossing bales. From there, I soon graduated to a position of honor–the stacker who rode on the wagon itself.

This role took strength, quick feet, and even quicker thinking. I had to grab the bales as they were tossed onto the wagon from both sides, then stack them in an order that allowed me to get as many bales on the wagon as possible without the risk of them toppling over on the rough trip through the field to the barn. After I had zigzagged from one side of the wagon to the other grabbing bales and stacking them, the wagon eventually filled, and I literally stacked myself into a corner and up to the top of the pile. Then I rode atop the load to the barn and prayed I had stacked well enough that I wouldn't get maimed or killed if the haybales avalanched off the wagon. I'm proud to say that my loads never once crumbled.

Our haymaking got progressively less organized during my teen years. A man named Jerry helped take in the hay before Dad hooked up with his buddy Dell. Jerry was getting up in years and becoming less and less capable of doing the hard work. He often promised to provide "helpers," men he would pay a few dollars for tossing the bales onto the wagon, but then they wouldn't show because Jerry forgot to call them.

Things got to the point where I almost single-handedly brought in the hay. Dad had taught me how to hook up the mowing blade to the tractor and cut the field, then hitch the rake to another tractor and scrape the hay into rows for the baler, which I also learned to operate. So I might cut the hay all day Monday, rake it all day Tuesday, then bale it all day Wednesday–all the while praying that Jerry would have his helpers there Wednesday afternoon to toss the bales.

Of course, they wouldn't show, and Jerry himself came less often each year. So after I cut, raked, and baled, Dad hauled a wagon with his pick-up while I threw on every bale myself, jumping up every ten bales or so to stack. Eventually, realizing Dad and I would have no help, I devised a system that involved hitching the wagon to the back of the baler. Dad did the baling, and I stood on the wagon and grabbed the newly tied bales as they came out of the baler and stacked them until I ran out of room on the wagon.

Dad never stopped marveling at my idea for hitching the wagon to the baler. For him, this was the absolute definition of genius, and his own son had thought of it. When I came home from college with good grades, Dad often said, "Well, that's exactly what I expect from the boy who was smart enough to hook the wagon to the baler."

But I wasn't smart enough to suspect then what I understand now–that Jerry merely *promised* to hire helpers. Why would he pay them when the little boy who hauled one bale at a time in a toy wagon would do the work for free?

***

When I was eighteen and ready to go off to college, I wanted to buy an old Dodge Dart that I saw for sale along the road a few miles from our home. Mom didn't want me to get it.

"You have no idea what it costs to put a car on the road," she said.

"Buying it, insuring it, repairing it, and keeping gas in it," I said with youthful smugness, knowing the theoretical costs of a car but having absolutely no concrete, practical knowledge of what it took to own one.

Needless to say, I didn't get the car and wouldn't own one for another ten years. I didn't even have my driver's license at the time. Mom didn't want me to get it while I lived at home. I finally got my license when I finished college and came home for the summer. Mom let me practice in her car (a real breakthrough for her) but would not ride with me when I practiced or took the test. My Aunt Mary Lynn took me during one of her visits from Texas.

Actually, I flunked the verbal test for the learner's permit the first time I took it. The test was based on a booklet of Pennsylvania traffic laws. I was twenty-two, a college graduate with honors, and had tested well since first grade, so I didn't study the booklet and barely opened it, thinking that it couldn't be that hard for a smart guy like me.

When the officer asked me to explain the term "yield," I froze. I pictured a yield sign in my head, and I tried to remember what Mom or Dad did when they approached one, but my brain was mush. I got none of the ten questions correct, and the officer (who had undoubtedly seen hundreds of thick-headed sixteen-year-olds pass) rolled his eyes and sent me home to study. I was crushed, never having failed a test in my life.

If Mom was disappointed, she had the good grace not to criticize. "You'll take it again," she said. "There's nothing wrong with passing on the second try." I studied like my life depended on it that night, took the test again the next day, and got ten correct out of ten. Two weeks later, after practicing under the gentle guidance of Aunt Mary Lynn, I passed the driving test. To my astonishment, the examiner remembered seeing me play high school basketball a few years before. "You really could rebound," he said as I gripped the steering wheel in the proper ten-two position.

He didn't even make me parallel park.

***

Chapter 11
Ceremony

Driving past Hyndman High School, I see a message board announcing upcoming basketball games against rival schools from the towns of Rockwood, Shanksville, and Turkeyfoot. Southwest central Pennsylvania certainly sports some odd town names.

I lived in the village of Madley, got mail through the post office in Buffalo Mills, and went to school in Hyndman. Madley is also a town in the Herefordshire area of England, as well as a somewhat uncommon British surname. Many British settlers traveled this area in pioneer days, which could explain the name. But when I was about seven, I invented a story about two people arguing along the roadside when someone walked by, saw them, and said, "You people here argue so much, we'll have to call this the Village of 'Madley.'" I gave myself a good laugh with that story.

In Hyndman itself, there are sections of town with goofy names like Hogback and Frogeye, but even more inexplicable is Hollywood, the part of town where the mayor lives.

Here are twenty-three Pennsylvania communities in and around Bedford County, one from every letter of the alphabet except X. (I've driven through Xenia, but it's in Ohio.) These are all real and within a hour's drive from Madley. Listening to them spoken aloud is almost like a lullaby from my childhood: Acme, Burning Bush, Cypher, Dunkard, Eichelbergertown, Fallentimber, Grindstone, Hunker, Isabella, Jerkwater, King, Lovely, Mench, Normalville, Ohiopyle, Paisley, Queen, Riddlesburg, Scalp Level, Tire Hill, Urey, Vinco, White House, Yount, and Zullinger.

Come to think of it, why does a town as small as Hyndman need a mayor?

***

Hyndman is pronounced "Hymen" by its natives, dropping the "d" consonant sound and shifting the vowel in the concluding syllable from a short "a" to a short "e" so that the name sounds like . . . well, we know what it sounds like. Today, it's a quiet town of about one thousand citizens on Route 96 six miles south of our farm and ten miles north of the Maryland border. But in its heyday in the mid-1800s, Hyndman was one of the fastest-growing communities in Pennsylvania with a variety of industries, five hotels, and even an opera house for local entertainment. News of Hyndman's rich history would have shocked my sleepy-eyed classmates and me back in high school, but no one ever even told us.

The first settlers were Irish immigrants who gave the name Londonderry to the general area from Madley to the Maryland state line. The town of Hyndman itself was originally known as Bridgeport, officially assigned that name in 1800. Later, the part of town north of Wills Creek was dubbed New Bridgeport. While a couple of "bridges" span the creek in town, a "port" didn't exist. The port part of the name came from a boat-building business in the early years.

What the town did have, however, was a railroad line. My main experience with the railroad was sitting on a southbound school bus, waiting for what seemed like hours for the train to pass and let us continue on to school. I remember counting cars on the passing trains, sometimes more than one hundred. I wasn't a huge fan of school, where another dull day awaited, but being any place beat the school bus where danger lurked–someone tossing their used chewing gum in my hair, spraying me with a squirt gun laced with bleach, or coming up with yet another interesting nickname to torment me. School bus kids were demons most of the time, and being stopped for a train whipped them into a frenzy.

Of course, most of the abuse came my way as one of the youngest kids on the bus. When I got older and big enough to take care of myself, most of the other kids didn't bother me. Or I simply rode my bike six miles to school as soon as the weather topped forty degrees.

Apparently, the railroad had a much greater purpose in the history of the town than simply giving me hellish moments on the school bus. The trains first made their way to Bridgeport on April 10, 1871, an event that brought the residents cheering into the streets–marking a new phase of progress for the town.

The railroad superintendent was a thirty-three-year-old man named Edward Kennedy Hyndman (a great name but a century too early). Town folks in Bridgeport and New Bridgeport were so taken with Hyndman that they united their two communities and named the combination after this impressive young man.

Hyndman (the man, not the town) is an amazing story. His birthplace was Mauch Chuck (another in a long list of strangely named Pennsylvania towns). He became a civil engineer in his teens, a railroad supervisor at age twenty-five, and a devoted husband and father of two sons soon after. In 1880, he resigned from the railroad and became active in the coal industry at a time when Pennsylvania was the world center of coal production. By his mid-thirties, he had amassed an impressive fortune, then returned to his first love, the rails, becoming the president of the Pittsburgh Junction Railroad.

After only a brief time back in the railroad business, Hyndman died of unspecified causes in 1884. He was only forty-six years old. His death was sudden, but the town that bears his name has been gamely hanging on through fires and floods ever since, refusing to pass away.

Possibly the greatest shortcoming of my high school education was learning nothing about Edward Kennedy Hyndman in any of my classes. Such an interesting character would have made a lively addition to our history curriculum. After all, he brought the railroad in its full glory and unified both sides of town under one name. Instead, our history classes were filled with war stories, presidents, and dates to be memorized. (I've forgotten most of those dates–although I do remember what year the War of 1812 started.)

Hyndman, the man, was omitted from education at Hyndman, the high school. The town's *name*, however, did have a lasting impact, forever condemning me to explain that it *only sounds like* a sensitive part of the female anatomy.

***

A mile or so north of Hyndman, there's a hairpin "S" curve on Route 96. I notice they've put up a warning sign and flashing light, but the curve wasn't well marked in my youth. Stories often circulated in school about some local kids who challenged out-of-towners to drag races, only to brake as they approached the curve and watch the clueless interlopers go right through the guardrail and land more-or-less harmlessly in the field beyond.

Mom, of course, took this curve at about three miles per hour–all the while fearing that her car might flip over and burst into flames anyway. I think she always dreaded a newspaper headline that would read, "Mother's Recklessness Causes Own and Children's Death." I could have jogged backward faster than Mom took this curve.

I did manage one driving adventure here. My classmate Marlene and I had been selling doughnut holes one rainy Saturday afternoon as a class project to raise money for our senior trip to New York City. She lived a couple of miles up the road, and we had been friends almost since infancy. By our senior year, she was class president while I was treasurer, which meant we got stuck with unloading the doughnut holes no one else wanted to sell.

We were returning home from a wet and mostly unsuccessful day of sales when we encountered the "S" curve on our way north. By then, the rain had stopped, but the road was still wet. Marlene seemed to be driving a reasonable speed as we entered the curve, but the car suddenly fishtailed one way, then back the other way, as Marlene fought to correct the skid.

We must have spun back and forth seven or eight times. I remember the sounds more than anything else–the screeching tires, of course, Marlene's hands pounding on the steering wheel again and again, her grunting from the effort. We were lucky that no one was driving southbound because her car came to rest in the wrong lane pointed the wrong way. Marlene quickly got us back to the correct lane, then pulled over to the side of the road.

We sat still for a few seconds, breathing hard. I looked down to see that I had grabbed the dashboard with both hands. When I unclenched and pulled my hands back, the dashboard had finger dents an inch deep. They quickly disappeared like a boot print filling with warm mud.

"Are you okay?" Marlene asked me, staring straight ahead.

"Yeah," I said. "Are you?"

"I'm okay," she replied.

Then she looked me full in the face and said, "Please don't tell anyone about this."

"I won't," I said.

She gripped my arm almost as hard as I had the dashboard. "Promise?" she asked.

"Promise," I answered.

The rest of the drive home was uneventful, and I kept my promise . . . until this moment. Marlene was a wonderful friend, and I hope she won't be mad at me for blabbing now.

***

We did make it to New York City for our senior class trip–quite a journey for rural kids from southern Pennsylvania. Many of my classmates stayed home, but I couldn't pass up a weekend of what I thought would be quasi-adulthood away from home. I had only seen New York on TV, and a trip there certainly beat shoveling cow manure or feeding the chickens.

Friday's bus ride to the big city took about seven hours, the longest single drive I'd ever taken in my life. My only other visits to an actual city had been three Boy Scout trips–twice to see Pittsburgh Pirates baseball games and once to Washington, DC, where I caught a glimpse of Nixon's motorcade but didn't actually get to see the president himself.

The bus ride to New York itself was worth the trip by itself. The first half, I played cards and monopoly with friends. When we got tired of games, we napped. I sat with Glenda Walters, a childhood crush who I still carried a torch for even if I would never admit it to her. When she leaned over and rested her head against my shoulder, I basked in the fantasy that we were newlyweds on our way to our honeymoon. My parents met on a bus, and that context made the romantic feeling of the moment intense–at least for me.

We stayed at the Picadilly Hotel in New York. Like a country bumpkin, I would have been happy spending our entire stay going up and down the hotel's twenty-five floors in the windowed elevator with a view of the city. Instead, I checked into the room that I shared with my classmates Derrick and Jamie.

After ten minutes, we decided to visit the room next door where three of our other classmates were staying. When I walked into their bathroom, I saw a big surprise in the tub. They had smuggled a huge stockpile of alcohol into their room. They each only had a small suitcase, so I have no clue how they carried all the booze with them. The tub was literally piled full of beer cans, wine bottles, and fifths of whiskey. At barely three in the afternoon, they were already drinking and apparently had been for much of the bus ride.

We had chaperones on the trip, of course, two teachers selected by the students ourselves–and we had chosen wisely. The history teacher/wrestling coach and the art teacher/drama advisor had been rumored to be a couple throughout the year, but they kept their relationship a secret from us and, it would seem, the school administration. They spent most of the trip locked in either his or her room together, so they never even saw the tub full of smuggled booze.

The extent of my drinking up to that point had been a few sips of wine at dinner with my family or as part of communion at church. I've never developed a taste for alcohol, probably due to my Uncle Jeddy's homemade West Virginia dandelion wine. That stuff was so rancid that it turned me off of alcohol forever, so I didn't sample the contents of the bathtub.

The highlight of my second day in New York was seeing a prostitute, being approached by a drug dealer, and recognizing a celebrity. A more worldly classmate pointed out the prostitute. To me, she looked like a friendly woman with too much make-up and a too-short skirt. The drug dealer was a kid about my own age who walked up to Derrick, Jamie, and me and launched into an immediate sales pitch.

"Hey, dudes, wadda ya need?" he chanted. "I got bennies, dexies, uppers, downers, blow, smack–grass if you're a virgin."

I blushed when he said "virgin" because he clearly meant me. The only appropriate response I could think of was "No, thank you."

Derrick was more blunt. He simply said, "No."

Jamie, on the other had, was more of a free spirit. "How much?" he asked, reaching for his wallet, but Derrick and I each took an arm and dragged him away, despite his mild protests and those of the young dealer we left behind.

The celebrity was a Columbia University student named Richard Thomas–much better known as "John Boy" on the TV show *The Waltons*. He walked along the street with his head slightly lowered just like a regular guy. I couldn't recognize a prostitute, but I knew "John Boy" when I saw him, and not just because of that beauty mark on his cheek. I really liked the show about a young would-be writer growing up rural and poor with too many siblings. I related to his character–but that didn't mean I liked being called "John Boy" as often as I was.

As soon as I recognized him, I said to Derrick and Jamie, "Hey, there's Richard Thomas."

"Who?" they asked.

"You know," I said, "John Boy."

Other people on the street recognized him as well. A few people called out, "John Boy! John Boy!" Thomas lowered his head even more and quickened his pace. A pack of ten people jostled behind him. So he started running. Not only did the pack run with him, but they overtook him, chanting, "John Boy! John Boy!" over and over.

Thomas managed to break out of the crowd and leap into a waiting taxi. The pack actually pounded their fists on the cab roof before it sped off down the street. I stood transfixed as the spectacle unfolded. Just as he made it to the cab, Thomas looked up, and we made eye-contact. I saw fear and anger in his eyes–a sad sight. If being called "John Boy" occasionally annoyed me, how must he feel to be called that by shouting strangers for the rest of his life?

In the evening, about a dozen people went to see the new movie *Alien*. Some friends called it the scariest movie ever made. I love a good scare, but I chose real-life drama when Glenda invited me to stay in her room while everyone else went to the movie.

Counting the previews and the walk time to and from the theater, Glenda and I had more than three hours alone together. We played cards and talked about our college plans and life goals. I've forgotten the specifics of what we said, but I still clearly remember the emotion of that evening. Being alone with her in a hotel room hundreds of miles from our parents was intoxicating. We even stretched out on the bed together and held hands. I couldn't have been happier–although we carefully avoided mentioning her college boyfriend.

If we'd had another hour together, we might have even touched our shy lips together for a first kiss. But her roommates destroyed the mood when they barged in after seeing *Alien*, their eyes wide from the movie-induced terror and the contact high they got when everyone else in the theater started smoking pot during the opening credits. Distracted by retelling the movie, they didn't even notice that Glenda kept hold of my hand even with other people present.

When I awoke Sunday morning, I noticed that Derrick and Jamie were not in their beds. Then I heard strange noises in the bathroom. When I entered, I saw them engaged in an oddly intimate act. Derrick, on his knees with his head over the toilet, vomited an orange liquid that I recognized as the contents of a tequila bottle from our neighbors' bathtub. He was straining so hard to vomit that he reminded me of last night's description of the alien in the movie. Jamie was bent over beside him, holding Derrick's forehead with one hand and lightly stroking his back with the other.

"It's okay buddy," Jamie said softly. "You just let it out. You'll be okay."

Before this trip, I had never seen the two of them even talking with one another. They were from different sides of the track, literally. Derrick's father worked a white-collar job of some kind in Cumberland, and Jamie's dad ran a gas station not far from the high school. Derrick was an athlete while Jamie was the best art student in the class.

I asked if they needed anything, but they waved me off. Then, to my amazement, they traded places. Jamie puked up his tequila as Derrick comforted him. They went on trading places for half an hour, and I made sure no one else came into our room. The other guys on our trip probably would have labeled them "a couple of queers" for comforting each other. I understood the closeness of the moment they shared, even if I didn't understand the drinking that led up to it. I felt thankful, however, that my stomach was empty. If I had just returned from breakfast, I might have thrown up too after hearing those horrible sounds echoing around that toilet bowl.

Everybody made it out to the bus for the ride home–although more than a few of my classmates looked as wrung-out as Jamie and Derrick. Sunday in New York was spent seeing as many tourist sights as we could before the bus left for home late in the evening. We rode the Staten Island Ferry and climbed to the head of the Statue of Liberty. We took a bus tour to see Radio City Music Hall, the Empire State Building, and the United Nations. Then we took an elevator to the top of one of the tallest buildings in the world, rising more than three hundred feet higher above the street than the quarry on Wills Mountain rose above our farm down in the valley.

I remember thinking how small the world below looked from the observation windows. If the entire cast of *Alien* had walked by (monster included), I couldn't have recognized them. Being that high was like being on a star ship or another planet. When I stood still, I sensed the building swaying a few inches in the wind and felt a tiny bit afraid that the World Trade Center would fall down with me inside it.

I finally saw *Alien* at college. Some friends and I rented one of those new-fangled VCR thingies and played it in our dorm lobby at midnight. Just as the creature burst from John Hurt's chest, a woman I barely knew dug her fingernails so deep into my arm that I screamed as loud as anyone on screen.

***

Londonderry Elementary School, which I attended from grades four through six, is about a mile from downtown Hyndman at the bottom of a pretty hill known as Hogback. During recess in elementary school, all the boys played baseball on the athletic fields. My baseball skills were mediocre at best. I loved the game but didn't have time to go to town and play. I always had way too much farm work, and we didn't have enough neighbors to get a game going.

I practiced by hitting the ball by myself. I went behind the house and faced west, toward our neighbor's house. The yard was pretty narrow (barely twenty feet wide, but two hundred feet long) with our garden on one side and the road and creek on the other. I tossed the ball up fungo style and swung away. My target was the pear tree in straight-away center field. If the ball rolled to the tree, I gave myself a double. Hitting the tree on the fly was a triple, clearing it a home run.

After I took my swing, I dropped the bat and ran after the ball. Then I'd run back and take another swing. Hit . . . run. Hit . . . run. Hit . . . run. I could do it for hours, like a hamster on its wheel or our dog running circles on its chain in the front yard. My only problem was hitting a "foul" ball a few feet to the left into our garden or to the right into the weeds–or worse, the creek. I lost dozens of balls (and got dozens of cases of poison ivy) in those weeds over the years. Twice I even watched balls float off down the creek.

Once, in a fit of power I didn't know I possessed, I hit the neighbor's house with a towering home run. It slammed into their siding a few inches to the right of a window, leaving a slightly dented scuff that no one ever noticed. I'm just thankful they weren't home at the time.

Despite my extensive solitary batting practice, I was one of the last ones picked to play in our elementary school recess baseball games. When finally chosen, I got stuck in deep right field and at the bottom of the batting order. I pretended this assessment of my skill didn't bother me, and I longed to surprise everyone with a home run. We called it a "piner" because any ball that went on the fly into the pine trees at the base of Hogback was officially a home run.

The last afternoon of school in sixth grade was spent outside because no one could concentrate in the classroom. A big male teacher pitched for both teams because he could get the ball over the plate consistently. When I finally came to bat, I took a good swing at the first pitch and cracked the ball deep into the pine trees, farther than any previous piner anyone had witnessed. I heard the teacher who threw the pitch mutter "holy shit" as I sprinted toward first base.

No one could believe it. Even as I rounded the bases, some of the kids on the other team tried to hold me back or knock me down. They didn't want me trespassing on their star athlete territory. My role had always been limited to classroom star. I had to barrel through them on my way to home plate.

The term "piner" is now pretty ironic. Our lovely little elementary school that was built in 1931 and its athletic fields have been sold to a home-improvement company. The whole place is now a lumberyard.

***

On the road into Hyndman is a bridge over Wills Creek that I always called the "humming bridge." The grated metal would hum as we drove over it. I loved the sound and especially the tickling vibration coming up through my butt when we crossed.

But I don't get the same thrill when I drive over it today that I did as a kid. Either the vibration isn't as strong, or I need a lot more to thrill me now than I did then.

***

In the spring of my junior year of high school, I was selected for membership in the National Honor Society, our school's greatest academic honor–our only academic honor that I can remember. The main perk of selection was that members got to read morning announcements over the public address system before classes started, which was wonderful not so much for the prestige it carried but because it got us out of the boring half hour of homeroom before the day's official education began.

Election to the society was supposed to be kept secret from new members, but word had a way of leaking out. The faculty advisor, Mrs. Andrews, contacted the parents of each new member a few weeks before the assembly so that they could attend and surprise their child. I knew I'd get in when Mom asked me that morning, "Is that what you're wearing today?" I smiled because I had picked my worst flannel shirt that morning to gauge her response.

"This?" I replied. "I just put this old thing on to feed the chickens." Before catching the bus, I went back up to my room and put on the nice sweater Mom had given me for Christmas. At the assembly, my name was called along with four of my other classmates. Considering our class had only fifty students, I guess that put us in the top ten percent. I walked up on stage and lit a candle held by Jan, the senior president of the society (also the daughter of the basketball coach and a cheerleader I sat with a few times on the basketball bus coming home from away games). Jan put a ribbon holding the wooden honor society key around my neck and surprised me with a kiss on the cheek in front of the whole school, more intimacy than we'd ever shared on the dark basketball bus.

After school, Mom and Dad took me out to an early dinner at a steak house to celebrate. Mom nagged me until I wore the wooden key around my neck, so I drew a few funny looks from the retirees having their dinner at four in the afternoon.

During the last week of school that year, we five new honor society members met to elect officers for the coming year. I was surprised to be elected president by decree before any other officers were even nominated. Besides running our meetings (with loads of necessary help from Mrs. Andrews), the president's main duties were emceeing the new-member induction assembly and giving a speech at graduation.

I probably got elected because I didn't mind giving the graduation speech–which went pretty well that year. Although the speech itself is something of a blank, I do remember that no one tossed rotten eggs at me, and I didn't throw up or accidentally say any swear words. The assembly for inducting new members, however, was something entirely different.

I had a great time planning the assembly, and the other members liked my ideas. Because the "four pillars" of the society were character, scholarship, leadership, and service, I suggested each of the other senior members give a speech about the pillar of their choice. They agreed–as long as the speeches were less than three minutes. I also suggested that the ninth-grade chorus sing during the assembly and that we all wear graduation gowns to give the event a formal atmosphere.

Everything went well as the assembly began. I had changed into dress pants and nice shoes to wear under my robe rather than the jeans and sneakers I wore to school that day. When I walked in, leading the formal procession toward the stage, a few of my basketball teammates snickered, but I didn't crack a smile. I spoke with confidence, welcoming everyone and leading our recital of the Pledge of Allegiance and introducing the afternoon's proceedings.

My fellow members' speeches were going very well, and Mrs. Andrews was beaming at us from the back of the auditorium, proud of our maturity and preparation. My buddy Chris spoke about character, and my long-time unrequited love interest Glenda talked about scholarship. As my childhood friend and neighbor Marlene was finishing her speech on leadership, I ran the rest of the program through my head to make sure the event continued smoothly.

Let's see, I thought to myself. *Leslie has her service speech next. Then the ninth-grade chorus sings a couple of songs. Then I'll read the list of names for provisional tenth-grade members who will stand and be recognized. Then we'll induct the eleventh-grade members, the principal will say a few words, and I'll finish everything by inviting new members and their parents to the library for refreshments.*

I tapped my right front pants pocket to make sure I had the list of provisional tenth-grade members–but the pocket was empty. I checked the left pocket, and it was empty too. I sat stock-still and took a deep breath. Where was the list? *Don't panic,* I thought. *Re-trace your steps. I got the list from Mrs. Andrews earlier in the day, folded it, put it in my pants pocket . . . my jeans pocket . . . the jeans I changed out of when I put on my dress pants . . . the jeans that at this moment are locked up in my gym locker.*

Now I panicked. I had no idea what to do. I stared yearningly at Mrs. Andrews's proud, happy face. I had never noticed how lovely she was until that moment–the moment when my poor planning was about to completely disappoint her. I sent out a powerful telepathic message to her: *I don't have the list . . . I don't have the list,* but she kept smiling her proud smile. She didn't know my locker number or combination anyway. Even if I could send the complicated string of numbers to her telepathically, she couldn't very well go into the *boy's* locker room.

What could I do? Telepathy wasn't going to work. And I couldn't stand at the podium and mumble, "Umm . . . this is the part of the program when I read . . . umm . . . *was going to read* the list of . . . umm . . . provisional ... you know ... members and stuff. But . . . ahh . . . what happened was . . . ahh . . . the list is . . . you know . . . in my . . . ahh . . . gym locker. You know . . . in, like, the . . . umm . . . *locker room.*" I would have sounded like a six-year-old.

Then I remembered one of the aphorisms I had said a few weeks ago during morning announcements: "If you won't do something, don't expect anyone else to do it for you." This was my problem, and I had to solve it.

As Marlene finished her speech, I turned to Leslie and whispered, "Don't panic. I'll introduce you, and then I have to go and get the list of provisional members. If I'm not back by the time you finish, introduce the chorus for me."

She whispered back, "Where are you going?"

"The list is in my gym locker. I'll be back. Don't panic." Then I smiled and put my hand on her arm, the most physical contact I had with a girl since Jan kissed my cheek at the ceremony the year before. "Your speech will be great."

After I introduced Leslie, I walked right by my chair and headed out the back of the stage and through a side door into the hallway. My last glimpse of the audience was Mrs. Andrews's face as her smile melted away and her eyes widened at my apparent desertion.

Once in the hallway, I faced a problem. Some minor construction blocked the doorway leading directly to the locker room. My options were either cutting through the back of the auditorium to another hallway or going through a nearby exit, around the outside of the building, back inside through the front doors, then to the locker room and back around the outside. I didn't want to go through the auditorium because that would make everyone turn and stare at me during Leslie's speech. Besides, Mrs. Andrews was back there, and I didn't have the time to stop and explain things to her–or the guts to walk by her.

So I headed outside. I must have been a strange sight sprinting around the school in my gown and dress shoes. I smiled and waved to an elderly couple out for a stroll near the school and ran by as they stared at me. To my relief, no one was in the hallway or the locker room. After one false try when I couldn't remember my combination, I got my locker open, grabbed the list from my pocket, and re-traced my route around the building, passing the couple from behind and startling them as I murmured, "Excuse me."

After a brief moment of panic when I thought the outside door was locked (only jammed) I made it back into the hallway, took a deep breath, checked to see that my gown was still on straight, smoothed my unruly hair, and walked through the back of the stage and took my seat. I made the entire trip to my locker and back in about two and a half minutes. Even from up on stage, I noticed Mrs. Andrews's shoulders relaxing when she saw me return.

The moment I sat down, Leslie finished her speech, so I bounced up again and strode calmly to the podium to introduce the ninth-grade chorus. As I turned from the podium, I saw that my fellow members were staring at me with concern, so I smiled reassuringly at them. When I sat, however, my heart hammered as sweat beaded my forehead. Luckily, I had all of the chorus's rendition of "We've Only Just Begun" to catch my breath before going back up to the podium to read the treasured list of provisional members clutched in my fist. The entire school wrestling team couldn't have extracted that list from my hand at that moment.

We finished the assembly without further incident. I lit the new members' candles and put keys around their necks, but I didn't kiss anyone on the cheek. I'd had enough excitement for one assembly. Besides, I didn't want to risk a slap on the face in front of the whole school.

When we arrived at the library for refreshments, Mrs. Andrews ran to me and asked, "What happened? Did you get sick? I was so worried." She and the other members listened as I told them my tale of running around the school to get the list. Then we all collapsed on the chairs with laughter and relief.

The new members and their parents were on their way, so we all got up and met them at the door, shaking their hands and offering our congratulations. As the last parent filed in, she shook my hand and thanked me.

"For what?" I asked.

"I'm so glad you got up in the middle of the ceremony to open those windows behind the stage," she said. "We were so hot in that auditorium until you did that. You cooled the place right down."

***

Mrs. Mortenson had a reputation as the toughest and most humorless teacher in the school, and I had my share of tangles with her. Once she assigned a short story for us to read, saying in an offhand way, "This is a difficult story. Most of you won't even be able to get all the way through, and no one will really enjoy it." That was all she needed to say to bring out my stubborn streak. I read the story happily and pretended to enjoy every second of it–a horrific tale of a martyr being put to death for his beliefs.

In Mrs. Mortenson's ninth grade English class, we were also assigned a book report presentation, my first speech. I read *Jonathan Livingston Seagull* by Richard Bach, selected partly because it was the shortest on the reading list, but mostly because Mrs. Mortenson had said it was probably too difficult for anyone in our class. I jumped at the challenge. I read it and was prepared to give my report about how the book taught us to reach beyond the traditional limits and authority and be the greatest seagull–or human being–we could be.

Rather than sending us up alphabetically or calling on us arbitrarily for the speeches, Mrs. Mortenson wanted us to volunteer. For some reason, this again brought out my stubbornness. I refused to volunteer, thinking that she would eventually call on me. As the hour progressed, all of my classmates grudgingly volunteered and gave their speeches. When I was the only one remaining, I glared at Mrs. Mortenson defiantly, expecting her to call my name. This went on for a very long ten seconds with everyone in the silent room staring at me.

Finally, she broke our battle of wills and said, "Okay, we're done." Then she started on the next assignment.

After class, I went to Mrs. Mortenson's desk, all of the defiance drained out of me, and told her in a small voice, "I didn't get to do my speech."

"You had the same chance as everyone else," she said, "but you chose to squander your chance." I got a zero for the assignment and a C+ in English that term, my lowest grade of the year.

"Perhaps you will learn a lesson from this incident," Mrs. Mortenson told me.

A few years later, Mrs. Mortenson sat with me for an hour after school giving me very perceptive feedback on the speech I would deliver at graduation as president of the National Honor Society. Now I teach college public speaking courses and have written a guidebook for giving speeches.

This was one of those rare times in school when I really did learn a lesson, thanks to Mrs. Mortenson and a fictional seagull.

***

Chapter 12
Thing

A few miles south of Hyndman, on my quest to find a photocopier for Grandma's papers, I pass an automotive repair shop with a big sign that reads, "Pete's Tires." Long ago, a few of my classmates went by with some paint late one night and changed the sign to "My Pete's Tired." I didn't get the joke then, but now, twenty-five years later, it finally hits me–"Pete," as in "Peter," as in "penis," as in "My penis is tired." I'm a little slow, but I'll get most jokes if you give me a quarter century.

Near the Maryland border, the road twists through a series of hills. I get my speed up to about sixty because I remember a couple of very special places up ahead. Just over the rise of some small hills, the road dips quickly. As a kid, those dips were the highlight of any trip to Cumberland. When Mom or Dad hit them, my sisters and I in the backseat felt our stomachs rise and fall as a weird, almost electric sensation passed along the base of our spines. I don't know the technical term for these feelings, but we called them "hiney splitters" because we had the feeling those dips divided our butts right in half. Every time we drove through this area, all of us would squeal with glee and shout, "Hiney splitter!" breaking the monotony of even the most boring drive.

For the next hour, I stop at every convenience store from Hyndman to Cumberland, buy lots of beef jerky and diet Mountain Dew, but find no copier. Eventually, I end up twenty miles away lost in Cumberland when I finally spot a large grocery store that's open. When I dash through the cold rain to get inside, I'm almost overjoyed to see an old, beat-up, coin-operated photocopier looking lost and lonely next to the service desk. I spend the next half hour and five dollars in change copying the words that Grandma wrote when I was barely three years old.

***

The rainstorm on my way back from Cumberland reminds me of a summer evening when I was fifteen. I had ridden my bike into Hyndman to play basketball, but on the way home, the sky quickly darkened. I still had five miles to go when a sudden and powerful thunderstorm broke out. Already soaked, I stopped at a gas station to call home and listened to ring after ring because my parents hated answering the phone during lightning for fear that the electric charge would leap through the phone line and into their ear, causing a fried brain and instant death.

When he finally answered the phone and heard my situation, Dad said, "Keep riding. Maybe we'll come for you–maybe we won't." Then he hung up. What else could I do? I got back on my bike and peddled through foot-deep puddles and drops so big that I could barely keep my eyes open. About halfway home, Dad pulled to the side of the road, and I tossed the bike into the back of his pickup. I was so wet that Dad wouldn't let me sit up front, so I climbed in the back and huddled there the rest of the way home.

***

When I'm almost back to the farm, I take a left onto Tar Water Hollow Road at Gravelpit, and a mile later see a sign for New Life Bible Camp. I mostly enjoyed the parts of four summers that I spent here during my teenage years. We played lots of sports, sang lots of songs–and a few girls thought I was cute and smart and funny. But the camp's religious philosophy taught that we should think of God first, others second, and ourselves last. I've always had an altruistic nature, but the camp drilled into me the idea that doing anything for myself was sinful because that selfish behavior didn't serve God or my fellow human beings. More than twenty years later, I'm still trying to shake that idea and take care of myself.

The camp also taught some monumentally screwed-up ideas. I remember a fellow camper asking about Jews and little babies who had never heard of Jesus.

"Do they all go to hell?" she asked.

"Well," the counselor replied, "Jesus does take care of little babies, but Jews are definitely going to hell, and so are Arabs, Chinese, Black Africans, Indians–the ones from India and on the reservation–unless, of course, they accept Jesus into their hearts, in which case they can turn from their sinful ways and be washed in the blood of the lamb."

This counselor was some college guy only a few years older than I was. His summer job was sending about three-fourths of the world's population to hell. Each time I heard, "blood of the lamb," I pictured Jesus with gray skin, a long black cape, and vampire teeth–ready to leap off the cross and chomp someone in the neck. That's not how I wanted to think of the Jesus I knew from reading the New Testament, and I fretted that I would go to hell for having such a sinful Jesus-as-vampire vision.

Another counselor bragged about her years as a hard-drug addict who fornicated with strangers and stole from her parents. Jesus had saved her from that life. After listening to her, I felt a little inadequate and defensive that my life was so ordinary. Her point seemed to be that any conversion from "mostly normal" to "saved" wasn't as important as one from "horrible" to "saved." I thought she had simply traded one addiction for another–heroin for Jesus, her own personal hell for the right to condemn others to hell.

One day at lunch, the head counselor threatened to ship one boy home for "taking the Lord's name in vain." The boy had mumbled, "Gosh darn it" because his hot dog was cold. The head counselor got so worked up that he spilled his lemonade onto my tray. He apologized, and I said, "You are forgiven" in a failed attempt to lighten the moment with a little humor. He turned on me and snapped, "I don't need your forgiveness because I've already been forgiven by Jesus."

A definite anti-woman thread ran through much of the preaching at New Life Bible Camp. Most of the female counselors had very minor roles, in keeping with the Apostle Paul's admonition that women be quiet in church. The head counselor even told us that a woman could only truly serve God by getting married, obeying her husband, and bearing children. A woman on her own was so unnatural, he told us, that single women got pet dogs not for companionship or protection but for sex because they didn't have men in their lives. I didn't know the word yet, but I still recognized misogyny when I heard it.

The camp even had its own brainwashing theme song, "New Life in Christ," which I can still remember:

> New life in Christ, abundant and free,
> What glories shine, what joys are mine,
> What wondrous blessings I see.
>
> My past with its sin, the searching and strife,
> Forever gone, there's a bright new dawn,
> For it's new life in Christ.

Before New Life Bible Camp, my sisters and I had gone to Camp Sequanota, an hour's drive away, for a week each summer. I enjoyed Sequanota much better than New Life, but my parents liked the idea of us being only a couple miles down the road. Sequanota was a church camp, but religion was more of an interesting background theme rather than the myopic focus that hung like a bad smell at New Life.

The worst thing that ever happened at Camp Sequanota was that I once lost my glasses. For three days, I staggered around with limited vision but still had a great time hiking and swimming and playing a ball game called "foursquare" that no one at home knew how to play. Still, my parents would be very upset if they had to buy a new pair of expensive glasses simply because I misplaced them. Just when I started scripting a lie about an epidemic of stolen glasses, another camper found them on the soap dish in the shower. I guess that says something about our hygiene habits that summer. We were having so much fun that we didn't wash for three days. In fact, our funk probably made those three days even more fun than if we'd been clean.

New Life Bible Camp, of course, had regimented bathing times each night before its next attempt to get us all "washed in the blood of the lamb." The camp motto could have been "Cleanliness is next to Godliness is next to Fascism."

Camp Sequanota even had a better song than New Life Bible Camp: "They'll Know We Are Christians By Our Love," by Peter Scholtes. With our counselors' blessings, we revised the original so that it focused more on love and less on God. Here are the parts that I remember best:

> We will walk with each other, we will walk hand in hand.
> We will walk with each other, we will walk hand in hand.
> And together we'll spread the news that love is in the land.
> And they'll know we are Christians by our love, by our love,
> Yes they'll know we are Christians by our love.
>
> We will work with each other, we will work side by side.
> We will work with each other, we will work side by side.
> And we'll guard each ones dignity and save each ones pride.
> And they'll know we are Christians by our love, by our love,
> Yes they'll know we are Christians by our love.
>
> We are one in our spirit, we are one in our love.
> We are one in our spirit, we are one in our love.
> And we pray that all unity will one day be restored.
> And they'll know we are Christians by our love, by our love,
> Yes they'll know we are Christians by our love.

You could substitute "Christian" with "Buddhist," "Muslim," "Jew," "Hindu," or even "American" and "Iraqi"–and this would still be a great song. Or insert "human" or even "sentient" if you want to get technical, and this could be a great theme song for the whole planet or even the universe. We'll be known by our love–what a perfect theme to live by. My teenage spiritual quest was always much more about love than getting saved or condemning anyone else to hell. In fact, it still is.

When I went to college, I joined a few Christian organizations, but I didn't last long. Early in my sophomore year, I mentioned that I enjoyed studying Islam and Hindu beliefs in my religion classes because they helped to put my own faith in perspective. That statement drew lots of blank stares from the Christian group members. A week later, I discovered that my comment landed my name on a list of "backsliders" who needed to be prayed for lest they tempt the fires of hell. The prayer list included President Carter, among others–pretty good company. I went to very few meetings after that, and when Dad died halfway through my junior year, I stopped going altogether.

I just didn't see the point any longer.

***

New Life Bible Camp was also the scene of the most traumatic medical crisis of my young life. A week before camp when I was fifteen, I took a walk in the woods. At one point during the walk, I unzipped my fly and took a pee. I didn't know it at the time, but I must have touched some poison ivy not long before relieving myself.

The next morning, I woke with my hands, arms, and lower legs covered with the familiar rash and blisters of an allergic reaction. I'd had bad cases of poison ivy many times before, so I knew I faced two weeks of itching, creams, sprays, and weeping blisters all over me. When I went to the bathroom that morning, however, I encountered the shock of my life.

I stood over the toilet and lowered my pajama bottoms. When my penis popped into view, I nearly fainted. It was swollen to twice its usual size–and not in the good way. The shaft felt lumpy with blisters, and the end was puffy and enflamed. It looked like the hammerhead shark in our biology textbook. As I stared with horror, the thing suddenly began to itch. Then, as I peed, I experienced a burning sensation like nothing I had ever felt before (or since). I nearly lost my balance and peed all over the floor.

That morning at breakfast, Mom saw the rash on my hands and gave me a tube of lotion to ease the itch.

"Mom," I said haltingly, "I think this case of poison ivy is worse than usual."

"Is it farther up your arms and legs?" Mom asked.

"Sort of," I replied. "I got it on my . . . umm . . . thing."

"What thing?" Mom asked.

"You know," I replied without meeting her eyes, "*my thing*."

"Oh, *your thing*," Mom said, finally getting the point. "Well, how did you do that? Were you rolling around naked in the woods or something?"

"No!" I protested. I had done my reading on poison ivy. I knew the rash-inducing particles could be transferred from one part of the body to another. "I got it on my hands, and then . . ."

"Were you playing with yourself?" Mom asked.

"No!" I responded, honest for once about this subject. "I took a pee in the woods yesterday. It must have happened then."

Whatever doubt Mom had about my explanation, she kept it to herself. "Well," she sighed, "let's call the doctor."

I got a shot in the butt that day from a very cute young nurse with a very large needle. As I lowered my pants for the shot, I kept my little hammerhead concealed. For some reason, I thought that the poor nurse might faint at the sight of such a monstrosity. It didn't occur to me that she must have already seen plenty of penis problems in her brief career. Like most teenagers with embarrassing conditions, I assumed no one else in the world ever had such a problem.

A few days later, I went to New Life Bible Camp for a week. The shot had cleared up the rashes on my arms and legs., but, unfortunately, my smallest extremity was more stubborn. For the entire week of camp, I fidgeted uncomfortably and spent lots of time in the restroom scratching where I shouldn't have been scratching. My only relief came during swim time when I lounged in the shallow end of the pool, basking in the soothing cool water and chatting with cute girl campers who had no idea the terrible secret lurking just beneath my swimming trunks.

I couldn't tell any of the camp counselors about my problem because they certainly would have told me God was punishing me for lust. But if God really punished teenagers for that, then there must have been many more rashes under many more swimming suits than my own. In fact, considering what I saw some of the counselors doing that summer, they probably had rashes all over their bodies.

By comparison, my little hammerhead wasn't so bad.

***

My right rear tire looked low this morning, but the air I added didn't hold very long, and now it's completely flat. I drive slowly to the house to pay for my stay in the cabin and to visit with Janet and Fred, also hoping to back my car into the shed and change the tire out of the pouring rain.

When I knock on the door, Janet invites me inside where it's dry. I need to change the tire soon before it gets too dark, but I really enjoy talking with Janet, and I'm very intrigued by the house. On my previous visits, I'd only been in the remodeled kitchen. Janet tells me that Mom visited here once and asked, "What have you done to my beautiful kitchen?" Janet's kitchen looks a million times better than when Mom lived here. We had wood paneling, clunky cupboards, and a drop ceiling with florescent lights. But Mom always had her own unique decorative style.

***

Our long, slender living room went through an odd transformation during my childhood. I vaguely remember early in my life the walls being a solid color. Then, for reasons that are beyond explanation, Mom hung "wallpaper" in the living room. But she didn't use traditional wallpaper, opting instead for contact paper–the sticky plastic sheets with removable backing used mostly for tacky arts and crafts or to line shelves and drawers.

Mom decided to do the entire living room with contact paper. She couldn't find enough of one pattern, so she did the two long walls in a light shade of fake wood paneling contact paper. On one short wall, Mom used a psychedelic paisley print, dominated by orange and yellow. And on the other end wall, she put up a stone and mortar pattern. The whole effect made the room seem about half its actual size, as though the walls were crashing in as I sat on the couch Saturday afternoons and watched old science fiction movies on TV. It could get downright creepy at times with Martians on TV and the walls dancing in the periphery of my vision.

The contact paper was also filled with tiny air bubbles that I liked to smush around to different places all over the walls on rainy summer days. I moved my favorite bubble the entire length of the long wall over the course of about two years, picking up smaller bubbles as I went along until the thing was as big as a silver dollar. The paper's edges were forever curling and peeling away from the ceiling until Mom started fixing them with Elmer's glue, giving the top of the walls a nice lumpy texture. The walls made for especially good fun when visitors came over and squinted in our outlandish living room like they had grabbed someone else's eyeglasses by mistake.

***

After we talk for a while, Janet gives me a tour of the house. She has remodeled the living room so that only the shape and window placement remind me of the room I knew. Thankfully, Janet long ago tore out the contact paper and painted all four walls. But for a "living" room, the place feels full of ghosts. Janet seems to have the same feeling, and she suddenly stops talking and looks around the room, lost in a memory.

"My mom and I came to visit your grandma in this house once," she says. "Must have been about 1961. I was just a girl. This living room," she lifts a hand to take in the space, "was jammed full with four cribs."

She doesn't have to tell me who occupied those cribs, but I have trouble imagining myself as one of the infants dozing in this very room four decades ago. My own ghost is haunting me today.

Mom had four children in diapers at the same time after her two oldest children were already grown and out of the house. She was thirty-five when Tam and Pam were born and thirty-seven when June and I came along. She probably felt old enough to be the mother of the women giving birth with her in the hospital maternity ward. As frightened as those teenaged mothers must have been, they were young and had only one kid to take home. Mom was twice their age and had four of us screaming and crying all day and half the night.

It's no wonder she was goofy enough to put up that mismatched contact paper all around the living room. If her state of mind was not always perfectly sound, I'm sure the four of us helped to drive her to it.

***

Janet tells me that rats as big as cats rule the basement. I laugh and tell her that I met their ancestors years ago. One peeked at me in the shower once and ran away when I threw a shampoo bottle at it. I saw so many rats in that basement that I used to stomp my feet five times at the top of the stairs before I turned on the light, just to give the critters a little warning.

The fuse box for our house was in the basement behind the furnace. To get to it, you had to wriggle sideways six feet along the nine-inch gap between the side of the hot furnace and the cement wall until you got to the back of the furnace. From there, you reached up with one hand to open the fuse box, held a flashlight at an impossible angle with the other hand, unscrewed one fuse at a time, and examined it to see if it was "good" or "shot." When you discovered the shot one, you crammed your hand into a pocket that was smashed against the concrete wall, extracted a new fuse, and screwed it into the hole where the shot one was.

This was Dad's job, definitely not his favorite. He hadn't been home to supervise the installation of the furnace many years before, and he told me how angry he was to discover that the installers had pretty much blocked access to the fuse box. As a short, thick-chested man, Dad had a terrible time squeezing into the tiny, filthy space and reaching the fuse box mounted near the ceiling. So when a fuse blew in our house, everyone knew Dad would be an unhappy man.

In my bedroom, I had one of those little greenish-blue glowing nightlights that plugs directly into an outlet. One boring afternoon when I was thirteen, I decided to see how my nightlight worked, so I got a butter knife from the kitchen and pried the thing apart. I found no answers after examining its mysterious innards for a few minutes, so I reassembled the pieces, used masking tape to hold it together, and plugged it back in. It immediately sparked, popped, smoked, and smelled like torched rubber. Naturally, it blew a fuse. I reluctantly told Dad, and he spent ten minutes cursing through the contortionist act of changing the fuse.

When I went back upstairs, I took the nightlight apart again to see if I could put it back together correctly this time. I liked having that nightlight, and I couldn't give it up without one more try at fixing it. I was either optimistic or stupid–or both–as I held it near the outlet and pushed the prongs in slowly, one millimeter at a time, praying silently that it would not blow the fuse again, thus causing Dad to blow his fuse.

They say sometimes God's answer to prayer is "No." This was one of those times. While God was saying "No," the nightlight was saying, "Spark, pop, smoke, stink." I slowly descended the stairs to tell Dad that I had blown the fuse again exactly the same way. The only thing that saved me was the brainstorm I had when I saw him sitting in his recliner reading the paper.

"Dad?" I said quietly. He lowered the paper slowly, peeking over the top to reveal a smudge of soot still on his cheek.

"I think it's time I learned how to change the fuses," I said.

***

As different as Janet's remodeled downstairs is, the upstairs looks as though it has hardly been touched. Janet shows me my old bedroom, which they plan to convert into a walk-in closet. That seems like a good idea because the room is so much smaller than I remember, maybe ten by twelve. It seemed so big to me as a kid. This was the place where I could get away by myself, listen to the radio, read, and dream.

My room still has the same brown paint that I put on the walls at age fourteen. Mom decided that the room needed to be painted, and she even let me select the color. I picked brown because it reminded me of the woods. So one Saturday afternoon in the middle of the summer, Mom and I were painting the room when I stepped too close to the vent in the floor and dropped right into it–crashing through the ceiling and landing with a thump next to Grandma's kitchen table.

Luckily, Grandma wasn't there at the time. If I had landed on her, a long and distinguished life would have come to an end right then. Even if she had been on the other side of the room, I probably would have startled her so badly that she might have aged another year or two.

Mom peered down through the floor at me, and Dad came running into the room. I thought they would be mad, but both of them were very concerned. I brushed myself off, cleaned up Grandma's floor, and went back up to help Mom finish painting–mostly on the side of the room away from the hole where the vent had been a few minutes earlier. One of Dad's friends came the next day to patch Grandma's ceiling, but the hole is still here in my bedroom floor, covered with the same "temporary" sheet of plywood that Dad nailed over it. I tell Janet the whole story of how a clumsy teenaged boy made that hole.

Every upstairs room looks smaller now than it did back then, and all the doors are the same old painted planks of wood that look like shanty doors. They'd bring a hefty price at a New England antique shop. The guest room where I stayed when I came home from college looks especially tiny with barely room for a bed and dresser.

This guest room has a stairway to the attic, the mysterious and forbidden place that I snooped in many times as a willful and curious child. It's the only place in the house that looks exactly the way I remembered it–cramped, dirty, and fascinating (partly because it was forbidden). Janet and Fred replaced the roof above the attic, so the only difference in here is that there's no hatchway out to where we had our TV antenna.

***

Back in the days before cable came to the valley, we had an enormous television antenna on the roof of our farmhouse. The guy who delivered our milk (back in the days of milk delivery) did TV repair on the side, and he helped us install the antenna at the very peak of the roof, way off near the edge. We had to climb up through the attic hatchway and tightrope walk the sharp ridge of the roof about twenty feet to get to it.

Even with the antenna, our reception was far from ideal. NBC from Johnstown came in best. CBS from Altoona was watchable but often faded out. ABC from far-off Pittsburgh had a faint picture but no voice, and PBS from Penn State University had a faint voice but no picture.

When I got to college, we had cable TV in the dorm lobby. *Seven* stations actually came in clearly, putting me in television heaven. The college had its own public access channel that showed announcements such as, "Dance This Friday in the Student Center." I felt so TV-starved that I would watch one of these announcements, then say, "Wow, that was a good show!"

Back on the farm, we were sometimes unfortunate enough to get rain, snow, or wind strong enough to spin the antenna or knock off a wire–and then all we got was a screen full of nothing on every channel. When this happened, we had to do an emergency repair job. Even with so few stations, four kids were devastated with no TV.

Emergency antenna repair was one of our biggest family projects. I climbed onto the roof and inched my way to the antenna. Dad poked his head up through the hatchway to watch me. (Before I turned twelve and was taller than Dad, these roles were reversed.) One of my sisters stationed herself at the bottom of the attic stairs, another at the top of the main stairway, and a third in front of the TV.

After I had replaced the loose wires, I would reach up and rotate the antenna a few degrees one way or the other and call to Dad in the hatchway, "How's that?"

Dad called, "How's that?" to the sister at the bottom of the attic stairs, who in turn called, "How's that?" to the sister at the top of the main stairs, who called, "How's that?" to the sister in front of the TV. That sister called back something like, "A little better . . . keep going," and the bucket brigade of voices continued back up person by person to the antenna for the next adjustment.

We kept going until the television reception got as strong as we could get it on each station and then started getting fuzzy again. At that point, the call became, "Worse . . . turn it back."

"Worse . . . turn it back."
"Worse . . . turn it back."
"Worse . . . turn it back."
Then I'd make another adjustment.
"How about now?"
"How about now?"
"How about now?"
"How about now?"
"Perfect!"
"Perfect!"
"Perfect!"
"Perfect!"
And then we were finished.

Mom's role through this whole process was to stand outside, winter or summer, rain or shine, and worry that I would take a deadly fall. She fulfilled this role very well, worrying herself into such a frenzy that she would start chanting, "Please God don't let my baby fall, please God don't let him fall, please God don't let him fall," so loud that I often politely asked her to stop because she made me nervous.

But at age sixteen, I really did fall off the roof. Mom's chanting distracted me so much that I turned to look at her, lost my balance, and tumbled down the steep pitch of the upper roof. From there, my momentum rolled me quickly over the flat part of the roof above my sisters' second-floor bedroom and off its edge, sending me down about seven feet to the porch roof. I bounced a couple of times, then went over that edge and thudded onto the grass in the front yard.

Mom screamed and ran to me, but I was okay. I had a few bruises and would wake up the next day with a headache, but youth and flexibility protected me. I climbed back up on the roof (against Mom's protests) to finish fixing the antenna. Looking around when I got back up there, I saw how lucky I'd been to fall in the direction I did. If I had gone the other way, the top part of the roof gave way to thin air rather than two layers of roof that divided the house and my fall into thirds. In the other direction, I would have dropped about twenty-five feet directly onto the hard ground and almost certain death–just so we could watch our handful of channels.

***

Chapter 13
Choice

I spend so much time sharing stories with Janet that darkness begins to descend. When I do finally back my car into the shed, the air is so inky that I can barely see to change the tire. To my relief, Fred arrives from the house with a big flashlight and offers to help me change the tire.

Dad always made a point of refusing help, no matter how much he might have liked that help–his way of being polite. Naturally, I refuse Fred's help with the tire, but I am happy to have him shine the flashlight so I that can see what I'm doing. I'm determined to change the tire faster and with more skill than an Indianapolis 500 pit crew. Most of the guys I grew up with considered me a little strange because I had no interest in working on cars. I still don't know much about cars–but one thing I can do is change a tire. I have the flat off and the spare on in five minutes, muscling the jack and lug wrench and tire around despite the throbbing pain in my pinkie finger, all the while keeping a running commentary going with Fred to prove how easy this job is for a manly man like me.

When I'm down on my knees lowering the car with the screw-jack, it hits me that I helped Dad change a tire on this exact spot about twenty-five years ago. Dad always backed cars into the shed to change the tires, raining or not. I'm amazed at how clear my memory holds the moment. Something about the shed's dirt floor–the rich brown dirt in the flickering beam, the moist, gritty feel against my bare hands, the fecund scent–makes me imagine that Dad is alive and real behind the flashlight.

***

When I finish changing the tire, I notice a man standing in the road studying the rising waters of Wolf Camp Run. He pulls a disposable camera from his coat pocket and snaps a few flash pictures of the stream. He's short, in his thirties, and vaguely familiar. When he sees me coming out of the shed, he turns and begins talking.

"They really screwed up this creek back in '96," he says. "I told them a dozen times that they were just making it worse."

I nod, and he keeps talking, telling me that the county authorities dredged the creek poorly after the flood a few years ago, and he's been waiting for a rain like today's to show how badly they damaged things. He says that he lives half a mile upstream, that the dredging cut away several yards of his property he was never compensated for.

"The county is too chicken to admit screwing up," he says.

Suddenly, I remember him: Ken, a neighbor a couple years younger than I. We weren't close, and the last time I saw him was a week before I left for college. He was sixteen and had taken his father's car speeding up the road by our house. We heard him slam on the brakes near the shed, and then we crowded around the kitchen door to watch him get out of the car, move around the front to the passenger side, bend to pick something up, and walk slowly to our porch with a white bundle in his hand. It looked like a pillowcase filled with laundry.

He knocked, and Dad opened the door. Ken looked surprised that our whole family–Dad, Mom, Grandma, my three sisters, and I–had gathered in the kitchen to investigate the commotion. This was an event for us, something to break the rural summer monotony. More than a little fear and shame mixed with Ken's surprise. He held up the white bundle by a scrawny set of yellowish-pink legs, and I suddenly recognized it as one of our chickens.

"I'm really sorry, Mr. Sheirer," he said to Dad. "I ran over a chicken. I feel really bad, and I want to pay you for the damage."

"That's okay," Dad said, taking the chicken from him and placing it on the kitchen table. "We'll have this one for dinner."

When I tell Ken who I am, his eyes widen in recognition as we shake hands. I can't resist revisiting the chicken story. After a moment, he remembers, chuckles, and blushes.

"Dad was really impressed that you came to the door and owned up to it," I tell Ken.

"I was scared, but your dad was a good guy," he says.

He goes back to snapping pictures of the creek. His blush fades. He tells me his own father is in the hospital dying of cancer. I remember Ken's father as short and stout, much like Ken–a lot like Dad. It's hard to imagine these strong men so weak and frail, dying.

Ken doesn't show much emotion. He climbs the bank and invites me to get into the picture.

"I'll show these to my dad," Ken says as the camera flashes. "He's the one who made me admit running over the Millers' cat and the Emerichs' dog that summer. Your chicken was the last straw."

"It really wasn't a big deal," I say. "We were going to eat that chicken sooner or later."

Ken laughs. "It was a big deal to my dad. He didn't let me get near his car for a year after that."

***

The rain has been intense all day, and the warm temperatures have made for significant snowmelt. The conditions are perfect for a flood. There's a rich history of flooding in this area. Fred and Janet showed me pictures of the most recent flood in 1996. The waters broke over the banks of Wolf Camp Run and almost took out the barn. In 1984, a flood hit Hyndman so hard that it devastated several sections of town.

Every time it rained for more than two days in a row, Grandma talked about the 1936 flood, the worst ever recorded in this area. She told us that the snows had been very heavy that winter, over three feet on Wills Mountain. In March, the weather turned warm and snowmelt soaked the ground. Then it rained nearly seven inches in three days. Roads, bridges, and the railroad were washed out, and the farmlands heavily damaged. The flood was so severe that part of Wolf Camp Run eventually settled thirty feet to the north of its previous path.

Ironically enough, March 1936 also saw a devastating flood hit Northampton, Massachusetts, the town where I lived before moving to Connecticut. I wonder if Grandma heard about the Northampton flood even as she worked hard to recover her own land. Did she send her heart out to those suffering New Englanders whose descendents would one day be my neighbors?

I can picture Grandma standing on the porch on a day like today and staring at the sky. "Did I ever tell you about the '36 flood?" she would have asked anyone within earshot.

***

The flood that I remember most happened late in the summer of 1977 while I slept in the trailer outside our house. Rain fell all night, but that wasn't unusual. Because it rained at least part of half the nights each summer, I barely noticed. But when I stepped out of the trailer that morning, my foot plunged into six inches of water. The creek had crested its banks and engulfed the road. Our fields were scattered with several good-sized ponds, and at the cabin, water flowed to the porch.

When I got to the house, the phone lines were already buzzing with news of flood damage. I heard that Janet's father's Volkswagen Beetle had washed down the creek. No one had any idea where it was, so I decided I'd find the car and be a hero. I crossed the railroad bridge and walked north toward Janet's house along the edge of the flooded creek, looking for a dark green VW Beetle.

Halfway to Janet's house, I stepped into what I assumed was a shallow run-off of water about ten feet from where the swollen creek thundered along. To my great surprise, the run-off turned out to be a trench seven feet deep. I plunged into water over my head before I knew what had happened. Luckily, my foot landed solidly on the bottom, and I bounded upward by reflex and scrambled out of the trench in a few seconds. If I had been pulled another three or four feet toward the creek, the current might have captured me and sucked me downstream. I've always been a mediocre swimmer at best, my heavy bones weighing me down, and I would have had the fight of my life to keep from drowning less than a few hundred yards from my own home.

I changed clothes in the trailer because I didn't want to admit my dunking to Mom and Dad. The VW was found a few days later about three miles downstream, a surprisingly long trip considering I had been looking for it within sight of its usual parking spot. Our family's only loss in the flood was the pipe that Dad and I had painstakingly suspended along a cable from a small spring on the steep creek bank near the cabin. When the Beetle didn't turn up right away, I joked that it would probably be found somewhere near the Atlantic Ocean with our spring pipe stuck through the window.

Dad didn't laugh. He was devastated by the loss of the pipe because he had been so proud of it. We had worked very hard to tap the hidden spring that produced some of the best water in the area. People drove from miles around to fill a few bottles to take home for drinking. This was back before everyone drank bottled water, but if Dad and I had set up shop with that spring water, we could have made a fortune.

A few weeks later, we tried to hook up another pipe to the spring. Dad and I spent a whole day on that steep bank, up to our knees in mud, struggling to wharf off a basin to capture the water again. But too much of the creek bank had been swept away in the flood. When we finally gave up, Dad wiped the mud from his hands and looked up at me, tears in his eyes.

"Why do things like this always happen to us?" he asked.

I still don't have an answer for his question.

***

When I drive back to the cabin after changing my tire, I see that the water from Little Wills Creek has begun flooding the road. I drive through a foot of water to turn into the cabin's yard. To be safe, I put the car into four-wheel drive and back it right up against the porch.

Before going inside, I decide on a whim to step to the side of the cabin and pee in the yard.

Dad was fond of peeing outside. I'll happily pee outside when I'm hiking or driving a back road with no rest stop in sight, but Dad simply didn't like climbing the stairs to our second-floor bathroom. He often rose from the kitchen table–where he and Mom read, talked, drank coffee, and played cards most evenings–took a few steps off the porch and around the corner, and then peed along the side of the house. After a few years, he created a teardrop shaped patch of dead grass where his urine had saturated the ground. I made a similar patch by peeing out the back door of the trailer where I slept during the summer.

Once inside the cabin, I settle into the futon, watching flood warnings on the television, thinking about what Jenny might be doing tonight, and wondering if Trackers float like VW Beetles.

At some point during the night, I wake for a moment and think I hear a very loud car going by the cabin … but the noise doesn't recede because there's no car. It's Little Wills Creek, raging with whitewater as loud as a river. I go back to sleep with visions of the cabin floating downstream with me inside–sort of like Dorothy riding a liquid tornado to Oz.

I wake at six on my last morning here and pad to the front door to look out. I'm half expecting to see water up on the porch and my car bobbing in the surf, but there's just enough light to tell me that the creek hasn't flooded. In fact, I can see that it has receded a bit. I guess there won't be a repeat of the 1936 flood after all.

***

Dad had a habit of repeating himself. At dinner, he would ask, "How was school today?" and we'd answer, "Fine." Then someone might relate an interesting story from the school day. Not ten minutes later, Dad would break a quiet moment of chewing and swallowing with another question: "Was school good today?" We'd roll our eyes but answer as if this were the first time we heard the question because we knew Dad would deny he'd asked it before.

I seem to have inherited this tendency. My ex-wife used to get upset with me for "not listening" because I might ask her the same question more than once during an hour. Students, too, give quite a few blank stares and puzzled looks when I tell them for the second or even the third time some basic point. I usually pretend that I'm repeating for emphasis.

***

Dad was pretty laid-back, a trait I've also inherited from him, but he sometimes sported a strange sense of humor. One of his favorite gags was popping his false teeth out at me. I was five the first time he did it, and he terrified me. I had no idea some adults had dentures. My teeth didn't pop out, so it rattled me that Dad's did. He got quite a laugh out of that trick for several years, startling me every time.

He also enjoyed cracking his nose. He'd put each hand on either side of his nose, fiddle with it for a few seconds (claiming he had to get the bones just right), then wrench it quickly to one side, making a snap so loud I could feel it in the pit of my stomach. Dad eventually taught me the secret to the trick. He really made the sound by snapping his thumbnail on his front teeth while he twisted his nose. His hands hid the whole operation, so it looked very realistic.

I've inherited Dad's off-center sense of humor as well. I crack my nose for hundreds of people each year, most of them captive-audience students in my classes. I love hearing them groan just like I did when I first saw Dad do it. Of course, I eventually let them in on the secret as well, passing on Dad's comic legacy.

Dad would definitely have enjoyed how I used to bend my right-hand pinky finger into creative shapes for entertainment purposes. Unfortunately, this trick was no sham. The finger had been dislocated so many times playing basketball that the tendons and ligaments no longer held it in place. It hurt like crazy to bend it around like that, but I had a great time alternately delighting and repulsing everyone I knew with my pinky trick. Now I can't do it anymore, thanks to the three screws implanted to fuse the joint straight, but at least I have a good surgery scar to keep people groaning.

By the way, Dad also repeated himself a lot.

***

Dad had a deep and abiding love for the Pirates and Steelers, Pittsburgh's baseball and football teams. He suffered through their bad times and celebrated their eventual successes. Those teams certainly had more bad times than good. I clearly remember Dad hurling curses at the television during one of his team's many defeats. I felt bad for him when they lost but even worse for Mom because Dad was usually inconsolable the rest of the day. These early sports disappointments prepared me well for my current life as a Boston Red Sox fan.

I eventually celebrated a few Steelers Super Bowl victories with Dad, but the 1971 Pirates World Series victory against the heavily favored Baltimore Orioles was my favorite. As much as Dad enjoyed that triumph, he told me it didn't compare to the Pirates beating the unbeatable Yankees on Bill Mazeroski's series-winning, game-seven home run in 1960. Dad actually got misty-eyed when he talked about those days.

Recently, I found myself thinking about the connection between my birth and that World Series. I went to the library and found an encyclopedia detailing the history of major league baseball. The Pirate-Yankee series took place in October 1960, and I was born in May 1961. That's a seven-month gap, and I wasn't born two months premature. But go back a month or two before the World Series, and it's entirely possible that I was conceived in celebration of the Pirates clinching the National League pennant that fall.

***

When I was about ten, Dad decided to make maple syrup. He bought a book on how to go about tapping the trees and was as excited about the project as I'd ever seen him. We had plenty of maple trees, and Dad had a good time carving and drilling the wooden taps out of branches. He hung dozens of buckets around the farm and collected gallons of sap that he poured into two ten-gallon pressure cookers that Mom used for canning. The cookers cost $35 each, a hefty sum in the early 1970s.

Dad stoked a very hot fire in our outside fireplace for the sap-filled cookers. My job was to keep the fire going while Dad stayed inside to read the newspaper and dream of maple syrup. After about an hour, I heard a very loud sizzle from the fireplace and called for Dad. Just as he arrived, we heard a second sizzle.

The roaring fire had burned through most of the old iron stovetop and the bottom of the two expensive pressure cookers, releasing the liquid into the flames below. Dad lost all of the sap he'd gathered, two of Mom's most expensive kitchen tools–and his taste for maple syrup.

After the incident, we never tapped a tree again, and Dad sweetened his pancakes with apple butter.

***

As a teenager, I overheard Grandma talking about the time Dad shot off one of his toes. I was dumbfounded that something so significant had happened to my own father, and I knew nothing about it. So I secretly quizzed an aunt and two older cousins, piecing the story together.

When Dad was about seventeen and hunting with his brothers, he stumbled, and the rifle in his hand fired a bullet right through the end of his left boot. When he removed the bloody boot and sock, his second toe fell to the ground, blown apart at its base. Dad spent three months on crutches while his foot healed, and everyone had a grand time teasing him.

I'd never seen Dad barefoot during all those years of living in the same house. When he wasn't wearing work boots or shoes, he always wore socks or bedroom slippers. I didn't even consider asking him to show me his foot. If he'd wanted me to see it, I'm sure he would have shown me a long time before. I sensed his defensiveness about the foot, so I kept my mouth shut and my eyes open.

My patience was eventually rewarded. Dad and I were watching a baseball game on TV one hot summer day when he began rubbing his stocking feet. This caught my attention, and I nearly gasped when Dad pulled off his left sock to scratch his foot. On the pretense of getting us each a glass of iced tea, I got up and walked toward the kitchen–but quickly detoured behind his recliner to get a good look at his bare foot before he put his sock back on.

The foot looked fine in every respect–except that it had only four toes, one big and three little. Over the decades since the injury, Dad's third and big toes had come to an understanding and grown together. If I didn't know that a normal foot had five toes, I probably wouldn't have noticed anything unusual.

When I returned from the kitchen, Dad's sock was back on, as usual. I wish now that I had asked Dad about his foot. In the next life, I hope he'll give me a good look at it, and in exchange, I'll show him my half-dozen surgery scars.

***

His voice was a bad combination of loud and nasal, adding another level of irritation as he taunted me for a third time: "Whatsa matter, farm boy? Are ya chicken?" Remembering that voice still makes me cringe twenty-five years later.

My sister Pam's boyfriend Mark was twenty, two years older than she and four years older than I. He was a big, obnoxious city jerk who liked to tease me for a variety of reasons: because I was younger, because I did well in school, because I spent my summer vacation helping Dad tend crops and cut firewood for winter. Of course, I would learn a few years later in my first college psychology class that he teased me primarily because he didn't like himself very much, but I didn't have that perspective at age sixteen. Instead of sympathy for his emotional weakness, I mostly felt disgusted with him.

Mark had spent a good portion of the evening proving his manhood by beating Pam arm wrestling several times–his idea of the perfect date. He toyed with her each time, pretending to be working hard as she pushed with her tomboy strength. Then he pounded her arm down on the coffee table and leaped to his feet in celebration, pumping his fist in the air and prancing around the living room, singing a bad rendition of Queen's, "We Are the Champions." Pam would too quickly forget her pride and the sting of defeat and tell him how strong he was and how he was her hero–an early example of the kind of mistake I would eventually see too many strong women make with weak men.

So Mark and I took up positions on either side of the little wooden coffee table and planted our elbows. He gave me his best evil-eye and assured me that I was "goin' down, sissy-boy" as he wrapped his fat hand around my bony one in the macho soul-brother handshake of arm wrestling.

We were both close to six feet tall, although he weighed more than two hundred pounds (at least fifty more than I did in those long-ago teenage years), but I noticed his soft and doughy middle. He had quickly given up the one time he condescended to help Dad and me load firewood into the old pick-up, claiming a football injury as he limped back inside the house. Dad and I just smiled and kept working. In contrast to Mark, I was thin but strong from years of outdoor work alongside Dad.

Mark pulled away from my hand three times to make adjustments, claiming that he didn't want me to cheat with an illegal grip. Pam was clearly rooting for him, but the fan support evened out when Dad walked into the room and saw what was going on. One corner of his mouth turned up slightly, and he gave me a wink. I didn't need a word from him to know that he wanted me to kick Mark's ass from one end of the living room to the other.

Finally satisfied with his grip, Mark counted, "one-two-three-go," jamming "three" and "go" together to try and catch me off guard. His pale arm vibrated with more strength than I'd given him credit for. My arm quickly became a knot of muscle, matching his every push with equal force. Realizing that this wouldn't be the easy victory he anticipated, he lifted his elbow, a clear foul, and nearly put me down. With the same strength that could throw a wet bale of hay into the barn loft, I recovered and bent his arm back an inch per second, gradually pushing him toward defeat. With his arm nearing the table, he pulled away and jumped up, claiming a cramp and rubbing his arm with a hurt look on his face.

Dad and I exchanged "what-a-jerk" looks as Mark stalked out of the room, Pam following closely behind. "Good job," Dad said. I thanked him and was about to say something bad about Mark when Dad did a curious thing. He got out of his chair and knelt down on the opposite side of the coffee table. "Wanna try me?" he asked as he put his thick arm on the table. "Okay," I replied automatically, used to saying yes to any request from Dad.

Dad once told me while we rested in the middle of some outdoor project how glad he was that I worked with him on the farm because my older brothers hadn't always helped. My mouth fell open because I hadn't known I had a choice–although I would have chosen to join him anyway. It wouldn't have occurred to me to refuse to go out and repair a fence with him or pick a dozen ears of corn for dinner. Likewise, it never crossed my mind that I could refuse to arm wrestle with him, so I locked my hand into his.

I thought Dad would beat me without much trouble. All my life, I had been a bit ashamed of not being more like him. He was only five feet, seven inches tall but very strong, a man with well-defined pectorals long before tax accountants and soccer-moms went to the gym five times a week. His arms seemed as big around as my legs, his neck as thick as my chest. He played semi-professional baseball and was a star on his high school football team, playing a mythic position called "scatback," where he could either overpower or outrun any opponent. In contrast, I was a gangly kid, with a body built for basketball but a temperament for chess. Dad came to every home game to see me rebound and play defense, and he didn't seem disappointed that I scored fewer points than most of the other sons.

Because Dad was so strong and vital and alive, I could easily forget that only five years earlier he had suffered a near-fatal heart attack. One winter afternoon during fifth-grade math class, I heard the school principal summon my sisters and me over the loud speaker. Mom picked us up and drove us to the hospital where Dad had been taken that morning shortly after we left for school. We were assured that he would be okay, but I was shocked to see his usually wind-burned bronze skin so pale next to the hospital-issue sky-blue pajamas and starched white bed sheets.

A few weeks after that, Dad came home. But he couldn't go back to his job as a construction steamfitter or work around our farm. In fact, we put a hospital bed in the living room because he wasn't even allowed to climb the stairs to the bedroom where he had suffered his heart attack. For six weeks, Dad slept in our living room, watching television, reading the paper, and mostly being miserable because he couldn't get outside and work. Eventually, the color returned to his face, and he began venturing to the porch and up the stairs. Soon he started sleeping in his own bed again, and a cousin came and hauled the living room bed back to the hospital.

Dad never returned to his real job, but he always found plenty to keep him (and me) busy on our farm. We got by on his veteran's benefits and disability from the union, and Mom eventually got a job as a clerk in the gift shop of an authentic recreated pioneer village. Mom wore what we called "granny dresses" to work three days a week while Dad focused most of his attention on cutting wood to feed our furnace now that coal was a bit beyond our means. Tending a few cows, chickens, and a garden always kept us well stocked for food, and Dad soon grew strong again, his muscles thickening over the course of a few years.

To my surprise, Dad didn't force my arm down right away. In fact, I held my own very well. At first, I just tried to avoid having my hand slammed down instantly, but soon I realized that I had a chance to win. Pushing with all my might, I thought my nose might start to bleed from the intense pressure. When I looked at Dad, I saw him straining too. His eyes bulged in a way that I had never seen before, and sweat formed on his upper lip. When I looked at his arm, the arm I had so long admired and wished that mine resembled more, it looked wrinkled and creased near the crook of his elbow. The muscle didn't leap out as I had seen it do so many times while he worked his chainsaw. His hands, I noticed for the first time, had age spots.

At that point, I once again saw Dad in the hospital that day five years earlier, pale under the harsh lights, looking small and frail to my eyes for the first time. Suddenly it dawned on me that Dad might not be the strong man he had been, that the strain of arm wrestling might be too much for him–even just arm wrestling his skinny, semi-sissy, teenage son. I realized that I might be hurting him, making his damaged heart work too hard–maybe even killing him.

I faced a choice. I could let myself weaken a fraction so that he could win quickly. Such a tactic might be easy because we were so evenly matched despite his heart condition–my growing youthful power and his mature adult strength. If I eased up a little but kept the strain showing on my face, he probably wouldn't even know that I was faking it. Or I could bear down with all my might and try to put him down as fast as I could. I wasn't sure that I had the strength to carry out this plan, but I knew I could give it a try.

Something important hinged on my decision as I moved toward my manhood and Dad faced the decline of his. Should I let him win so that he could keep his pride, or should I try to beat him and see if his pride in me would overcome his own disappointment?

***

Five years after that pivotal arm wrestling match, Mom called me at the tiny college apartment I shared with three other guys. "Oh Johnny, Johnny, Johnny," she sobbed over and over until my aunt took the phone from her to tell me that my father had died that afternoon while plowing snow outside our home, this heart attack so swift and severe that he died before he could even shut off the truck or reach for his medicine. Everyone was relieved that he was taken without pain while doing work he enjoyed. At the funeral home, when someone remarked how natural he looked in his casket, I said that he had never looked so dead before. Then I quietly went to a rest room and cried for half an hour.

When I think back on that evening of those two very different arm wrestling matches so long ago, I'm still not sure what to make of my decision to pin my father's arm to the table. It had taken all of my strength. I can still see the moment of surprise as he watched his arm being bent down by the son he had carried home from the hospital. Did the years between my infancy and that evening seem to him as compressed and impossibly brief as the years between that evening and today, more than two decades later, seem to me? Did he think to himself, *Good lord, this boy is stronger than I am. When the hell did this happen? Why didn't I notice?* When his expression quickly turned to pride, did he really feel it, or was he using it to mask his own disappointment in himself at that moment? Or did he think, *I probably won't live much longer if my own son can beat me arm wrestling?*

I am now not far from my father's age when he had his first heart attack. I tell myself that I don't have his risk factors. My last cigarette was one I swiped from my father's pack a few years before I arm wrestled with him. I'm the first man in my family line to have a job where I go to an office rather than a work site. I get my exercise on a stationary bike and a pec-deck. I drink bottled water and eat ground turkey instead of my father's beer and steak.

Every now and then, when I can't sleep at night, I ask myself why I didn't let my father beat me at arm wrestling. I've told myself for years that he would have known if I had faked it and would have lost respect for me because he would have believed that I had lost respect for him. But doubt comes creeping. I beat my sister's jerk boyfriend because I wanted him to know that I was stronger, more important, more valuable, a better person than he was. I've always been called laid back and low key, just like my father–but at that moment I burned to let Mark know that he wasn't my equal.

When I sit in my office or teach my classes or ride my stationary bike and live my civilized life, can I allow myself the thought that I beat my father simply because I wanted him to know that I could?

***

Chapter 14
Ghosts

In junior high, we were told that parents in pioneer times often had lots of children to help with the burdens of farm work. When I learned this interesting fact, I thought, *Hmmm . . . some things never change.*

As a kid, our garden seemed to be simply a torture device designed by my parents to punish me. The potatoes were the worst. Each year, we planted more potatoes than one family could use in a decade—rows and rows of potatoes, more than half of our huge one-acre garden. We saved a few bushels of the best potatoes from each year's crop to use as "planters" for next year's crop. Every "eye" on the potato could grow a new potato plant, so we cut the planters into chunks, one eye to a chunk. By the end of the summer, each planter turned into about eight new potatoes.

The day before potato digging, Dad used the lawn mower to cut the plants themselves right down to the ground. I followed him and raked the cut plants into a pile, lifted them into the wheelbarrow, and took them out to feed to the farm animals, dividing them between the chickens and the cows.

By seven o'clock the next morning, Dad would have the garden tractor out and ready. The plow had a special attachment to hold a concrete block so that the extra weight would force the plow deeper into the soil, but the block didn't get it deep enough for Dad's taste. He had each of us kids take turns sitting on the block atop the plow, adding an extra seventy to one hundred fifty pounds (depending on the age and chubbiness of the child), enabling the plow to reach even the deepest spuds two feet below the surface.

As the potatoes rolled out of the dirt behind the plow, my sisters and I followed along with thirty-five-gallon buckets that we filled with potatoes, knocking as much dirt off as we could and separating the cut and damaged ones for immediate use. I had the added role of designated bucket-hauler. When my sisters called my name to announce a full bucket, I ran to them and lugged their buckets to the backyard where Mom had set up her potato-processing station.

She had saved every milk crate she could get her hands on because they were great for washing potatoes. I dumped the potatoes into the milk crates that Mom had stationed atop a bench, and Mom unleashed a vigorous spray from the garden hose. The dirt rolled like a mudslide, and in no time at all, the potatoes looked perfectly clean. Of course, they still weren't clean enough for Mom. She had me dump each clean-looking crate of potatoes into an empty crate to expose the dirt that was missed in the first washing. After Mom sprayed again, I dumped them into fresh crates twice more until they were spotless.

Once the potatoes were clean and dry, I dumped them into bushel baskets or burlap sacks for long-term storage–or sometimes straight into one of the five old refrigerators that I had buried on their backs three feet deep in various places around our farm as make-shift root cellars. Amazingly, those refrigerators could keep any crop from spoiling in the summer or freezing in the winter, and the potatoes would be safe for as long as we wanted. I often took a bucket out to one of the refrigerators in the middle of winter, kicked the snow off the door, and pulled out enough potatoes for that evening's dinner.

Potato digging went on all day. At around noon, we took a break for lunch, usually sandwiches that Mom had made the night before. Of course, we also had carrots and tomatoes from the garden. We drank gallons of Kool-Aid and sat around the yard looking at the many crates of potatoes we had already picked and the expanse of garden still pregnant with unseen spuds. Grandma joined us and poked the ground with her garden hoe, pronouncing her assessment of that year's crop. "Good bunch of taters," she would say.

Then Dad would stand up, clap his hands together, and ask, "Wadda ya say we get this job done?" and we staggered back into the garden until we finished sometime around dark. Then we wolfed down a hot meal of venison or fried chicken, corn on the cob, and, of course, fresh mashed potatoes. Afterwards, we each took a bath or shower, went to bed, and had nightmares of human-sized potatoes chasing us through the garden.

***

We also ate wild dandelion. Grandma often sent me to yank some from the ground while the flower was still yellow before it went to seed. She seared the leaves in ham grease, added little chunks of bacon and served it as a hot side dish. I mentioned once out of politeness that I liked it, and, unfortunately, Grandma never forgot. Each time I came home from college, she cooked dandelion. "It's your favorite," she'd say. I ate the big serving she loaded onto my plate, then asked for seconds, not wanting to hurt her feelings, but the truth was I had slowly come to despise those bitter little greens. And, I confess, it felt strange to make a side dish out of a weed that grew in the yard.

***

We had only two holiday food traditions in our household, not counting Thanksgiving turkey. One was sauerkraut on New Year's Day because Grandma was convinced it would make us prosperous for the coming year. Needless to say, I have not continued this tradition as an adult. Maybe that's why I'm still paying off my student loan.

The other tradition was far worse: eating oyster stew on Christmas Eve. I have no idea where this tradition originated. I only know that oyster stew is one of the worst foods a child could possibly be required to eat.

I sat at the kitchen table for an hour, nibbling crackers, sulking, and letting my oyster stew congeal–long after everyone else had finished their bowls. Finally, in a moment of desperation, I tipped the bowl to my mouth and gulped it all down as fast as I could, twisting my tongue to the side of my mouth in an unsuccessful attempt not to taste the vile stuff. Then I sat for five minutes with my eyes closed, trying not to move because even the slightest shift might make me throw up. When the nausea finally passed, I joined my family around the Christmas tree.

Mom would ask me, "Now that wasn't so bad, was it?" and I lied to her through the horrible taste that lingered in my mouth.

"No, Mom, I guess not."

***

Four of the words I dreaded most in life were Dad calling us kids together on a summer afternoon and saying, "Let's go mushroom hunting!" His suggestion made everybody else happy, but signaled misery for me.

I loved being in the woods, but my problem was finding the mushrooms. I could look straight at one and not see it because the grayish-brown mushroom blended with the grayish-brown soil. Searching for something I couldn't see made the whole activity frustrating and depressing. To this day, I still don't know how my parents and siblings could find these annoying little fungi. My sister June, with her coke-bottle glasses, could find them–even Grandma's ancient eyes could find more in ten minutes than I could in my whole life.

My frustration didn't end there–eating them was no picnic either. Mom sliced and batter-dipped the mushrooms, then fried them in a skillet. The greasy fog of frying mushrooms could bring me to the point of vomiting. It wasn't the smell exactly. If batter-dipped chicken had been frying, I'd have been thrilled. It was the fact that, no matter how hard I looked for them, the mushrooms had eluded me so many times. I sat through those meals sullenly chewing on a piece of buttered bread until my parents got sick of me and sent me to my room.

To this day, I still despise mushrooms and will avoid them whenever I can. Not long after I started my job at Asnuntuck, Bob, the academic dean who hired me, invited me to his home for dinner. Rather than asking what I liked to eat, he asked me if I didn't like any foods.

"Just mushrooms," I said.

"Really?" Bob replied. "The next time you see my car, take a look at the license plate."

I walked to the parking lot right after I left his office. His personalized plate read, "FUNGI." He raises mushrooms in his backyard as a hobby, I soon learned. Apparently, he grows some of the best mushrooms in the area. In his office, he has a large poster that shows all the different types of edible mushrooms. Bob told me Morels (*morchella deliciosa*, to be specific), the ones that terrorized me in my youth, are a highly prized delicacy.

When I went to his home for dinner, mushrooms were served as a side dish, rather than as an accent to the rack of lamb he and his wife had skillfully prepared. The meal was delicious, and after I told him my story about the psychological trauma of hunting mushrooms as a child, he didn't fire me for not sampling his homegrown delicacies.

***

For a couple of seemingly normal rural folks, Mom and Dad were pretty creative with their children's names. They showed very little of their creative potential with my older brothers' names–Norman Leon and William Ronald, Jr. (a.k.a. Ronnie). But after those two grew up and my parents faced their empty nest, they decided to bring into the world my two older sisters, Tamela May and Pamela Kay (a.k.a. Tammy and Pammy or Tam and Pam).

Those names would have been enough to get my parents some strange looks when introducing their kids. But Mom and Dad weren't finished. Twenty-six months later, another set of twins arrived (this time an accident). They gave my twin sister and me the cute names June Marie and John Mark. I thought the playground teasing that the names "Junie and Johnny" inspired was as bad as it could get.

Oh, but I was wrong.

When I was fifteen, Mom finally revealed that our original names were not June and John. Those were the names we were given about three months into our little lives after my parents got tired of the grief people heaped upon them for our *original* names. Although they have long ago been destroyed and replaced, our original birth certificates revealed my parents' true sense of the absurd.

At birth, our names were Jack and Jill.

***

I've noticed that Jim uses the phone at Jenny's house whenever he wants. He simply picks it up and starts dialing. I could never have done that as a child–or as a teenager, for that matter. My sisters and I were allowed to use the phone only in extreme circumstances. Mom controlled the phone, and I don't remember making more than a dozen calls from home before my eighteenth birthday. If someone called me, Mom glared at me while I whispered into the receiver. After three minutes, she told me to hang up and stop hogging the line.

If I needed to find out about a tenth-grade homework assignment, for example, Mom herself made the call and talked to the mother of one of my classmates.

Mom (into phone): Hi Helen. This is Thelma Sheirer. Sorry to bother you . . . How are you? . . . Good, good . . . Just fine, thanks. Hey, listen, I hate to bother you, but John forgot what chapters his history test is on. Could you please ask Marlene? . . . Thanks. (to me) She's asking Marlene. (into phone) Chapters eight and nine? Okay, I'll tell him. Thanks. (laughing) Oh, God, yes! John too. All of my kids. They'd forget their heads if they weren't screwed on. (more laughter) Okay, well thanks a lot Helen. Sorry I bothered you . . . You too. Bye-bye.

The next day, Marlene asked why I didn't call her myself. Rather than reveal that I wasn't allowed to use the phone, I told her Mom wanted to feel involved in my education. Then I'd slink away, embarrassed that Mom treated me like a six year old.

Ironically, Mom's attitude toward my phone use changed a few years later when I was in college. If I went more than a week without calling her, she scolded, "Is it so much trouble to pick up the phone?"

***

We had party-line telephone service, meaning four neighboring houses each had a different phone number but were somehow on the same line. Mom often picked up the phone, listened for a second or two, then said, "Oh, sorry, Margie. No, no rush." Then she'd hang up and wait for half an hour to be sure our neighbor had finished her call.

Now it seems like every home has a phone line for the parents, one for each kid over six, one for the Internet, one for the fax machine–not to mention about six cell phones, each with its own goofy song instead of a standard ring. Jim would probably think I was telling a whopper if I tried to explain party lines to him.

Grandma was quite fond of the party line. One of her favorite activities was lifting the phone as quietly as possible to see if anyone else was talking. If she was lucky enough to pick up while someone was in the middle of a call, she pressed the receiver to her ear and covered the mouthpiece with both hands, listening intently. She could do this for hours, but I'm not sure what she heard that kept her attention. Once, when no one else was home, I picked up the phone to find a couple neighbors chatting. They were so focused on the weather and the activities of distant relatives with names like Bertha or Hephzibah and the fate of Tiny-Joe's ailing pick-up truck that I got bored after about a minute and hung up.

***

As Grandma's hearing failed, she had someone from the phone company install a high-volume earpiece on the phone. This newfangled contraption helped her enjoy the phone even more. Her favorite conversation partner was my Aunt Nellie, Grandma's daughter-in-law, who had been married to Dad's brother, Uncle Harvey, until his death when I was about ten.

We had loved Uncle Harvey, a funny man who had a wonderful farm back in the woods with lots of animals and a pond for swimming and fishing. But we weren't always fond of Aunt Nellie because she gave us the two Christmas presents every kid knows are obligation gifts: socks and underwear. We gritted our teeth every Christmas, smiled, sang out, "Thank you, Aunt Nellie," and kissed her on the cheek for Grandma's benefit.

After Uncle Harvey died, Nellie and Grandma became the best of friends. "The Merry Widows' Club," Dad called their get-togethers, and Mom would laugh. Not too many years later, Dad would spin in his grave as Mom became a charter member of that particular club.

When the phone rang, Mom (usually) or Dad (only if Mom wasn't home) answered it. I could hear Nellie through the high-volume receiver saying "Heeeyyy-looowww" in a cloying, annoying way. Mom or Dad's face fell as they put down the phone to get Grandma. Then she and Nellie would spend the afternoon on the phone, talking so loud that everyone in the house could hear both sides of the conversation. Their most common topic was, of course, the faults of everybody in the family, usually including people within earshot of their booming voices.

***

My parents seemed to be very good friends and life partners, if not often affectionate or romantic. In fact, I don't even remember ever seeing them kiss or hearing them argue, but they must have done both at one time or another. The closest I ever saw Mom and Dad come to a full-scale blow-up happened when I was about seven. We kids were playing in the yard when Mom came running out of the house with Dad trailing behind her. She hissed between clenched teeth, "I'm leaving this place, and I'm never coming back! Never!"

We stared at her as she hustled into the car, tore out of the driveway and down the dirt road leading away from our farm. This was a woman who didn't get her driver's license until her early forties. She never drove fast, but this day she raced down the road in a plume of dust. My sisters started to cry and ask Dad what had happened. I sniffled, trying to be strong and stoic but dying inside at the thought of Mom never coming back. Dad kept repeating softly, "Don't worry kids. She'll be back," but Mom was nearly to the end of the road. I knew in my little heart that if her car went out of sight, I'd never see her again.

With a few yards to spare, Mom's car stopped. She sat still for a full two minutes while we mumbled through our tears, "Mom's gonna come back . . . please come back." Then her car slowly started to back up.

Mom hated backing a car, so this took incredible will on her part. She backed about one hundred yards to our cabin, a journey that took her nearly five minutes of fits and starts. Dad hardly breathed the whole time–partly hoping for Mom to come back, partly worrying about the car's rear bumper. She turned around in the cabin yard and drove home to the waiting embraces of her children.

As she walked up the steps to the house with four kids crying and laughing and hanging from her, she shot a vicious look at Dad who had kept his distance from our celebration.

I never learned what had made Mom so upset. By the next day, my parents restored their normal peace. But that moment when Dad saw the look that Mom gave him on her return, his face turned pale, and he immediately walked to the shed where he spent the next couple of hours rearranging his tools.

***

Mom's first husband died in a motorcycle accident while she was pregnant with Norman, my oldest brother, in the late 1940s. Although we still sometimes visited Mom's first mother-in-law (we called her "Grandma Mason"), no one ever talked very much about her first husband. In fact, I don't even know his first name.

I once saw a photograph of him while snooping through some things Mom had left lying out on the kitchen table. My sister Tam told me that the man pictured in his military uniform was Norman's father.

Although I only looked at his face for a few minutes, the dead man in the photo haunted me. I spent a great deal of time wondering about how I might have been different if he were my father. I would look different, certainly, but would I be better looking or worse? Dad was a good-looking guy, but so was the man in the photo. I might be taller because Dad was only five feet, seven inches. Would I still think the same thoughts and feel the same feelings if I had been born this different-looking person named John Mason instead of John Sheirer?

The one thing I knew for sure was that I would have liked having a name like Mason that people could spell and pronounce correctly on the first try.

***

Grandma was a brilliant woman, but she sometimes had trouble remembering what happened an hour before. She could, however, tell stories with vivid detail about events that took place before our old farmhouse had indoor plumbing. Her favorite subject was "Old Billy Hessong," a friend of the family long ago when Grandma was a young wife and mother. He rented the family log cabin and helped my grandfather take in crops, tend the farm animals, and cut trees for lumber and firewood.

Throughout my childhood, I heard so many of Grandma's stories about Old Billy Hessong that I became convinced I knew him. He died a decade before my birth, but I felt in my little-boy imagination that I had been by his side for dozens of adventures.

The Old Billy Hessong in her stories was both larger than life and completely human. He was a war hero many times over, a great prankster and master storyteller, a crafty woodsman who could live off berries and shrubs for as long as he liked, and a legendary hunter who bagged more deer and bear than anyone in local history. Grandma's tales also revealed a man with human flaws. Once he disappeared for a year and didn't tell anyone where he went, leaving one day without a word, then returning as if he'd never been gone. She even once told us that he slipped tiny slivers of lead into the ginseng roots that he sold to city slickers–more lead, more weight, more money.

As a child, I thought Grandma was the oldest person in the world. She had lived on our farm for more years than I could comprehend and had been a widow longer than my own parents had been married. Her stories seemed to be from another age of the earth, and I pictured them in the grainy black and white of distant memory. I once asked Grandma if she knew Lincoln, a question that did not go over well with her. Her grumpiness was legendary, and my sisters and I knew not to cross her. She scoffed at our first experiences with girlfriends and boyfriends, calling our early romances "silliness." She refused to carry a cane but walked around our farm leaning on a garden hoe, occasionally chopping at the ground to prove to anyone who might be watching that she could still work as hard as she always had.

She also had a soft side, which, unfortunately, her grandchildren didn't really appreciate. She often walked through the door connecting our kitchen to hers and ran her fingers through our hair while we ate our breakfast. We flinched at her affection and wolfed down our cereal before running to catch the school bus that wasn't even due for half an hour. She made us pick bushels of vegetables for any visiting relative– even though they had overflowing gardens of their own at home. With the railing in one hand and her garden hoe in the other, she climbed to the tub in our upstairs bathroom to take a bath every week. When she kissed us each night before she went to bed, and we called out, "Goodnight Grandma, see you in the morning," she walked away murmuring, "Oh, if I live that long. It's a horrible thing when a body gets old . . ." her voice trailing off as she shuffled away to her bedroom.

One night while sitting at the kitchen table, she told me the story of how Old Billy Hessong had a stroke and spent the last twenty years of his life unable to walk or talk, confined to my little upstairs bedroom–in the very same bed where I slept each night.

Of course, Grandma told me this particular story right before my bedtime when I was nine years old, an age where the borders between fantasy and reality are blurred, to say the least. As I lay awake in bed that night, I was unsure of only one thing: *Could the ghost of Old Billy Hessong read my thoughts?* That his ghost existed, I was certain. That his ghost was there in my bedroom, I was certain. That his ghost could see and hear me, I was certain. That his ghost had been present in my room every night of my life up to that point, I was all too certain.

Hello ghost of Old Billy Hessong, I thought in my terrified brain that night as I stared at the ceiling, taking care not to look around the room for fear of seeing his ghost–or to close my eyes, giving his ghost the opportunity for a sneak attack. *I've heard lots of stories about you from Grandma, Mr. Ghost, and I feel like I know you. I'm very sorry you had a stroke and had to stay shut up in my room in this bed for twenty years until you died. I wish you could have gone outside to hunt bear and collect ginseng roots. I like you very much ghost of Old Billy Hessong. I hope you like me too. I'll try not to close my eyes and fall asleep tonight, but if I do, please, sir, please don't kill me.*

In case his ghost couldn't read my thoughts, I repeated the whole speech in a strangled whisper, loud enough for any ghost to detect, but soft enough for my sisters, parents, and grandmother asleep in various rooms of the house not to hear.

Eventually, I did drift off to sleep that night, and, to my amazement, the ghost of Old Billy Hessong didn't kill me. I survived the next night as well, and the night after that, and every night that I slept in that little bed in that little room until I packed up and went to college at age eighteen. Over the years, I came to a truce with the ghost of Old Billy Hessong. In exchange for him not killing me in my sleep, I would occasionally mull over his stories, reflecting on his life and keeping him alive in my memory and my dreams. Not long after I left home, my twin sister June (who apparently either never heard Billy's story or didn't believe in ghosts) dropped out of college and took over my room, replacing Billy's stroke-bed with her own.

As I have grown into adulthood and early middle age, the stories of Old Billy Hessong have faded. I no longer feel the same sense of having known him that I felt as a child. When I think about him now, I mostly think about how childhood imaginations can be strange and amazing things. But Old Billy Hessong's story has never completely left my thoughts, and recently I've begun to think of him and Grandma in a new way. I've realized that no one takes a casual friend into her home for twenty years. Such an act requires an immense commitment of time and resources, to say nothing of the psychological dedication of giving your life over to the long-term care of another human being. He must have had some family to care for him after his stroke. There must have been a hospital or institution that could have taken him in. But instead, Grandma, a young, recently widowed woman with a house full of kids, brought this bed-ridden man into her home.

I needed more than thirty years to understand something that I couldn't at age nine. Only one kind of person would take in someone and provide twenty years of care. After decades of Grandma's Old Billy Hessong stories bouncing around the edges of my consciousness, I've finally realized that my prim, prudish grandmother and Old Billy Hessong must have been lovers.

No one in my family, least of all Grandma herself, would have mentioned their relationship. My family's gossip was one of two types: rumors about people outside our family that could possibly be true, or rumors about people within the family that were extremely unlikely. Something that might be true about someone in the family simply wasn't proper gossip material. The fact that Grandma's relationship with Billy was never mentioned around our house serves only to give it more credence. The whole situation was probably something that all of the adults knew about but simply did not discuss when they gathered around the Thanksgiving dinner table while I sat eavesdropping on the grown-ups from the kids' table in Grandma's adjoining kitchen.

Now that I'm an adult too, the whole situation makes me see Grandma in a different light. She's no longer just the grumpy family matriarch holding court at mid-summer family reunions–"Grandma Sheirer" as she was known to nearly everyone in the area. I now also see her as "Annie," a young woman who had fallen in love, married, bore five children, outlived three of them, became a widow at the tragically early age of forty-two, built bombs and bullets in a World War I munitions factory, founded her own one-room schoolhouse, discovered love again, and then lived a different tragedy when her new love soon fell victim to a debilitating long-term illness.

Not long after Dad died, Mom told me the story of moving into our home when she married Dad after her first husband was killed. Dad brought her and her toddler son to live in his childhood home down the hall from my bedroom where Old Billy Hessong lay slowly dying. For the first few months, Grandma wouldn't even speak to Mom, who assumed it was because, in those days, a young man marrying a widow with a child was a minor scandal. Now I know the real reason Grandma was cold to her. Mom got a second chance at a full life and true love after her first husband died–Grandma's second chance turned into a lifetime as noble widow and two decades as nursemaid to a broken man. Grandma and Mom only became real friends after Dad died and Grandma saw her as an equal in widowhood.

If I could go back to my childhood knowing what I know now, I would be less inclined to pull away from Grandma's touch and sneak to the other room when she repeated her stories for the fifth time. I would try to connect with her and her mysterious past, to let her know that I knew about her pain and that I knew she was so much more than the shriveled old woman she had become late in life. I would have let her know that she could tell me all about it, that I would keep my mouth shut. I'd have let her know that I loved her more for the secret we could have shared.

When Grandma was in her early nineties, she broke her hip–a death sentence at her age. She had been descending the stairs after her weekly bath. Near the bottom, she lost her grip on the railing and tumbled only a few feet, but that was enough. The doctors did what they could, but Grandma needed full-time care, much more than Mom could provide as she approached age seventy. So Grandma spent the last year of her life in the "rest home" operated by one of our distant cousins. Her mind and memory, so sharp for so long, quickly failed during that painful, final year, her stories replaced by crying and begging to go home.

Shortly before her death, I went to see her. By then I was nearly thirty, a full-grown man. When I told my confused Grandma who I was, she had trouble believing I wasn't the little nine-year-old boy who listened to so many of her stories. She seemed upset by her confusion, going from tears to slurred curses and back again in her frustration and pain as she writhed atop the bed. I rose to leave so that she could calm down and rest, but just for a moment her eyes cleared, and she was herself again.

"Billy," she said in a strong voice, grabbing my hands. "It's so good to see you again, Billy. Oh, I love you, Billy."

I assumed she thought I was my father, her son William, Jr., dead for nearly a decade then, or her own husband William, Sr., gone for more than fifty years. We held hands, gazing into each other's eyes.

After a moment, I said, "I'm glad to see you, Annie. I love you too." Then she sighed and lay back on her pillows and drifted off to sleep.

A month later, she died. I'm still not sure which Billy she saw that day. It's most comforting to think she had one last chance to say goodbye to a young and healthy "Old Billy Hessong."

***

Chapter 15
Both

By seven o'clock on January second, my last morning in Pennsylvania, I can hear the loggers from the cabin's porch. They're getting an early start again, undaunted by yesterday's rain that must have covered the mountain with mud. I know they have every right to cut the trees. They're working hard to make an honest living, but it still breaks my heart to think of what the mountain will look like this summer.

After eating some oatmeal and packing to leave, I take a quick walk on the hill, soaking in the view of Lybarger Church on one side and the house, barn, field, cabin, and mountain on the other. The quarry above is shrouded in fog. Maybe on my next trip, I'll camp overnight there and wake to see the view from inside the fog. Would the valley be as invisible as the quarry is from here this morning? If so, I'll wait for the air to clear, gradually revealing my childhood home.

***

The cabin's electricity goes out for a while, and I can't use the TV, radio, computer, hair dryer, or toaster. The hot water will be gone before long because I used it for a long shower this morning. For a brief moment, I feel like a real pioneer.

What must it have been like for the first settlers here? Everyday life would have centered around keeping a fire going at all times in the stove to heat the house, cook the food, and, probably once a month or so, take a hot bath. Only oil lamps and candles would illuminate the dark nights. There could be no phone to call if someone was lurking around outside. In the earliest days, the threat of Indians unhappy about white incursion would be constant.

Of course, even without electricity, I'm no pioneer. I have a battery-powered laptop computer, a cell phone, and a flush toilet. I have hundreds of people within five miles and a car to drive to those people in a few short minutes. And if an Indian shows up here, I suppose we can talk about all the Tony Hillerman novels we've read.

I had been using the blow dryer and the toaster at the same time when the power went off. That same combination will throw the circuit breaker at my house in Connecticut every time, but the cabin's breakers are fine. For a moment, I remember yesterday's rainstorm and consider the possibility that the rain and winds could have knocked a tree down onto a power line. But that would most likely have happened yesterday afternoon or last night–not mid-morning the day after the storm. Of course, I'd love to blame it on the Lords and their logging, but there are no power lines on Wills Mountain.

Unexplained electricity outages happened about once a month in my youth. My parents would say that the electric company must be "working on the lines" again. When the power comes back on as mysteriously as it went out after about half an hour, I remember that Janet mentioned something on the phone last week about the possibility of the electric company "working on the lines" during my visit. It's strangely comforting to know that some things haven't changed.

***

As I drive away from the cabin, I keep the camera on the car seat in case I see something that I want to photograph. But no matter how many photos I take, I'm never going to be able to capture what this place looks like and means to me after all these years. No matter how many words I write, I'll never be able to put on paper exactly what I've experienced here.

Coming here gives me a powerful and contradictory mix of emotions and memories–bits of pride at the hardworking farm boy I was, bits of embarrassment at the naïve hillbilly kid I was, and lots of confusion about how I got from here to where I am now. Not that I've made such huge steps up in life. I'm only a community college teacher, after all, someone snooty university types consider academic trailer-trash. But I've taken a very different course from what my life would have been if I had stayed here and not felt an overwhelming compulsion to leave that began at age thirteen.

***

The weather report for my drive back to Connecticut calls for freezing rain and snow, but it's only cloudy as I start home. In fact, the roads are dry. A few miles north of Bedford, I even see a ray of sunshine deepening the shadows on the gray and white hillsides. I've hit a calm window between the heavy rains of yesterday and the snow and ice that will surely be here tomorrow.

Along Route 220, large rock cliffs surround the highway where it was literally carved into the mountain in gashes as deep as the quarry on both sides. As a kid, I marveled at the amount of work it must have taken to carve this highway from the hills. I pictured hundreds of men with nothing but picks and shovels working for months or even years in burning sun, stinging rain, chilling wind, and blinding snow.

Dad later told me they did the work with explosives, backhoes, and bulldozers, but I still like my version. In fact, I could even imagine myself on the hillside, swinging a pick for the millionth time to chip away one more chunk of rock.

Back in high school civics class, we were taught that the American interstate highway system was built much more rugged than it needed to be for simple car and truck travel. The highways could handle vehicles as big as tanks or serve as airplane runways–all in the event that some outside force invaded American soil, and our government needed to mobilize its army quickly to defend the nation.

That makes a lot more sense than a million smart bombs.

***

I get a little chuckle when I see a sign telling me I'm driving on Bud Shuster Highway. My very first political activity came in 1978 working for Bud Shuster, the congressional representative from our district. Someone had arranged for several kids in my class to go to the polls on election day and hand out flyers and buttons for him. Some of the voters smiled and some scowled and shoved the flyers back at me.

Later, Grandma, a Democrat from way back who voted for Franklin Roosevelt four times, asked me if I knew that Shuster was a Republican. I barely even knew what that meant. I was just glad to get out of school for the day. Now I get the heebie-jeebies knowing I worked for a Republican. As penance, I've waved Carter, Mondale, Dukakis, Clinton, and Gore posters every four years since.

Bud Shuster served in congress from 1973 until January 2001 when he retired after being sanctioned by the House Ethics Committee for several problems, including flagrant violations of the rules governing the receiving of gifts. But it's no surprise to see a highway named after him considering he was the chair of the House Transportation and Infrastructure Committee for six years.

Bud Shuster's son, car dealer Bill Shuster, is the representative here now. Also a Republican, he won a special election to fill his father's seat. I remember playing basketball against him in high school. He was the only player on either team with a tan in the middle of winter because his family went on a tropical cruise for Christmas, something unheard of in my family. He was a decent player but a big crybaby who complained bitterly to the referees throughout the game. In one of the wittiest things I ever heard in a high school gymnasium, a Hyndman fan once yelled at him, "Don't like the officiating? Write a letter to your congressman!"

***

On the drive back to Connecticut, I see several places where timber has been stripped from mountains along the highway. These places look awful and barren, and I can't help but notice them. I used to shake my head when I saw something like this, then think, *what a shame* as I drove on. Ten seconds later, I'd be passing beautiful forested hillsides again, the treeless places out of my thoughts very quickly at sixty-five miles per hour.

When I come back this summer, Wills Mountain won't be a fleeting moment along the highway like these places are. From the farm and cabin, the mountain will be barren for several years. Everything will eventually grow back, but I'm not looking forward to waiting.

***

I thought I noticed a faint whiff of something foul when I put air in the tires half an hour into the drive back to Connecticut. The source was elusive, so I looked at my jacket, my hands, the tires–but I didn't think to look at my feet.

Two hours later, when I step out of the car to fill the gas tank, I see that the toe-end of my left shoe, a hiker with deep tread, is carrying about half a pound of cow poop. It must have gotten there as I took pictures of the barn just before leaving the farm.

So I spend about five minutes vigorously dragging my foot through the snow near the gas station, trying to get every speck of the stuff out of my shoe before I get back in the car. I must look like I'm doing a poor imitation of a tribal dance.

After a moment, I look up and notice a couple with two young kids staring at me. What can I do? I smile and wave and return to my poop-removal duties. It's work that has to be done.

***

The last thing I want to do while driving though upstate New York is stop at the highway rest area, but I have to. I bring in a book, lock the door, and sit down.

Soon someone comes in and sits in the stall next to me. He's wearing huge work boots that must be about size sixteen, so I name him "Mr. Boots." After a moment, he begins whispering very softly. I can't tell if he's whispering to me or to himself. I can't make out any of the words. I'm not even sure they actually are words.

Then I hear a strange crinkling sound, followed by repeated crunching and more crinkling. I'm confused for about half a minute, but then it hits me. Mr. Boots is eating chips while sitting on a public toilet.

Without warning, a chip falls to the floor and skitters a couple inches into my stall. It's one of those curlicue corn chips that I really like. We are both silent for about ten seconds.

"Are you going to eat that?" Mr. Boots asks in a clear, intelligent, almost refined voice.

"No thank you," I reply.

"Okay," he says, and reaches down to pluck the chip from the floor with a large, clean, well-manicured hand. The hand and the chip disappear from my view, moving upward.

A fraction of a second later, I hear the crunch.

***

Driving through Scranton is bad, but going from Danbury to Hartford on Route 84 may be just as bad. The three lanes are narrow and the traffic heavy. Concrete retainers line both sides of the highway, promising certain death for motorists who stray two feet outside the right or left lane. The speed limit is fifty-five, but people routinely hit ninety. Just as many trucks careen around here as they do in Scranton, even if Harry Chapin never commemorated them in a song. The reflective paint on signs is so worn I have trouble reading the words at night–and I always seem to be making this part of the drive at night on the way back from a long, tiring trip.

Signs here indicate that the left lane is for passing, the center for travel, and the right for slow vehicles–but that's a joke. On the way through Waterbury, I see a guy in my rearview mirror weaving through all three lanes and making a reckless nuisance of himself. I can smell his cigarette and hear him shouting on a cell phone as he drives by–even with my windows up. I'm certain now–drivers like this guy make this part of the trip worse than Scranton.

To my joy and amazement a few miles up the road, a cop had pulled this jerk over. I blow my horn in celebration as I pass. Maybe justice exists, if only on this small scale.

***

At thirteen, I realized for the first time that I would not remain at home forever. A friend at school asked me if I planned to "take over the farm" after high school. I couldn't even imagine doing that, but what else would there be for me if I had stayed? Would I have worked at a factory down the road in Cumberland, like a few of my classmates' older brothers? Would I have started some kind of business? What did I know about business? Would I have stayed at home until my parents finally ordered me to leave?

Like so many other young people, I left my home at eighteen, and the little farm that had nurtured me has long ago become a part of my past. When I ventured off to college, then graduate school, then the work world, the place where I grew up no longer seemed like home.

But once, in 1987, after I had my master's degree but was having enormous difficulty finding a teaching job, I sat in my little efficiency apartment preparing to go to my job at a fast-food restaurant. I could see the apartment's dirt basement through the kitchen's rotting floorboards. I had no car and went to my minimum-wage job by city bus, and the rent (which I didn't have) was due the next day. So I indulged myself in a little fantasy about what my life could have been like if I had stayed in Pennsylvania instead of leaving for college as soon as I possibly could.

I would have borrowed a few dollars from my parents after high school graduation and moved to Bedford to get a job–washing dishes in a restaurant, waxing the floor at the roller-rink, or bagging groceries at the Giant Eagle.

Maybe I could have worked at the *Bedford Gazette* newspaper, taking a class now and then at Allegheny Community College in Cumberland. I would have started in the print shop, getting sweaty and grimy each day, driving my cheap car back to my boarding house room each night to scrub the ink stains from my hands and ignore the tinny country music played all night on cheap transistor radios by my drunken housemates. All the older workers at the paper would have called me "Hey, Kid," but soon they would have learned that I could work as hard as any of them, thanks to my years on the farm.

One day I would have made a point of running into the youngest reporter there, probably an ambitious guy no more than thirty, on the way to the parking lot. I'd begin slowly, nodding and saying hello to him. After a week or so, I'd start a conversation–an easy topic such as sports. He'd be impressed that I knew a few of the Pittsburgh Pirates' batting averages. He might even remember me from last year's basketball game against Bedford. "You're the kid who played defense and rebounded, aren't you?"

Eventually, we might sit together at lunch in the cafeteria, and he'd notice that I could speak pretty articulately about why Carter wasn't nearly as bad a president as everyone seemed to think. Before long, he'd come around to the question I wanted him to ask: "Why is a smart kid like you working in the print shop instead of going to college?" I'd tell him that I was saving my money and taking some community college classes, but I really wanted to try my hand at writing for the paper someday. It would turn out that he had a throwaway assignment—some obscure regulation up for debate at a town meeting or the obligatory obituary—and he'd toss it my way.

"Do good work on this one, kid," he'd say, "and there may be more."

I wouldn't just do good work—I would do historically excellent work, better than he'd ever seen. He'd arrange a meeting with an editor, get me some part-time assignments. I'd keep working in the print shop and do the assignments in my free time until they'd beg me to join the staff as a full-time reporter, the pay twice what I'd been earning, writing anything I wanted.

I'd make enough money to get a reliable car and move from my boarding house to our cabin, where I would install a real bathroom, doing all the work myself with advice from Dad. I'd finish my associate's degree at Allegheny, then commute to Penn State part-time to earn my bachelor's in sociology and master's in journalism. Within a few years, I'd be a junior editor at the paper and buy the farm from my parents, letting them live there as long as they liked, rent free. They would swell with pride at how well I repaid them for all their work and expense in raising me. When I made big money as editor-in-chief of the paper at age thirty, I'd send them on yearly vacations wherever they wanted to go.

Meanwhile, I'd no longer be the nerdy high school kid who didn't date. Maturity and success would make me more attractive, and I'd be the most eligible bachelor in Bedford County. Glenda Walters, my unrequited high school love, would return from college to teach first grade at Hyndman Primary. We'd have a long courtship, marry when we were thirty-three, honeymoon for a month in the Australian outback, live together in the cabin, and buy back all of the property on Wills Mountain that the Lords had purchased from my family decades before. We would stay thin and athletic by climbing to the quarry at least one hundred times a year.

By age forty, the local Democratic Party would recruit me to run for Congress against Bud Shuster, the long-term incumbent Republican, but I'd turn them down because I liked editing the paper. My weekly syndicated columns would win the Pulitzer Prize and then be collected into a bestseller that would win the National Book Award. A two-book, six-figure deal would be offered for my memoir and first novel. Oprah would e-mail me. And my behind-the-scenes work would help a

Democrat from our district get elected to Congress for the first time in decades. The newly elected Gore administration would call about a White House speechwriting job.

How many of our kids Glenda and I would bring to the premiere of the movie based on my life was the only part of my fantasy I hadn't finalized when the phone rang to pull me back to my apartment in 1987. I was surprised that the phone still worked considering how long it had been since I had paid the bill. My student loan company was calling. They wanted to know when I planned to repay the $25,000 I had borrowed for the master's degree that wasn't getting me a teaching job.

I told them that John had died a few months ago. "Yes, very sad, all that potential wasted," I said. "Very sad, indeed."

Of course, things might have gone differently if I had stayed in Pennsylvania. I might have married a nice local gal who put on two hundred pounds and had seven kids in five years and who continued to get pregnant each time I so much as kissed her on the cheek. The boys would be in juvenile detention centers by age thirteen, and the girls would be pregnant by fifteen. I'd be a grandfather by age thirty-five. When I hit forty, the police would be hauling in my grandchildren because they would already be shoplifting or breaking windows at school. I would have ballooned up to three hundred pounds from the stress of constant near-foreclosure on the farm because all of my llamas had been swept away in a freak flood . . . three times.

And I wouldn't even have a creative outlet for expressing my troubles because I wouldn't live in a trailer park, so even Jerry Springer wouldn't invite me to be a guest on his show.

***

I'm glad I took the path I did–even though it led me away from the farm. I miss where I was raised and what I had growing up there. I had strong, loving, wise parents with a sense of humor. I had a close relationship with a grandmother who was the most powerful person in the family. I had sisters who drove me nuts but were always there for me. I had brothers who were physically distant but who connected me with the past. I had teachers who cared and did as much as they could with limited resources. I had a few close friends. I had the opportunity to experience, understand, and appreciate hard work. I had a close tie with the miracle of nature. I had the realization that money isn't as important as the world tries to make it. I had a real home for eighteen years. I had a looming, distant, omnipresent stone quarry to remind me then that

I could reach for something more and to remind me now that I have a past that matters. I had a cabin that would one day host my return.

But I still remember all the things I *wished* I had back then: brothers closer to my own age, more friends living nearby, more chances for activities with kids in town, more time spent goofing off and being a kid instead of working on the farm, a little adventure, a girlfriend–maybe a UFO visit or two.

Even though I did my best for years to pretend my odd upbringing didn't have anything to do with my adulthood, I realize now that the boyhood I had helped form the man I am. And I'm not a finished product, by any means. That upbringing will continue to shape me, partly for the better, partly for the worse–mostly for the better, I hope. My childhood was mostly happy and mostly normal, and I've mostly come to understand its wonders as well as its limits.

***

At the end of my journey, I pull into my driveway in Somers, Connecticut, miles and years from that little farm on Sheirer Road at the base of Wills Mountain in the village of Madley, southern Bedford County, southwest central Pennsylvania. I'm going to bring in my stuff from the car and call Jenny.

I can't wait to see her.

But even as I'm thinking about her, I'm already planning my next trip. From now on, when I pack for the cabin, I'll tell anyone who asks that I'm going "home." My trip to the farm after twenty years has taught me the most important lesson of my life, that I am blessed with two homes: the one I was born into and the one I went out into the world and made for myself.

I love them both.

***

Epilogue

One of Jenny's good friends died recently, and she asked me the other day what I wanted done after my death.

I confessed to her that I hadn't thought much on the subject beyond signing my organ-donor card.

"Would it be a health hazard to spread my ashes in the corners of all my classrooms?" I asked, only half joking. With the history of air-quality problems at Asnuntuck, my ashes could probably go unnoticed for years in the ventilation system.

I've given the issue some serious thought since then, and here's what I really want. (Gosh, I hope someone actually reads this book all the way to the end before I die and remembers this part.) Please, no funeral homes or processions or caskets or ministers who never knew me. A party at the college would be nice–with a few friends telling stories about what a knuckle-head I could be ... some students retelling the worst of my classroom jokes ... maybe even some folks reading from this book (multiple autographed copies for sale in the college bookstore).

As for my body, I want to be cremated and have half my ashes scattered somewhere at Asnuntuck (surprise me with the exact location). The other half could be taken up to the top of the quarry and sprinkled over the edge. My divided ashes would reflect the two most significant places in my life: where I am and where I've been.

And, I must admit, I would certainly enjoy trespassing on Lord Land forever.

***

Acknowledgments

I'm grateful to everyone who helped with this book. My heartfelt thanks go especially to these wonderful people:

To my sister Tam (Sheirer) Chomas for her recollections, family photos, and memorabilia (and for being a great sister).

To Tam's husband Dale Chomas for his research into our family history (and he married Tam anyway–go figure).

To my grandmother, Annie Katherine Stuby Sheirer, and her brother, my Great Uncle Clarence E. Stuby, for their writings on the history of our farm and the local area.

To Janet and Fred Willis for their hospitality and wonderful care of my childhood home and the cabin, as well as Janet's knowledge of local history.

To Cathy Jouzokas for insightful feedback and editing advice–and for telling me about her own experience growing up in her corner of the middle of nowhere.

To my colleagues, students, and friends at Asnuntuck Community College for their interest in my writing.

To Mark DeFoe, a wonderful poet and my first and only official creative writing teacher all those years ago in college. The front quote is from his beautiful book of poems, *Bringing Home Breakfast* (published by Black Willow, 1982).

To Bob Winston for his wisdom, friendship, dignity–and for not making me eat mushrooms.

To Suzanne Strempek Shea and Kevin O'Hara for their inspiring books and their quotes on the back cover.

And, especially, to Jenny for her understanding, caring, and love, her deep respect for and knowledge of nature, her patience while listening to my endless stories, her encouragement while I wrote these stories down, her sense of humor at suggesting that the title of this book should be revised from "mostly" to "halfway" normal–and to her sons Rob and Jim for helping me see through young eyes again.

I'm also grateful to the editors of these print and internet publications where portions of this book have been previously published, sometimes in different versions: *Artella, The Backpacker, Clever, Drifter's Oasis, Ethical Oasis, E: Thought, Foliate Oak, Free the Writer, Full Circle Journal, The Gloob, The Glut, The Green Tricycle,*

Holy Ignorance, Humor is Relative, Laughter Loaf, Lifewriter's Digest, The Ladies Room, The Littoral, Mocha Memoirs, The Nature of Writing News, Nice Stories, Nights and Weekends, Open Wide, Parenthetical Note, Perfectland, Pindeldyboz, Poor Mojo's Almanac(k), Pulse, Really Small Talk, Retrozine, Seven Seas Magazine, The Sidewalk's End, Slant, Springfield Journal, The Square Table, Storyhouse, Storymania, The Stump, The Surface, Under Obstruction, We Love Writers, The Wissahickon, Word Riot, and *Zine 5.*

    The section about butchering in Chapter 5 won first prize in the Southern California Genealogical Society's 2003 Writer's Contest.

    The section about Hyndman in Chapter 10 won special honorable mention in the Southern California Genealogical Society's 2003 Writer's Contest.

    The section about the lost list in Chapter 10 won third prize in the Seventh Annual John W. Paton Storytelling Contest sponsored by Russell Library in Middletown, Connecticut.

    A manuscript comprised of excerpts from this book was honored as a finalist for the Sante Fe Writers Project Literary Award.

    The back cover author photo is by Virginia Patsun. The front cover photo is by the author.

    This is a work of memoir, relying heavily on both memory and imagination. In some cases, people outside my own family have been partially fictionalized as amalgams of actual people, and names have been changed to protect anonymity. Resemblance to actual people, events, and places carries no malice. (Except for the guy who blabbed about Santa not existing–I still can't stand that kid.) Any errors are due to lapses in the author's memory and imagination.

***

About the Author

A teacher of writing, public speaking, and literature for two decades, John Sheirer (pronounced *shy-er*) has been twice honored by Who's Who Among America's Teachers. He holds a B.A. in from West Virginia Wesleyan College, an M.A. in from Ohio University, and has done doctoral study at Indiana University of Pennsylvania. Since 1993, he has been a full-time faculty member at Asnuntuck Community College in Enfield, Connecticut. He recently designed a memoir writing course to help students at Asnuntuck write about their own lives.

Over the years, he has also taught at Ohio University, Parkersburg Community College, Bowling Green State University, Mount Holyoke College, American International College, Springfield College, Manchester Community College, and Wesleyan University.

Between teaching jobs, he has paid the bills as a video store clerk, movie theater projectionist, restaurant cook and dishwasher, house painter, voice-over performer, college dorm director, farm laborer, journalist, proofreader, and public relations writer. For a brief time in graduate school, he even sold his own plasma to a medical lab.

In addition to twenty limited edition chapbooks of poetry, he is the author of these full-length books:
Saying My Name: Selected Poems, 1982-2002
From the Projection Booth: Three Screenplays
Free Chairs: Essays and Stories
Shut Up and Speak! Essential Guidelines for Public
    Speaking in School, Work, and Life

His essays, stories, poems, letters, photos, and educational materials have been published in print and online in the following publications, among others: *The Athens News, Brady Magazine, Chalkdust Online, The Christian Science Monitor, The Chronicle of Higher Education, Clean Sheets, Clever, Ethical Oasis, Faculty Shack, The Foliate Oak, Freshwater, Frogpond, Full Circle, Harper's, The Holyoke Transcript-Telegram, The Manchester Journal Inquirer, Laughter Loaf, Laurel Review, Lifewriter's Digest, Midwest Poetry Review, Mocha Memoirs, Modern Haiku, Naked Humorists, Nights and Weekends, Piedmont Literary Review, Pinedeldyboz, Raw Nervz, Seven Seas Magazine, The Springfield Journal, Still, Teaching and Learning, Teaching English at the Two-Year College, the Teaching Professor, Technocursed, Tennessee English Journal, Tinywords, Tundra*, and *The Writer's Life*.

His writing honors include a Pushcart Prize Nomination and selection as a Sante Fe Writers Project Literary Award Finalist. He has also received two Southern California Genealogical Association Writing Contest Awards, a John W. Paton Storytelling Contest Third Prize, three Red Moon Press Awards, a Haiku Society of America Merit Book Award, a *Woodnotes* best-of-issue award, a Tanka Splendor Award, an Ohio University Playwrights Festival Feature Award, and three *Writer's Digest* Scriptwriting Contest Honorable Mentions.

He lives in Somers, Connecticut, where he is an avid reader of memoirs, photographer, and hiker who does volunteer land preservation work with the Northern Connecticut Land Trust.

John can be reached at JohnSheirer@aol.com .

***